A Search for Equality: The National Urban League, 1910–1961

Jesse Thomas Moore, Jr.

The Pennsylvania State University Press
University Park and London

Library of Congress Cataloging in Publication Data

Moore, Jesse Thomas, 1936–
  A search for equality.

  Includes bibliography and index.
  1. National Urban League.   2.   Afro-Americans—Civil
rights.   3.   Afro-Americans—History—1877–1964.
I.   Title.
E185.61.M784   322.4′4′06073   80-24302
ISBN 0-271-00302-2

To Ann S. Kheel, Theodore W. Kheel, Lloyd K. Garrison, and the late Whitney M. Young, Jr., for their splendid dedication to the work of the National Urban League and the Urban League Movement.

Contents

List of Tables

Preface

This study attempts to chart those changes—psychological, educational, political, social, attitudinal, and geographic—that Negroes* experienced between 1830 and 1960. I wish to point out at the outset that the inclusion of data on Negroes of the antebellum, the Civil War, the Reconstruction, and the post-Reconstruction eras in no way is meant to suggest or imply that the ideological roots of the National Urban League (NUL) and the Urban League Movement (ULM) are traceable to nineteenth-century America. Suffice it to say that the NUL and the ULM were authentic products of the Progressive Era. But I do argue that sustained opposition on the part of the white population during the nineteenth century to full equality for Negroes led to the creation of racial advancement organizations. Moreover, the progress made by Negroes throughout the nineteenth century in nurturing racial pride and racial solidarity, not to mention their successes in education and community development, paved the way for the creation of the NUL and the ULM.

While anti-Negro sentiments changed only slowly, if at all, between 1830 and 1900, American society was changing in ways that would ultimately affect the nature and structure of Negroes' unending search for equality. American society was becoming more urban and industrial, and these changes came to have considerable impact on the Negro population. Urbanization and industrialization not only led to population shifts among Negroes but also led to the development of racial pride and racial solidarity among those Negroes who were urban residents. Moreover, urbanization and industrialization raised cultural levels and provided more employment opportunities and leisure time to the more fortunate and the best

*The term "Negro" is used throughout this study because this was the acceptable way of referring to Americans of African ancestry from about 1850 to about 1960. The term "black" came to have widespread usage after 1960.

educated among the Negro population. Those who had the leisure and the education to contemplate their situation soon realized their low status and undertook to do something about it. The result was a very rapid growth of racial advancement organizations in the last half of the nineteenth century. Most of the racial advancement organizations of the last half of the nineteenth century were all-Negro, while a minority of the post-1865 racial advancement organizations were interracial.

The founding of racial advancement organizations continued during the Progressive Era. This time, however, these organizations were not only national in scope, but they also addressed economic and social problems, and they called for full enforcement of the U.S. Constitution as regards Negroes' rights. The two most prominent and enduring racial advancement organizations created during the Progressive Era—the NUL and the National Association for the Advancement of Colored People (NAACP)—drew their leaders and members primarily from the ranks of urban intellectuals, the urban occupational elites, and the urban middle classes.

The whites and Negroes who supported racial advancement efforts and organizations did so because of their desire to defend, protect, and expand the constitutional rights of Negroes; eliminate those needless barriers that stymied racial advancement; and assist Negroes in acculturating to urban life styles and accepting the "Protestant work ethic" as their own guiding principle. Despite white support of racial advancement, the Negro founders of the NUL were not blind to the fact that most whites, including those in the NUL, opposed social equality between the races.

The fact that most of the whites engaged in racial advancement frowned upon social equality between the races did not prevent them from working with Negroes who rejected the racial caste system in American society. Scores of Negroes and whites agreed that the special needs of urban Negroes required immediate attention, and that urban problems cut across racial and class lines. Therefore Negro and white racial reformers turned to scientific social work, hoping to fashion the disparate groups into a distinctively American nationality. In short, the white urban racial reformers of the Progressive Era did not call for complete equality for Negroes, because they knew what was possible to achieve and what was not.

It is debatable whether the Negro and white NUL founders were wise in their choices of what was possible to achieve and what was not. Nevertheless, three views guided the Negro and white Urban League founders from about 1910 to about 1940: that scientific social work would assist Negroes in acculturating to urban lifestyles; that the proper use of scientific social work would contain racial, ethnic, and class conflicts within acceptable bounds; and that the emergence of an industrial democracy was inevitable.

The beliefs that scientific social work had the capacity to reshape racial and class attitudes and that an industrial democracy was inevitable were short-lived. Hence, during the 1920s and the 1930s, the Urban League altered its course somewhat by continuing its social service orientation, as well as enlarging its programs to include sustained political pressure, efforts to reform existing governmental structures, and civil rights. Indeed, as the program changes suggest, Negro intellectuals and other reform-minded racial advancement supporters kept abreast of changing historical conditions. This fact enabled them to capitalize on various opportunities, in 1910 and again during the 1940s and the 1950s, to launch programs that could conceivably change the society. Credit should also be given to countless numbers of Negroes and whites who, while not Urban Leaguers, did give of their time and energy to racial advancement causes.

The broad lines along which this study is cast do not permit an examination of the exceptionally fine work of scores of non-Urban Leaguers, a score or more of the League affiliates throughout the country, and a descriptive analysis of the services performed by a goodly company of dedicated individuals, many of them—affiliates and persons—worthy of a book-length study in their own right. Neither does space permit coverage of all of the activities that the NUL and the ULM have engaged in. In general the founding of the NUL and the ULM was an attempt on the part of Negroes and whites to legitimize racial advancement in the minds of countless numbers of Americans. Indeed, by the advent of the Progressive Era, the question was no longer whether the rights of Negroes needed defending, but only when, how, and to what extent.

Acknowledgments

An Edwin Earle Sparks Fellowship from The Pennsylvania State University and a Young Humanist Fellowship from the National Endowment for the Humanities enabled me to complete this study. I owe a great debt of gratitude to the staffs of the Franklin D. Roosevelt, Dwight D. Eisenhower, and the Harry S Truman Libraries. My special thanks to Peter Sullivan of the Manuscript Division, Library of Congress, for his assistance, and that given me by the library staffs of the Moorland Research Center, Howard University, and the Modern Military Records Division, National Archives. Finally, I thank the staff of the Rush Rhees Library of the University of Rochester for the splendid service offered me.

The suggestions and criticisms made by Stanley Engerman, Eugene D. Genovese, and Robert Hall were always perceptive and extraordinarily helpful. Four of my colleagues, William Hauser, Elizabeth Fox-Genovese, Abraham Karp, and Mary Young, gave me the benefit of their wise counsel. Special thanks are due Robert K. Murray and Ari Hoogenboom, who gave me both encouragement and expert advice. Mark Letcher helped with the Tables, as did Stanley Engerman. Claire Sundeen and Margaret Vacca, who typed and retyped the manuscript, displayed extraordinary patience and skill in producing the final copy. Professors Benjamin Quarles and Arvarh Strickland read the manuscript and offered many constructive criticisms. Mr. John Pickering of the Penn State Press has been most helpful and cooperative.

To my wife, Carol, and our son, Jay, I owe a great debt for their understanding and patience, and their painful silence during the writing stages of this manuscript.

1

The Background to Racial
Advancement Organizations

Wesley F. Craven, the renowned historian, has noted that as early as the 1630s, the whites in the Virginia colony made sharp distinctions between themselves and the Negroes. Whites in Virginia and in other colonies ultimately built a wall of caste around Negroes, followed by a system of white supremacy. The extent to which the seventeenth- and eighteenth-century Negroes resisted a racial caste system and white supremacy remains unclear because of a paucity of data. But it is clear that Negroes of the seventeenth, eighteenth, nineteenth, and twentieth centuries (including the 1970s) have experienced indignities ranging from indifference and paternalism to exploitation and hostility, because of the larger society's insistence on white supremacy. Whites of each century have periodically resorted to violence to keep Negroes in their place and to maintain a system of white supremacy.

Negroes have reacted in several ways: resentment, frustration, cynicism, surrender and adjustment (accommodation), or defiance. Few Negroes have embraced the concept of white supremacy. But the extent to which they have resisted or accepted it has rested on several factors. Educational and occupational mobility, or the lack of them, have conditioned Negroes' responses to white supremacy. The place of geographical residence—rural or urban, Northern or Southern—is another variable in determining why some Negroes have resisted a second-class status while others have not. The psychological perceptions that Negroes hold of themselves, and particularly whether or not they view themselves as Americans, have also influenced their acceptance or rejection of a racial caste system and white supremacy.

This chapter has several major purposes. It discusses urbanization's impact on the antebellum Negroes' perceptions of themselves and the larger society. This chapter also examines the role of Northern white philanthropists in underwriting training and education for antebellum and postbellum Negroes. Moreover, it assesses the reasons why some Negroes accommodated to white supremacy while others did not. It offers a systematic analysis of the antebellum urban racial ideologies that sought solutions to slavery and the noncitizenship status of the free Negroes, and the institutional structures created by urban Negroes that promoted racial advancement. Finally, it considers the positive and negative aspects of the racial ideologies of Benjamin "Pap" Singleton and Booker T. Washington, two postbellum rural-oriented Negroes who promoted racial advancement in an era of worsening racial relations.

I

Antebellum and postbellum Negro leaders, with few exceptions, refused either to surrender or to adjust to the subservient position assigned them and other Negroes by white society. Their efforts to promote racial advancement and their opposition to racial injustices paved the way for racial advancement organizations founded during the postbellum and Progressive eras. It is therefore necessary to examine the efforts of antebellum urban and postbellum rural Negro leaders in order to understand the historical dimensions of Negroes' search for equality.

Unquestionably, urban Negro leaders of the antebellum era opposed slavery, pursued citizenship, and challenged racial injustice. The postbellum urban Negro leaders sought to consolidate and perpetuate those rights granted them and other Negroes by the U.S. Constitution and by congressional enactments. Several factors account for antebellum and postbellum urban Negro leaders' opposition to racial inequality. Each generation, more fervently than its predecessor, subscribed to those ideals undergirding democracy—life, liberty, and the pursuit of happiness. The various educational opportunities pursued by urban Negroes created and enlarged the professional and Negro middle classes. It was primarily from these classes that newer and younger leaders were recruited. Education, along with urbanization, radically altered Negroes' lifestyles, and education and urbanization both contributed to Negroes viewing themselves in a more positive manner than either whites viewed Negroes or rural Negroes perceived themselves. Residing in the urban centers and in the towns of the North and South enabled scores of Negroes to put behind some of the most debilitating influences associated with plantation life, slavery, and rural life.

The role of Northern white philanthropists in introducing Negroes to the institutions of urban life was enormous. But while Northern white philanthropists, antebellum and postbellum, underwrote various types of educational opportunities for Negroes, they opposed social equality between the races. Philanthropists in Philadelphia headed the list of whites who aided the Negro in the transition from rural to urban America. Founded in 1789, the Society for Free Instruction to Black People (Philadelphia) offered courses in industrial and academic training.[1] By 1791, a school for Africans ran courses in reading, writing, arithmetic, and the household and mechanical arts.[2] A committee representing the Abolition Society reported twelve schools in Philadelphia (1803) offering various types of vocational-industrial and academic training.[3] Similar training programs were undertaken in other large cities of the North, notably New York City and Boston.

Residing in urban centers exposed Negroes to ideologies that were incompatible with slavery, noncitizenship, and racial inequality. The evolutionary and revolutionary ideologies that sparked the French and American Revolutions are cases in point. By the nineteenth century, urban Negroes increasingly believed that all men are created equal and are endowed by their Creator with certain inalienable rights, among which are life, liberty, and the pursuit of happiness.

The belief that all men are created equal has undergirded the Negroes' unending search for equality. This belief has also been largely responsible for the Americanization of the Negro. The moment that the "free Africans" perceived themselves as colored became an important historical watershed in the history of Negroes. The antebellum urban free Negroes viewed themselves as Africans or free Africans until about 1800. Subsequently they wished to be known as "people of color" or the "colored population."

Referring to themselves as colored was significant in several respects. If the antebellum free Negroes did not as yet consider themselves Americans, at least they no longer looked upon themselves as Africans. It was a clear signal to white America that a majority of the free Negroes neither held out hope nor had the desire to return to Africa.[4] The fact that the free Negroes looked upon themselves as colored rather than Africans meant that they would remain in America and intended "to be recognized, eventually, as citizens."[5]

The emerging Negro leaders of the antebellum communities were thoroughly in tune with the times and its people. Realizing that the goals of equality, citizenship, and equal justice were unachievable at the time, free Negroes nonetheless reminded whites that they would not abandon these goals. A proliferation of racial advancement organizations between 1830 and 1860 was a signal to whites that Negroes were preparing for a protracted struggle. The founding of these organizations also underscored the urban free Negroes' opposition to their low and undefined status.[6]

Urban free Negroes sought, among other things, a clarification of their undefined status. In 1830 Hezekiah Grice, a free Negro from Baltimore, and other prominent Negroes met and founded the Convention of Colored Men (COCM).[7] Convening in Philadelphia, the men discussed and considered what actions were required to end their status as noncitizens. As a reflection of their new identity, the group decisively rejected overseas emigration. Instead they supported the establishment of colonies in Canada for free Negroes and runaway slaves.[8] In attendance at this meeting were the Reverend Richard Allen, a founder of the African Methodist Episcopal Church (AME) and the Reverend Christopher Rush, a bishop in the AME Church, among other equally notable free Negroes.

One year later, the COCM convened in Baltimore. For a second time the delegates eschewed overseas emigration. The most important transaction at the Baltimore meeting was passage of a resolution that authorized Grice to seek legal counsel to ascertain the legal status of free Negroes.[9] Nothing came of this resolution because white lawyers in Baltimore and elsewhere refused counsel. This and the first meeting of the COCM were not total failures, inasmuch as they provoked discussion on or resulted in concrete strategies that conceivably could enhance the status of free Negroes and win freedom for the slaves. The COCM's racial advancement strategies were: pressure group tactics, legal defense, separation, and colonization in the Western Hemisphere.

The proliferation of strategies and ideologies coincided with the creation of new organizations within free Negro America. The Negro Convention Movement (NCM), begun in 1840, expanded upon the work begun by the COCM. Its founding was a clear indication that a national consciousness was identifiable within the Negro leadership, if not among the urban Negro masses. The creation of the NCM also meant that the white abolitionists and the free Negroes were divided on the issue of slavery and of equality. White abolitionists, with few exceptions, denounced slavery rather than racial inequality. Conversely, those Negroes in the abolitionist movement opposed all forms of racial inequality. The NCM not only reflected a growing impatience on the part of the free urban Negroes to the slowness with which their rights were recognized, but also indicated that separatism among urban Negroes was on the ascendancy.

Separatism was not an attractive ideology at the time of the NCM's founding in 1840. But this fact did not cause the separatist faction of the NCM to desist from urging Negroes to establish residence outside the United States. But not all separatists were emigrationists, as the events surrounding the New York State Convention of Colored People (NYS-COCP) indicate. One of the groups comprising the NCM, the NYSCOCP held its initial meeting in 1840. The final document produced by those in attendance at the NYSCOCP, written by Henry Highland Garnet, born a slave in New Market, Maryland, endorsed separatism. Garnet argued persuasively that Negroes had formed their own organizations because whites had refused to extend to them full political and economic rights.[10]

Negroes of almost every conceivable ideological persuasion backed the drive for full political and economic rights. Therefore the NCM attracted the attention of free Negroes in the United States and Canada. The founding of the NCM marked the first time that Negroes throughout the United States and Canada raised their voices in unison against slavery, and called for the franchise and citizenship for Negroes not in bondage. Separatism was also given a full airing.

The NCM did not endorse separatism. Frederick Douglass's stature among the antebellum free Negro communities was in part what prevented any single ideology or strategy from guiding the work of the NCM. Despite his belief in integration, Douglass rarely, if ever, denounced NCM members who advocated emigration or separatism or condoned violence as solutions to slavery and the problems of free Negroes. Initially Douglass and others like himself were convinced that slavery could be abolished and the rights of free Negroes could be won without a violent confrontation and a protracted struggle. By the 1850s, however, Douglass and other integrationists in the NCM had altered their thinking on how to pursue equality for all Negroes, and did not rule out the use of violence to overthrow the institution of slavery.

Throughout the 1850s, the NCM chided the federal government for supporting slavery and for not extending citizenship rights to free Negroes. The intransigence on the part of federal officials and the white-led abolitionist movement marked a further parting of the way between antebellum free Negroes and whites who opposed slavery.[11] As it turned out, free Negro leaders in the urban communities, both inside and outside of the NCM, eschewed moral suasion and turned to political action during the decade before the Civil War.[12]

The political action took two forms. One group of Negroes became actively involved in political parties whose main objectives were the abolition of slavery and/or the containment of the slavery institution. Another group resolved that full equality for themselves and others of African descent was unattainable in America because whites seemed incapable of supporting equality for all. Therefore the emigrationists and separatists made renewed appeals to Negroes that they leave the United States and establish residence in Africa or in the Caribbean.

Foremost among the emigrationists was Martin R. Delany. Born to free parents, Delany objected to slavery and inequality, as did Douglass and other Negro leaders. Delany, one of the earliest Negro intellectuals, had had medical and scientific training at Harvard University. Unlike Douglass and other integrationists, Delany urged that Negroes establish permanent residence in Africa (Liberia). Central to his ideology was the belief that there should be solidarity among peoples of African descent. Pan-Africanism, an ideology binding all peoples of African descent together, is sometimes referred to as Delany's brainchild.[13]

Delany and other emigrationists were somewhat shortsighted. While correctly perceiving the extent of the free Negroes' anger because of their second-class status, the emigrationists failed to comprehend the degree to which the free urban Negroes were already psychologically integrated into American society. The Negroes who emigrated to Liberia, for example, soon realized that they were Americans, not Africans. Hence they, like the European settlers in Liberia and elsewhere in Africa, went to great lengths to distinguish themselves from the indigenous people of Liberia.[14] For example, the Negro emigrants in Liberia held high the ideals of life, liberty, and the pursuit of happiness for themselves, if not for the native Liberians.

The Negro emigrants to Liberia and the American Negro subscribed to other American values, for example, education. Since education in Liberia is not relevant to this study, suffice it to say that the antebellum free urban Negro leaders endorsed both industrial and classical education as tools of racial advancement. Delany held that Negroes could avoid a servile role by pursuing industrial education.[15] The Reverend Samuel Cornish, born in 1795 in Sussex County, Delaware, of free parents, urged the establishment of schools, academies, and one general college that embraced the mechanical arts along with a thorough classical curriculum.[16]

Educational opportunities for the urban antebellum free Negroes were extremely limited, both in the North and in the South. Separate educational institutions, from the primary grades to the middle grades, were a necessity for Northern Negroes until about 1830. Negroes were barred from many public schools in the North until about 1830, and secondary education was denied them until the 1860s.[17] In the urban South, free Negroes maintained their own schools, because the South did not establish a public school system until after the Civil War.

Despite numerous obstacles, the antebellum urban Negro made remarkable strides in education. As of 1850, U.S. Census data show the following number of Negro students enrolled in schools: Connecticut, 1,364; Louisiana, 1,219; New York City, 1,418; and New Orleans, Louisiana, 1,000.[18] A close examination of the 1850 Census data also reveals that the ability to read and write was widespread among the antebellum free Negroes, as shown in Table 1. Table 2 gives a state-by-state breakdown of literacy and illiteracy among native whites and the free Negroes, as of 1850.

Any reduction of illiteracy among the antebellum urban free Negroes added to their determination to become American citizens and to pursue higher education. Opportunities for higher education were not readily

Table 1. Numbers and Percent Illiterate: Native White and Free Colored Populations According to Regions, 1850[a]

Region	Native White			Free Colored		
	20 Years Old	Illiterate	Percent Illiterate	Over 21 Years Old	Illiterate	Percent Illiterate
New England	1,495,437	6,281	.42	23,021[b]	1,878	8.45
Middle states	3,205,854	96,176	3.00	229,360	51,111	22.42
Southern states	1,029,570	209,003	20.30	94,619	19,989	21.20
Southwestern states	984,833	163,778	16.62	28,084	5,018	18.54
Northwestern states	2,675,557	265,415	9.92	58,157	12,399	21.44
Slave states	2,867,537	494,007	17.23	238,267	58,444	24.52
Free states and territories	6,649,001	273,939	4.12	196,314	32,078	16.55

[a]Data extracted from *Statistical View of the United States, 1850* (Washington: Beverly Tucker, Senate Printer, 1854), Table 157, p. 153.
[b]Number of free Negroes taken from *Statistical View of the United States, 1850*, Table 136, p. 131. There were 1,254 free Negroes residing in California and the territories in 1850.

Table 2. Percent Illiterate among Native White and Free Colored Populations; Total Number of Free Colored, Number Attending School, and Number Illiterate among the Free Colored Population, in Selected States, 1850[a]

	Native White	Free Colored		
States	Percent Illiterate	Total Number	Number Attending School	Number Illiterate	Percent Illiterate
Alabama	7.91	2,265	68	235	10.37
Connecticut	1.30	7,693	1,264	567	7.37
Massachusetts	2.79	9,064	1,439	805	8.89
New York	2.99	49,069	5,447	7,429	15.14
Ohio	3.12	25,279	2,531	4,989	19.74
Pennsylvania	2.50	53,626	6,499	9,342	17.42
South Carolina	5.71	8,960	80	808	9.82
District of Columbia	3.84	10,059	467	3,214	31.95
Louisiana	8.30	17,462	1,619	3,387	19.40
Maryland	4.98	74,723	1,616	21,057	28.18

[a]Data extracted from *Statistical View of the United States, 1850* (Washington: Beverly Tucker, Senate Printer, 1854), Table 147, p. 144; Table 136, p. 133; and Table 155, p. 152.

available to the antebellum free Negroes. Most white colleges would not admit Negroes. Hence a mere thirty-four Negroes had graduated from college by 1863, twenty-two of whom were Oberlin (Ohio) College graduates.[19] These thirty-four college graduates were symbolic in two ways: they were proof that Negroes could indeed pursue and complete college training; and they were the foundation of a Negro intellectual class.

Much of the opposition to segregated education in the Northern states was directed by the Negro intellectual class and the Negro middle classes. Their early pleas fell on deaf ears. But in 1855 the Massachusetts legislature banned segregated education. This revolution in education was not accomplished without the determined efforts of Benjamin Roberts, a Negro who was offended that his daughter had to leave her neighborhood and attend a segregated school; and William Bell, who successfully spearheaded a campaign to petition the legislature to end segregated education throughout the Commonwealth of Massachusetts.

Antebellum Negroes' assault on segregated public education was made possible by winning the ears of sympathetic whites and an expanding urban Negro population. The free Negro population numbered 434,495 in 1850. Concentrated primarily in urban areas, as shown in Table 3, free Negroes set about the task of founding schools, literary societies, reading rooms, churches, as well as self-help and racial advancement organizations. Each of these institutions enabled more Negroes than ever before to gain an elementary literacy. Antebellum Negro leaders knew that education,

Table 3. Population of Whites and Free Colored, Towns and Cities, 1850[a]

City	County	State	White	Free Colored
Alexandria	Alexandria	Virginia	6,390	1,283
Richmond	Henrico	Virginia	15,274	2,369
Columbus	Franklin	Ohio	16,605	1,277
Cincinnati	Hamilton	Ohio	112,198	3,237
Louisville	Jefferson	Kentucky	36,224	1,538
Nashville	Davidson	Tennessee	7,626	511
Detroit	Wayne	Michigan	20,432	587
Flint	Genesee	Michigan	1,608	26
New Orleans	Orleans Parish	Louisiana	89,364	9,905
Lafayette	Jefferson Parish	Louisiana	12,319	332
Atlanta	DeKalb	Georgia	2,060	19
Savannah	Chatham	Georgia	8,395	686
Darien	McIntosh	Georgia	262	36
Chicago	Cook	Illinois	29,640	323
Williamsburg	James City	Virginia	415	64
Cleveland	Cuyahoga	Ohio	16,801	224

[a]Data extracted from *The Seventh Census of the United States: 1850, An Appendix* (Washington: Robert Armstrong, 1853), pp. 3, 4, 258, 474, 366, 574, 575, 612, 705, 896, and 889.

community development, and racial advancement were inseparable. Hence the reading rooms, literary societies, and Negro-controlled churches not only became permanent fixtures but were deemed necessary in an urban environment. City and town life provided the antebellum urban slaves and free Negroes alike with invaluable experiences. The urban slaves learned skills and in some instances to read and write. Both the urban slaves and the free Negroes gained some experience in managing their own affairs.[20] Urban life also exposed both slaves and free Negroes to values, lifestyles, and ideas that were incompatible with slavery and inequality.

The movement of Negroes to the cities and towns enabled them to expose more forcefully the evils of slavery. Urban Negroes founded their own newspapers, and used the printed media to communicate with each other, as well as to air their views on equality to whites. They spoke in bolder terms and took more direct steps toward the goal of full equality than rural free Negroes did. The urban free Negroes also used the printed media to urge an end to employment discrimination based on race. Urban life required competition rather than paternalism, as employment discrimination stymied racial advancement. There are no hard data showing the success that Negro leaders registered in convincing unions to accept Negroes and employers to hire competent Negro laborers. But the geographical changes of the Negro population between 1810 and 1850—rural

Table 4. Free Colored Population of the United States, Selected States: 1810, 1820, 1830, and 1850[a]

States	1810	1820	Percent Change	1830	1850	Percent Change[b]
Connecticut	6,453	7,844	+ 22.0	8,045	7,693	− 4.0
Illinois	613	457	− 25.0	1,637	5,436	+232.0
Indiana	393	1,230	+213.0	3,629	11,262	+210.0
Iowa	—	—	—	—	333	—
Maine	969	929	− 4.0	1,190	1,356	+ 14.0
Massachusetts	6,737	6,740	+ 0.4	7,048	9,064	+ 29.0
Michigan	120	174	+ 45.0	261	2,583	+890.0
New Jersey	7,843	12,460	+ 59.0	18,303	23,810	+ 30.0
New York	25,333	29,279	+ 16.0	44,870	49,069	+ 9.0
Ohio	1,899	4,723	+149.0	9,568	25,279	+164.0
Vermont	750	903	+ 20.0	881	718	− 19.0

[a]Data extracted from *Statistical View of the United States, 1850* (Washington: Beverly Tucker, Senate Printer, 1854), Table 42, p. 63.

[b]Any population growth within a ten-year period in excess of 18 percent suggests there was in-migration into the states.

Note: +Increase; −Decrease

to urban and South to North—suggest that the cities held out greater opportunities than rural areas. Table 4 documents the population shifts of Negroes between 1830 and 1850.

The 1850 Census shows that about one-fifth of the roughly 50,000 Negroes then residing in New York City "were born in the present slave states."[21] Some of the migrants to New York City were already skilled or semiskilled laborers, but a much larger group came without any marketable skills. In 1850 one in every fifty-five employed in New York City was a skilled worker.[22] A similar pattern existed in New Orleans, where free Negro male workers or about one in every eleven was employed in a job requiring some training. Table 5 shows the occupational distribution of Negroes (free male Negroes) in selected cities, states, and occupations for the year 1850.

The skilled worker, the college graduate, and the small business owner were the elites among the antebellum Negroes. But even they, like the masses, were subjected to discrimination and suffered from general patterns of racism. Accordingly, additional racial advancement and self-help organizations were formed, because the Negro elites had the resources to challenge their low status. The rise and proliferation of racial advancement organizations indeed signaled urban Negroes' resistance to patterns of discrimination that permeated the industrial world. It should be pointed out that except for the presence of skilled Negro laborers in New Orle-

Table 5. Number of Free Colored in Selected Occupations: Connecticut, Louisiana, New York City, and New Orleans, 1850[a]

Occupations	Connecticut	Louisiana	New York City	New Orleans
Apprentices	1	11	2	4
Architects	—	1	—	1
Barbers	39	46	122	41
Cabinetmakers	10	—	—	—
Boatsmen	5	39	28	37
Carpenters	4	521	12	355
Clerks	4	63	7	61
Doctors	—	6	9	4
Druggists	—	—	3	—
Engineers	—	4	—	—
Jewelers	—	5	3	5
Lawyers	—	—	4	—
Tailors	9	86	23	82
Mechanics	2	77	3	52
Musicians	5	4	24	4
Shoemakers	41	99	23	92
Printers	1	—	4	—
Teachers	—	15	8	12
Ministers	2	77	3	64

[a]*Statistical View of the United States, 1850* (Washington: Beverly Tucker, Senate Printer, 1854), Table 70, pp. 80–81.

ans, Charleston, and a few other Southern cities, the cities of the North held out greater opportunity to Negroes. Hence Negroes migrated northward in search of jobs, education, and a greater chance of freedom. Table 6 presents the increases and decreases of the free Negro and the escaped slaves in the states and territories of the South, North, Midwest, and Far West between 1850 and 1860.

Negroes' movement to urban centers and their growing interest in abolitionism, integration, separatism, emigration, and democracy should be further underscored. Each of these ideologies promoted group, ethnic, and racial consciousness. While the antebellum free Negroes did not realize their objectives of abolition, citizenship, and equality, they did experience partial success in uniting "the communities represented and in [coordinating] their efforts to attain equal rights."[23] Equally important, they set the stage for new efforts that became the struggles of the post-Civil War Negroes. Finally, a number of strategies and ideologies—protest, separatism, Negro-white cooperation, integration, mediation, and winning the cooperation of white labor—which have undergirded twentieth-century racial advancement efforts and organizations, all had their origins in the antebellum era.

Table 6. Free Colored in Selected States, 1850 and 1860[a]

States	1850[b]	1860[c]	Percent Change[d]
Free states:			
California	962	4,086	+325.0
Illinois	5,436	7,628	+ 29.0
Indiana	11,262	11,428	+ 1.0
Massachusetts	9,064	9,602	+ 6.0
New Jersey	23,810	25,318	+ 6.0
New York	49,069	49,005	− 0.3
Ohio	25,279	36,693	+ 31.0
Pennsylvania	53,626	56,949	+ 6.0
Connecticut	7,693	8,627	+ 11.0
Michigan	2,583	6,799	+ 62.0
Slave states:			
North Carolina	27,463	30,463	+ 11.0
Virginia	54,333	58,042	+ 7.0
Louisiana	17,462	18,647	+ 7.0
Maryland	74,723	83,942	+ 12.0
South Carolina	8,960	9,914	+ 11.0

[a]Data extracted from *Statistical View of the United States, 1850* (Washington: Beverly Tucker, Senate Printer, 1854), Table 42, p. 63.

[b]Ibid.

[c]*The United States on the Eve of the Civil War: As Described in the 1860 Census* (Washington: U.S. Civil War Centennial, 1963), Table 1, p. 61.

[d]Ibid.

Note: +Increase; −Decrease. Increases in the free colored population in the states in excess of 13 percent were the result of in-migration.

II

Some 186,000 Negroes participated in the military campaigns or other efforts that contributed to the destruction of the Confederacy. The collapse and defeat of the Confederacy indeed compelled a change in Negro-white relations. Two of the antebellum free Negroes' goals—abolition and citizenship—were realized. But their hopes of equality seemed a far-off dream. A Civil War did not drastically alter Negro-white relations. The ratification of the Thirteenth, Fourteenth, and Fifteenth Amendments, and congressional enactment of civil rights legislation, made the Negro and the ex-slave citizens with well-defined rights.

The actions of the Congress, the defeat of the Confederacy, and the changed status of Negroes neither ushered in full equality nor expunged from the mind of most white Americans the belief that Negroes were inferior beings. The white supremacist attitudes associated with antebellum America were enduring legacies that could not be erased or eliminated overnight.

The systemic and aberrational aspects of the Negro condition were also legacies that would endure for generations to come. The African's enslavement was a general indication of the European and white American's perception of people with dark skin. Overt forms of racial discrimination had contributed to unstable family life among antebellum free Negro families. Slavery had disrupted family life and had made Negro males and females anything but men and women. These conditions, systemic and aberrational, had to be addressed before Negroes could unite in the search for equality.

The internal and external factors that stymied postbellum racial advancement were complex. Internally the Negroes lacked the leadership required to press for a full enforcement of the Constitution. Regional racial ideologies contributed to Negro disunity, although different ideologies were appropriate for the era. Financial instability and the absence of solid institutional structures prevented the union of urban and rural Negroes, Northern and Southern Negroes, and the intellectuals, the middle classes, and the masses. Between 1865 and about 1890, urban and rural Negroes placed too much emphasis on the political system's capacity to resolve the race question. Northern and Southern Negro leaders were also incorrect in believing that education and the ownership of property could win white acceptance of Negroes as the equal of Anglo-Saxons. But in the final analysis, sustained white opposition to equality, rather than any Negro weaknesses, was what stymied postbellum racial advancement.

The white fear of social equality sparked opposition to any form of racial equality. This same fear also governed Negro-white relations in the political and economic worlds. The postbellum Negro leaders sought to make the best of the situation, debating the value of integration, separatism, emigration, protest, agitation, and education of various sorts. Of the issues debated by these leaders, education attracted the most attention.

The postbellum Negroes' exposure to education is well worth examining. In the wake of the Civil War, the Congress established the Freedmen's Bureau, which among other tasks endeavored to provide educational opportunities for the ex-slaves. Appointed Commissioner of the Bureau on May 19, 1865, General Oliver Otis Howard set forth its overall educational policy:

> The utmost facility will be offered to benevolent and religious organizations and state authorities in the maintenance of good schools for refugees and freedmen until a system of free schools can be supported by reorganized local governments. It is not my purpose to supersede the benevolent agencies organized in the work of education, but to systematize and facilitate them.[24]

Hence the Bureau's tasks were to promote education for the freedmen, to work cooperatively with the Northern philanthropic societies that promoted Negro education, and to work with Southern whites and Negroes. Northern white philanthropists did not seem at first to be concerned with

Southern whites' view of what type of education the Negro should receive. Hence the success of Negro education from 1865 to 1870 rested with the Northern philanthropists rather than with the Freedmen's Bureau. In 1865 Congress appropriated money to the Bureau for the repair and rental of schools. Monies required for recruiting students, for books and supplies, for transporting students, and for teachers' salaries came from Northern philanthropists. Monetary assistance was also forthcoming from scores of freedmen's benevolent societies.

The cooperative efforts of Bureau officials, Northern philanthropists, and the benevolent freedmen's societies provided educational opportunities for Negroes in South Carolina between 1865 and 1870.[25] Ex-slaves assisted the Bureau officials in the operation of the schools and took full advantage of this new opportunity. Bureau officials, white philanthropists, the benevolent freedmen's societies, and the ex-slaves in South Carolina and the other Southern states witnessed many positive results from their combined efforts. Reuben Tomlinson of Philadelphia, who was the State Superintendent of Education for South Carolina, wrote to his immediate supervisor, J.M Alvord, Superintendent of Education for the Freedmen's Bureau, that: "It would be difficult to find schools even in the North conducted with more system and intelligence than are displayed in the schools of the City of Charleston."[26] Commenting on the schools of rural South Carolina, Tomlinson remarked that: "[The] inability of the colored people in the rural districts to assist in the support of the schools, owing to the failure of the crops and other causes, is not nearly as great as we had reason to think it would be."[27] Moreover, the ex-slaves and other Negroes in South Carolina and in the other former Confederate States paid liberally according to their means for instruction for themselves and their progeny.

But neither the Bureau nor Northern white philanthropy had a sustained interest in educating Southern Negroes. Perhaps their interest waned in response to Southern whites' opposition to teaching the ex-slaves to read and write. Sensing that the mood of the people toward educating Southern Negroes had changed, the Congress too reduced appropriations to the Bureau.

As early as 1867, Southern whites began debating what type of education Negroes should receive. The withdrawal of Northern white philanthropists from Southern education allowed the Southern whites more say in the Bureau-run schools, and also opened discussions on industrial education. Some Bureau officials were none too happy at what was occurring. Edward L. Deane, Tomlinson's successor, wrote during July 1870 that:

> . . . the work of educating the freed people is but in its infancy. We have only made a commencement, hereafter it must depend upon State Authorities. . . . I

am painfully aware of the futility of our efforts when measured against the ignorance and stupidity of the County School Officials and the comparative indifference of our legislature to this cause. I therefore close my connection with this
work with gloomy forebodings, seeing no favorable promises for the future.[28]

Deane's predictions proved correct. The white South's opposition to
teaching Negroes to read and write hardened, the Bureau's work among
them came to a halt, and Northern white philanthropists largely withheld
their support from the Southern Negro elementary and secondary public
schools.

White Southerners opposed the work of the Bureau, the direct involvement of Northern white philanthropists in education, and liberal education
for Southern Negroes for several reasons. Many believed that any education for the ex-slaves promoted ill feeling between the races. Others
seemed convinced that the Bureau schools, largely staffed by Northern
whites, were vehicles to propagandize the ignorant Negroes into believing
in racial equality. But the chief reason that Southern whites opposed education and schools for Negroes, according to Tomlinson, was their wish to get
rid of the Northern teachers because they taught politics in the schools.[29]

White Southerners believed resolutely that public education would politicize Negroes. This politicalization, many white Southerners believed,
directly threatened white supremacy. Such fears not only conditioned the
white Southerners' views of Negro education but also left their mark on
the thinking of Bureau officials. In 1869 the Bureau's staff in South Carolina, led by Alvord, suggested that industrial education be given greater
emphasis in the schools' curriculum. (But in 1866, Alvord had praised the
curriculum, writing that the Bureau's aim was to teach the freedmen to
read and write.[30]) The Bureau's endorsement of industrial education for
Southern Negroes not only pleased whites but also paved the way for
rural-oriented Negroes who championed industrial education as the panacea for deteriorating Negro-white relations.

Southern whites generally did not seem concerned about the curriculum
offerings in the Southern Negro colleges. And not much pressure was put
on Northern white philanthropists to relinquish control of these colleges.
A plausible reason for white Southerners' unconcern about these colleges
and what was taught in them was that their enrollments were so small that
Negroes as a group could not be politicized. Liberal training commenced
at Straight University (New Orleans) in 1870; Shaw University (Raleigh,
North Carolina) in 1870; Fisk University (Nashville, Tennessee) in 1871;
and Atlanta University (Georgia) in 1872.[31] These are but a few of the
colleges and universities that were founded by Northern white philanthropists, Negroes, and the Bureau.

The Southern Negro colleges and universities offered both classical and industrial training. From the outset their boards of trustees, presidents, and faculties opposed the formation of a caste system in education and in American society. Negroes trained at and employed by the Southern Negro colleges, and those who had attended colleges and universities in the North, argued that a race without the background of education needed "an equipment no less inferior than the race which has had five hundred years of education in the past."[32] Indeed they, and scores of Northern whites to a lesser degree, opposed any racial ideology that implied the restriction of Negroes to industrial training, or the withholding of political rights from Negroes until such time as they earned the right to them. The Northern and urban-oriented Negro leaders believed that the direst future awaited America unless the ex-slaves and the pre-Civil War free Negroes were led by highly trained and intelligent leaders.[33]

The extent to which the Northern and urban-oriented Negro leaders fully understood the stark realities of postbellum rural and Southern America is unclear. But it is clear that they generally applauded the humanitarian efforts of Northern white philanthropists to uplift Negroes. The founding of Hampton Institute in 1868 by General Samuel C. Armstrong is a case in point. It should be noted at the outset that Armstrong did not found Hampton Institute and promote industrial training in order to arrive at a political accommodation with the white South. Neither did the founding of Hampton Institute necessarily point to a new direction in the type of education most suitable for the ex-slaves and other Negroes. Armstrong saw the founding of Hampton Institute and its industrial education program as a humanitarian effort to assist Negroes in the transition from slavery and noncitizenship to citizenship and life in an urban-industrial society.

Such a transition required both immediate and long-term efforts. Perhaps industrial training was an immediate solution, or at least many Negroes and whites saw it as such. But a gradual erosion of Northern and federal support of full equality for Negroes, and sustained Southern white opposition to any and all forms of social, economic, and political equality ultimately left Negroes throughout the nation to their own ingenuity.

Two "leaders," both of a Southern and rural orientation, offered programs that conceivably could advance the Negro cause in the South without seriously contributing to any further Negro-white disharmony. The first "leader" was Benjamin "Pap" Singleton, whose movement symbolized the separatist and internal colonization wing of postbellum Southern Negro ideology. Born a slave in Nashville in 1809, Singleton undertook the founding of settlements for his people on government lands in Kansas.[34] He eschewed both politics and integration as tools of racial advancement. He embraced economic uplift and physical separation from whites as desirable goals for Negroes to pursue.[35]

Singleton's racial ideology was unrealistic. The Negro population could not physically disengage itself from white America and remain in this country. Economic power without corresponding political power was an illusion. Yet between 1870 and 1900 other Negroes, as did Singleton, urged the establishment of all-Negro settlements in the Western Hemisphere, and also the pursuit of economic uplift.[36]

Booker T. Washington followed in Singleton's wake. He advocated economic uplift and industrial training. Unlike Singleton and the Negroes who preached separatism, Washington sought Northern white philanthropists' help in underwriting industrial training programs. In an effort to allay Southern whites' fears that teaching Negroes to read and write would politicize them and lead to calls for social equality, Washington urged Southern Negroes not to attempt to exercise their constitutional rights.

Washington believed that industrial training for the Negro would be less offensive to the white South than political power, liberal education, and social equality would. A student of Southern history and one who was keenly aware of the Negro-white hostilities that were ever-present in Southern society, Washington correctly pointed out that the Civil War and the Reconstruction eras had strained relations between Negroes and whites, and that the Reconstruction era had not prepared either group to coexist as equals. Therefore he proposed that Negroes eschew any claims to political and social equality. A pragmatist, Washington courted the friendship of the Southern white planter-industrial classes, knowing that they admired the skilled Negro artisan. He assumed that the Negroes' ultimate fate rested in the hands of the planter-industrial classes. Skilled Negro artisans, Washington resolved, would be attractive to the planter-industrial classes who could use Negroes in transforming the South from an agricultural to an industrial society.

It remained to be seen whether or not the planter-industrial classes would be the Negroes' friend and protector as Washington envisioned they would. Further, it was unclear that the type of industrial education then being offered Negroes would be useful to whites in their efforts to industrialize the South. Education of some sort, however, had to be given Southern Negroes and whites if the South was to be industrialized.

Washington's racial ideology offered something to whites and Negroes alike. But it was an overstatement on Washington's part to claim that any objective history of industrial education would illuminate the Negroes' role in defining its aims and shaping its methods.[37] Industrial education's goals and methods were shaped and defined well in advance of the time that the white South and Washington saw it as peculiarly suited for the Negro. Washington was also incorrect in arguing that the idea of introducing industrial education in America, for the purpose of solving the problem created by the liberation of nearly four million slaves, was first clearly conceived and carried out by General Samuel C. Armstrong.[38] As stated previously, Armstrong did not attempt to solve the Negro problem but to perform a humanitarian deed for the ex-slave. Therefore a more careful examination of industrial education's introduction into America is required than that offered by Washington.

Industrial education in America was an evolutionary process, commencing before the Civil War. Western Europeans borrowed the innovative educational concept from the Russians, who, during the 1830s, experimented with teaching students to work with the hands as well as with the mind.[39] Americans patterned their industrial programs after those of the British, Germans, and other Europeans. Northern white philanthropists had underwritten industrial-vocational training for some Negroes better than a century before the founding of Hampton and Tuskegee Institutes. And the antebellum Southern planter class had made industrial training an integral part of plantation life.[40] In the final analysis, Armstrong's and Washington's major contribution to postbellum Negro advancement was not that of proving industrial education's worth, but that of interesting Northern philanthropy in underwriting it in a formal setting for the freedmen.

Manual and industrial training offered Northern Negroes between 1830 and 1860 influenced programs of the postbellum era. As early as 1832, Richard Humphreys of Philadelphia bequeathed a sum of money to found the Institute of Colored Youth. This school trained the descendants of the African race in "school learning, in the various branches of the mechanical arts and trades and in agriculture."[41] It is doubtful that Armstrong and other postbellum whites who supported and underwrote industrial training for Negroes in the South were unaware of antebellum efforts, or that their concerns for the unskilled did not also extend to the white masses.

Training the white masses to enter industry was what led to the development of industrial-vocational education, as Jane Addams's commentary shows. Before the 1840s, according to Addams, the schools concentrated on training boys for the clergy, medicine, and teaching. Captured by the business owners about the time of the Civil War, schools in the North shifted emphasis, as children were taught the virtues of obedience, promptness, and accuracy. By the 1880s the manufacturers wanted schools to train individuals to enter industry who were already fitted for a particular job.[42]

In one sense, Washington's views of industrial education coincided with those of the post-1880 manufacturers. Washington saw in industrial training the mechanism for instilling discipline and self-confidence in the exslaves. In another sense, Washington's use of industrial education differed from that of the manufacturers. Washington's program of industrial education at Tuskegee was to give Negroes an old type of artisan training, a type of training that did not meet the expectations of manufacturers who wanted workers trained for a particular type of job in industry. Washington and the whites who underwrote industrial education in the South believed that it had the capacity to make Negroes productive citizens, and to improve and stabilize family and community life among the ex-slaves.

Washington's pronouncements during the 1890s on the Negroes' place in American life, unlike his earlier statements on industrial education's value to Negroes, gave industrial training a political basis not found at Hampton Institute and the other industrial schools. By the 1890s, his racial ideology revolved around more than industrial education for Southern Negroes. It also was an attempt to arrive at an accommodation with the white South on issues such as the extent of Negro participation in the political process and what white Southerners would be willing to concede to Negroes who disavowed any claims to social equality.

Washington's program of racial advancement, as of 1895, rested on the premise that where the want of time and money prevented broader culture, Negroes as a group required training that had special meaning for their present existence. But at no time did he oppose liberal and higher education for all Negroes, or eschew politics as a solution to the racial problem. He simply stated that politics and agitation ought not to be the race's chief strategies for winning a fairer measure of justice and equality than they enjoyed.

Unquestionably Washington believed that it was unprofitable for Negroes to engage in an intense struggle with Southern whites for control of the political institutions of the region. Yet he did not deny that integration was and should be a future target for Negroes to pursue. Washington of course was not above relying upon pressure-group techniques and legal defense to promote racial advancement, although he used these two strategies sparingly and clandestinely against white America.

Washington's racial ideology embraced future integration, legal remedies, racial consciousness, and a circumscribed form of Black Nationalism. These were goals shared by Negro intellectuals, the middle classes, and the pillars of the urban Negro communities. As it turned out, however, Washington's racial ideology came under intense attack from Negroes of an urban orientation, and from the rising Negro intellectual community and the middle classes.

Several factors explain why so many Negroes rejected Washington's racial ideology and his racial advancement program of industrial education. First, his ideology did not take into account the fact that increasingly Negroes were migrating northward, and that those already in the North were not engaged in an intense struggle with whites for control of the nation's social, political, and economic institutions. Neither did Washington show great concern for or much awareness of the fact that urban

Southern Negroes were prepared to resist the white South's attempts to exclude them from the political process; at least the middle classes and Negro professionals, if not the masses, were prepared to do so. Second, Washington's program of racial advancement made no provision for the training of a Negro leadership class—a class from which leaders of action and thought would emerge. Third, it was mere speculation on Washington's part to believe that industrial education would improve relations between Southern whites and Negroes. The legacy of slavery remained too fresh in the minds of both Negroes and whites to be ignored. Fourth, Washington's neglect of the future, as compared with his concern for the Negroes' present status, lent itself to the white South's racist schemes; his belief that the Negroes' political and economic rights would be defended and protected without their active participation in the political process proved to be sheer folly—and this became evident by 1908. Finally, Washington was incorrect in assuming that acquiring money and property would solve problems that touched the deepest human feelings and passions. However mighty, the dollar has never been almighty.

Despite these indictments against Washington, his racial ideology was not totally incorrect. If nothing more, it reflected the deteriorating race relations in American society. Washington's views on race relations had been shaped by both a slave and free experience. Washington, like so many urban and rural Negro leaders of the era, believed that full equality was unattainable at the time, and he was right. Washington, Singleton, and other postbellum Southern Negro leaders should be credited with endeavoring to free their race from the throes of hunger, poverty, ignorance, and despair. Their efforts not only paved the way for later racial advancement organizations, indirectly and directly, but also contributed to a growing awareness among younger Negroes that full equality would not be achieved without an intense and protracted struggle with the white majority. In the final analysis, Washington and other Southern Negroes of his generation did not lose sight of the fact that Negroes' most basic needs had to be met before any considerable number of them would join the ongoing struggle for full and complete equality.[43]

Washington, Singleton, and other Southern Negro leaders of a rural orientation developed ideologies grounded in an American tradition: the belief that democracy was nurtured and brought to fruition in an environment of educated and self-reliant men and women. Washington never doubted industrial education's capacity to produce self-reliant men and women. At the same time, Washington, "in a candid moment, could have agreed with virtually all of the long-range goals articulated in the [1905] Niagara Declaration."[44] In this sense, Washington's racial ideology was neither a marked departure from the racial reform movements that dominated the first four decades of the twentieth century, nor was it at odds with the egalitarian concepts that originated in the Age of Revolution. Washington, Singleton, and other Southern, rural-oriented postbellum Negro leaders' racial ideologies stand as watersheds. By the 1880s there was considerable evidence of a growing rift between urban and rural Negroes over what tactics and strategies should be relied upon in the search for equality.

The entry of Northern white philanthropists into the field of industrial education served to widen the rift. Not all Northern whites agreed with the white South's views about and treatment of the Negro. Nor did they all agree that industrial education was peculiarly suited to the Negro. The factors that influenced Northern white philanthropists to underwrite industrial education for the Southern Negro are indeed complex. First, the white South's most respected citizens convinced the nation, without too much difficulty, that the best way to solve the Negro problem was to leave the South alone.[45] Leaving the South alone meant that Northern white philanthropists would continue their educational work among Negroes, but would not meddle in the South's political affairs. Second, Northern white philanthropists subordinated all abstract and sentimental considerations of the Negro condition to a commiserating appreciation of Southern conditions. Expressed in another way, they did not object to Southern whites' efforts to deny the franchise to Negroes; Northern whites, like white Southerners, believed that the vote was not the right of any race as a race. Third, and most important, over the years Northern white philanthropists came to believe that most Southerners, both white and Negro, had to be elevated to the standards of the Northern Anglo-Saxon. They saw industrial education as fitting Negroes to join the ranks of industrial workers, as well as giving them the necessary tools to live and prosper in the South. They believed that individuals of exceptional talent should be allowed to compete in the industrial world without regard to ethnicity, race, or color, though they did not seek to impose their own racial views on the white South.[46] Thus industrial-vocational education would equip both unskilled Negroes and whites to join the industrial ranks of the nation.

Southern whites of the postbellum era generally saw industrial education in terms of its value to Negroes. Yet they paid only lip service to industrial training programs. Data from reports compiled by the Commissioner of Education, shown in Table 7, confirm this observation. It was Northern philanthropy that sustained Hampton and Tuskegee Institutes. Both schools trained Negroes who not only learned skills and trades but also worked among the Negro masses in an effort to reduce illiteracy and to transform them into independent and productive citizens. But the work of the liberal arts colleges in offering both classical and industrial training programs should not be overlooked. These colleges too were financed

Table 7. Number of Negro Pupils in Southern States Receiving Industrial Training in the Public Schools, 1899–1900[a]

States	Estimated Number of Pupils, 5–18	Pupils Enrolled in Public Schools	Pupils Receiving Manual Training in Public High Schools	Negro as Percentage of Total School Population
Alabama	301,300	142,423	0	46.94
Arkansas	130,740	84,317	0	27.94
Florida	77,640	41,797	5	44.21
Georgia	380,970	195,276	197	48.41
Mississippi	227,470	192,493	0	59.29
North Carolina	250,860	130,005	68	37.48
South Carolina	311,900	155,602	2	62.66
Missouri	55,420	34,540	250	5.74

[a]Data extracted from *Report of the Commissioner of Education, 1899–1900* (Washington: Government Printing Office, 1901), 2505.

largely by Northern white philanthropists, and their enrollments were nearly ten times that of the two industrial education schools. The Southern private Negro colleges were neither controlled nor influenced by Southern white racists. They graduated men and women schooled in American democracy who, like Negro graduates of the Northern white colleges, created institutions that challenged segregation, discrimination, and inequality in American society.

A majority of the studies that examine the Negro condition discuss the Negro organizations—antebellum and postbellum—and their pursuit of equality by relying upon such questionable categories as conservative, militant, radical, accommodation, and the like. These terms have had even broader application to the racial advancement organizations and leaders of the twentieth century. Yet these descriptive labels have so many different meanings for so many different individuals that they are pejorative or vague. It seems better to replace them with more precise descriptions.

Antebellum and postbellum Negroes sought to improve their status by relying upon these strategies and techniques: (1) revolt; (2) escape to the nonslaveholding states in the North, or to Canada; (3) colonization in Africa, or in the Western Hemisphere; (4) emancipation; (5) enfranchisement; (6) calls for protective laws and a definitive statement of their status as the free Negroes; (7) legal defense; (8) agitation; (9) pressure-group techniques; (10) education of various sorts; and (11) the formation of national and international organizations to promote racial advancement. None of these strategies seemed capable of neutralizing white opposition to full and complete equality for Negroes. Thus Negro leaders called for new programs during the 1890s. Urban Negro leaders achieved great success in nurturing racial pride, awareness, and consciousness. This emerging national consciousness among urban Negroes had enabled their leaders to speak in bolder terms and to take more direct steps toward the goal of complete equality than rural-oriented Negroes seemed prepared for.

2

Postbellum and Early Twentieth-Century Urban Reform Leaders, Organizations, and Ideologies

The urban Negroes of the postbellum era and the twentieth century continued the search for equality that had been launched by antebellum free Negroes. They posed questions about and sought solutions to inequalities that were sometimes unique to an urban environment. Yet urban Negroes addressed issues—segregation and discrimination—that affected the lives of all Negroes, South and North, rural and urban. Throughout the postbellum era and into the twentieth century, Negroes everywhere in the United States felt the effects of the Southern Negroes' gradual elimination from politics and the hardening racial attitudes that led to their being barred from skilled occupations. Yet the legally enforced segregation that ultimately became a way of life in the South shielded scores of Negroes from certain forms of employment discrimination found in the North. The separation of the races in rural and urban Southern America afforded Negro teachers, lawyers, doctors, and other professionals opportunities to practice their skills. A dual society also offered some protection to the skilled Negro tradesmen—plumbers, carpenters, barbers, and the like.

The Negroes residing in the cities of the North, like Southern rural and urban Negroes, faced racial discrimination and segregation at every turn, and needed to develop racial strategies to cope with them. Those strategies deemed suitable for rural Negroes in their efforts to survive and prosper in the midst of adversity were largely rejected by the urban Southern and Northern Negroes.

The purpose of this chapter is to examine the urban Southern and Northern Negro communities and to show how their leaders endeavored to fashion ideologies that addressed the urban Negro condition. It will also examine the influence of the Populist and Progressive eras on Negro thought. The role of the Anglo-Saxon, Jewish, and other reform-minded whites in shaping policies and creating organizations that addressed the problems of the urban Negro will be considered. This chapter discusses the role of Negro intellectuals, professionals, and the middle classes in promoting and nurturing racial consciousness, racial pride, and self-respect among the expanding urban Negro communities of the North and the South. Finally, it examines the reasons why some Negro intellectuals joined forces with white urban occupational elites to combat racism.

I

As mentioned in Chapter 1, migration from rural to urban areas of the North and South contributed to a further growth in numbers of Negro intellectuals, Negro professionals, and the Negro middle classes. Their vantage point in life inevitably gave them a different perspective of themselves and American society than could be detected among Negroes who either remained in rural America or were unskilled workers. Having taken full advantage of opportunities not available to most Negroes, these Negro intellectuals, professionals, middle classes, and skilled workers were more likely to object to their second-class status in society.

The extent to which the Negro migrants resisted Northern-style racial discrimination is unclear. But the evidence suggests that Negro migrants to the North between 1865 and 1900 were more easily integrated into the existing Negro communities than were the Negro migrants after 1900. Hence the possibility does exist that they quickly joined the ranks of Negroes who demanded changes, however modest, in Negro-white relations.

One historian characterized the Negro migrants to the North between 1865 and 1900 as the intelligent laboring classes.[1] This does not mean that every Negro migrant was of the intelligent working classes. Perhaps hundreds or thousands of the migrants were unskilled laborers. But they, like the intelligent working classes, left the South because of their dissatisfaction with the limited educational and employment opportunities available to them.

Northern white philanthropists funded educational programs for the migrants. Their efforts were supplemented by urban racial reformers, who underwrote educational programs and called for wider employment opportunities for the migrants. By the 1880s, scores of Northern whites capitalized on the reform zeal sweeping the nation, giving serious thought to ways of improving urban life for thousands of European immigrants and the Negro migrants.

The institutions created by urban racial reformers reflected the reform zeal that culminated in the Progressive Era. Sometimes the schools and social-work organizations served both the migrants and the immigrants; at other times they were exclusively for the benefit of the Negro migrants. The Institute of Colored Youth, founded in 1832 by Richard Humphreys of Philadelphia, added an industrial department in 1899. Subsequently instruction in carpentry, bricklaying, shoemaking, printing, dressmaking, millinery, and other trades commenced. Some 259 persons (108 males and 151 females) were enrolled in the industrial department as of 1901.[2]

Philadelphia's civic-minded Negroes and whites underwrote other training programs for the Negro migrants. The Reverend Matthew Anderson, a Negro, founded the Berean Manual Training School in 1899, following a study of Philadelphia's Negro population by Anderson and twenty public-spirited citizens. The Berean School assisted the migrants in making vocational and social adjustments to urban life by offering courses in chair, desk, and table making, tailoring, and shoemaking. In 1904 its Negro and white Board of Trustees altered the school's charter and began offering industrial training in cooking, carpentry, upholstery, sewing, millinery, and all kinds of manual and industrial employment, along with practical and liberal education.[3]

The fact that the Board of Trustees voted to alter the school's charter to be able to instruct Negroes in the industrial and manual arts is significant for two reasons. First, civic-minded Negroes and whites in the Northern cities were aware of the rising barriers against Negroes in the industrial world and therefore wished to train Negroes for employment opportunities that were open to them. Second, a majority of the nation's most respected Negroes and white citizens believed in industrial education's capacity to uplift Negroes. But the altering of the Berean Manual Training School's charter also had other implications. That the board of directors did not vote to end liberal arts training at the school indeed reflected the beliefs of Negro intellectuals and the urban middle classes that various types of education were required in the struggle for racial advancement.

Northern white philanthropists and civic-minded Negroes and whites supported various sorts of education for Negroes in the Northern cities with sizeable populations. New York City was a case in point. The training programs and schools established in New York City were generally interracial in character. Colonel Richard T. Auchmuty, a businessman with considerable interest in the problems of the working man, founded the New York Trade School about 1884. Located on First Avenue and Sixty-Eighth Street (Manhattan), this school readied men to enter certain trades as well as provided continuing education to those already employed in the crafts. Day and evening classes offered instruction in bricklaying, plastering, plumbing, carpentry, house, sign, and fresco painting, stone cutting, blacksmithing, tailoring, and printing.[4] No evidence was found to indicate that Negroes were barred from this school or that Auchmuty intended that it be open only to the white workers.

There were other individuals in New York City, who, like Auchmuty, were interested in the problems of workers. One person was Felix Adler, who was noted for his interest in racial, urban, and labor reforms. Adler founded the Workingman's School in 1878. This school provided instruction to the children of the poor and working-class parents, whatever their nationality, religion, or color. Manual training was integrated into all grades of instruction, from kindergarten through high school. The founding of the Workingman's School, like the founding of the New York Trade School, demonstrated that whites were not blind to the problems of urban life that cut across racial, religious, and ethnic lines. Moreover, their concerns for the poor and unskilled workers reflected the spirit of the times, which was that the "best" citizens had a responsibility to improve life for the less fortunate members of society. The belief that the "best" citizens had a responsibility to the poor and unfortunate members of society was institutionalized in the all-Negro and interracial organizations as well.

II

It seems necessary to examine the years 1880 to 1900 in order to understand the ideals, reforms, ideologies, and strategies for change that developed in the Progressive Era (to be examined in the following section). As one historian, Louis Filler, wrote: "Progressivism may be traced in a score of movements preceding the Progressive era proper. It expressed itself in uprisings and broader political movement."[5] Having written a definitive account of the times leading up to and including the Progressive Era, Filler elaborated further:

> In general, Progressivism . . . involved popular protest and unrest, and efforts to cross class and group lines for greater social impact. Progressivism . . . sought a common denominator for disparate elements of the American population. It is no accident . . . that the popular and the progressive became interwoven. Inevitably, however, they required a leadership, and that which had proclaimed itself of the populace found itself communicating with peers: a new elite.[6]

The individuals promoting racial advancement for Negroes emerged as part of this new elite, which included urban Anglo-Saxons, other whites, Negroes, and Jews.

The "Old Immigrant" American Jews were among the early pioneers for activities that could conceivably raise the status of those like themselves. On April 26, 1655, the board of directors of the Dutch West Indies Company informed the New Netherlands governor, Peter Stuyvesant, of its decision to permit Portuguese Jews to trade, sell, and reside in the colony (later New York State). These Jews, in return for those privileges, promised to support their poor without any aid from the company.[7] Jewish charities in America trace their origins from this agreement. From 1655 until about 1881, Jews created organizations to administer to the needs and to defend the rights of Jewish-Americans and the Jewish immigrants.

The influx of Southern and Eastern European Jews into New York City, commencing in 1881, led to the creation of additional advancement organizations. Some 600,000 Jews arrived at the Port of New York between 1881 and 1903. Most of these immigrants lacked the language, trade, and educational skills to be quickly assimilated into the already established Jewish communities in New York City. And owing to the fact that various industries and businesses would not offer employment to Jews, they found it difficult to find steady or permanent employment. The Jewish Agricultural and Industrial Society of New York (JAISONY) sought solutions to the problems facing the immigrants. It "undertook to distribute Jewish residents of New York City, who were willing to go, to other places, where work had previously been found for them."[8] The JAISONY and other Jewish-run organizations, as well as organizations headed by Anglo-Saxons, other whites, and Negroes, were among the scores of movements that preceded the Progressive Era proper.

Organizations with a broader constituency than that of Jews or Negroes made their appearance in New York City and in other cities before the turn of the twentieth century and the Progressive Era. One of these was the College Settlement of New York (CSNY), founded about 1898. Its primary goals were to elevate homemaking standards among the poor, to cultivate civic responsibility and an appreciation of books and education among all races and groups, and to improve the physical conditions of neighborhoods in which the poor and working classes resided. Begun on the Lower East Side of Manhattan, the settlement work sponsored by the CSNY, and the work undertaken by other agencies involved in the problems of the migrant, immigrant, the poor, and the urban working classes, moved north to Harlem, to Manhattan's West Side, and to Brooklyn.[9]

Settlement work was not pursued in the Southern cities to the extent that it was in the Northern cities. There were civic-minded Negroes and whites in the Southern cities, but racial barriers, required by law, prevented them from publicly joining forces to seek solutions to problems that were unique to Negro communities. In the Southern cities Negroes generally constituted the largest minority group, but this was not the case in the Northern cities. The fact that Negroes in the Southern cities constituted an angry minority led to the emergence of leaders who did not subscribe to Washington's or Singleton's prescriptions and solutions to the race problem.

Two Southern Negroes whose programs reflected an urban orientation were the Reverend W.R. Pettiford and the Reverend T.W. Walker of Birmingham, Alabama. Born in North Carolina and the son of freed slaves, Pettiford graduated from the Normal School in Selma, Alabama. In 1883, following a brief career as a teacher, he became the pastor of a congregation in Birmingham. Its membership at the outset numbered 150 persons. Pettiford learned that the "pulpit alone was inadequate to stimulate his people to higher ideals and self-restraint."[10] He urged members of his congregation to take an active interest in and become involved in politics. Pettiford set an example for his followers, serving as a delegate-at-large to the 1896 Republican Party's National Convention.

Pettiford also provided leadership for Birmingham's Negroes in other ways. He founded the Penny Savings Bank during the 1890s. Some four thousand of the roughly five thousand Negro bank depositors in that city used the bank. Pettiford was often mentioned as Washington's rival in Alabama, because of his concern for and service to the Negro community. Indeed he became known as the apostle of saving.[11]

The work of the Reverend T.W. Walker, pastor of the institutional church in Birmingham, Alabama, both supplemented and complemented the work undertaken by Pettiford in Negro Birmingham. He was born a slave and one of his earliest memories was that of being placed on an auctioneer's block. At the age of seventeen years, Walker moved from Emmore County (rural Alabama) to the ex-Confederate capital in Montgomery, Alabama. In 1881 Walker moved to Birmingham and began organizing small group prayer meetings; by 1884 he was an ordained minister. The founding of the Shiloh Baptist Church, known to its members as Walker's Church, stood as a monument to Walker's hard work and to the faith that his followers placed in him as a leader. Situated in an area where large numbers of Negro women worked regularly as maids, Walker organized them into a union when it was clear that they were not receiving adequate compensation for their work. He became their advisor on matters such as overwork and underpayment. The white employers did not take kindly to Walker's extrareligious activities. They fired the Negro maids upon learning that Walker had organized them into a union. In retaliation, the Shiloh Church placed the employers on its blacklist. In the end the white employers came to terms with Walker and the union, granting substantial wage increases to the domestic workers.

Walker's work in Negro Birmingham did not end with the unionization of domestic workers. He also founded within Shiloh Church a Christian

Relief Society, the Afro-American Benevolent Association, and the Tenth Legion (the Tenth Legion was comprised of individuals who pledged one-tenth of their earnings to the Church for its support and for investment purposes). The Christian Relief American Benevolent Association engaged in relief-type activities among those Negroes in Birmingham who required assistance.

Walker managed the Shiloh Church's money with skillfulness and a keen business sense. The same can be said of the money that he made as pastor of the Shiloh Church. Walker's personal economic holdings in the city of Birmingham were extensive. He operated a shoe store and a drugstore, and founded a relief association with sickness and death benefits, among other commercial enterprises. The one commercial venture that he began with personal and church money that proved to be unsuccessful was a coal mine. Despite this failure, Walker's contributions to Negro Birmingham were enormous. He advised Negroes in spending and investing money wisely. Walker became known as the apostle of spending.[12] In the final analysis, the value of Pettiford and Walker's work in Negro Birmingham was that it promoted racial pride, group solidarity, and racial consciousness.

The most striking developments in Negro America during the last thirteen or so years of the nineteenth century were neither the work of Pettiford, Walker, and others, nor the concern shown by whites (Jews, Anglo-Saxons, and others) toward the Negro condition. Rather, the most striking developments were white Americans' insistence on a permanent second-class status for Negroes, and the stirrings among Negro intellectuals and the urban middle classes that led to the creation of institutions that challenged segregation, racial discrimination, and injustices in every aspect of the society.

Space will not permit the citing of every organization founded by the Negro intellectuals and the middle classes. The most prominent ones will be given a brief introduction. The National Federation of Colored Men, comprised of lawyers, was founded in 1895 in Detroit, and called for social, political, and economic justice for all Americans.[13] Begun in 1896, the National Association of Colored Women was both a social service and a political body. It operated welfare programs, ran reformatories for Negro youth, underwrote homes for the aged and infirm, held classes in the domestic arts, and sponsored day-care nurseries for working mothers. Its members, who were primarily civic-minded and professional women, also protested against lynching and racial discrimination.[14] The one organization that was clearly representative of Negro intellectuals was founded by the Reverend Alexander Crummell, a graduate of Queens College, Cambridge, England. The American Negro Academy promoted racial pride, and preserved and disseminated the Negroes' past. Among the intellectuals holding membership in the Academy were William E.B. Du Bois,

Table 8. Negro Persons 10 Years and Over Engaged in Professional Occupations (of a group of 140 occupations), 1900[a]

Professional Service	Males	Females	Total
Actors, professional showmen, etc.	1,781	262	2,043
Architects, designers, draftsmen, etc.	52	—	52
Artists and teachers of art	150	86	236
Clergymen	15,366	164	15,530
Dentists	205	7	212
Electricians	184	1	185
Engineers (civil, etc.) and surveyors	119	1	120
Journalists	199	11	210
Lawyers	718	10	728
Literary and scientific persons	74	25	99
Musicians and teachers of music	2,736	1,185	3,921
Officials (government)	668	50	718
Physicians and surgeons	1,574	160	1,734
Teachers and professors in college, etc.	7,743	13,525	21,268
Other professional services	154	114	268

[a]Data extracted from *Special Reports, Supplementary Analysis and Derivative Tables, Twelfth Census of the United States, 1900* (Washington: Government Printing Office, 1906), Table 79, p. 252. This table represents only a partial list of the professional occupations in which Negroes were engaged in 1900.

William Grogman, president of Clark College in Atlanta, Archibald and Francis Grimke, and Kelly Miller, dean of Howard University.

Negro intellectuals also directed their energies toward political efforts, as their involvement in the Afro-American League (later the Afro-American Council) indicated. Founded in 1890 by T. Thomas Fortune, a newspaper editor, the League was for several years Negro America's chief vehicle for chastising white America for disregarding its constitutional rights. The League protested against taxation without representation (in the Southern states), discrimination and segregation in the use of public conveyances and facilities, and other detestable manifestations of racial injustices.[15]

Throughout the 1890s, the League and other racial advancement organizations were largely ineffective in either convincing or forcing white America to mend its ways. The Negro intellectuals and professionals were but one-tenth of one percent of the total Negro population in 1900. Table 8 shows the number of Negroes in some of the high-status jobs. Despite their small numbers, Negro intellectuals and scores of professionals could not be totally ignored by the white population, especially that segment which spoke of a fairer measure of justice for the poor and the downtrodden. The Negro intellectuals and the profession-als, like the middle classes, the urban Negro masses, and the migrants to the cities, were dissatisfied with life in America. What distinguished the Negro intellectuals from all other Negroes was their clear vision of what was required to advance the race. Their training and education equipped them to create and head organizations that could lead the way in the search for equality.

The Negro masses, however, lacked the training, leaders, and clear vision to realize their hopes and aspirations. Generally their response to their low status was in direct relation to the degree of segregation and discrimination confronting them. Hence it seemed only a matter of time before they and the Negro intellectuals would jointly wage war on segre-gation and discrimination. Indeed the Negro masses were aware of the occupational changes that were not in their best interest, and knew that hardening racial attitudes foretold even more dire consequences. Table 9 shows the changing occupational status of Negroes between 1890 and 1900. By 1900 it was increasingly difficult for Negroes to gain member-ship in the AFL unions, or to win employment in the skilled jobs. Hence Negroes had two options for dealing with the situation. They could either forge a union with civic-minded whites and hope that change would be forthcoming, or they could embrace separatism. Both Negro-white coop-eration and separatism received wide currency during the years known as the Progressive Era (1901–1914).

III

Writing of the Progressive Era, Louis Filler concluded that: "The con-cept of 'progress' seemed important to the crusaders of the early twentieth century, in the same way that justice and religious faith had once moti-vated and inspired earlier social movements."[16] If this is the correct per-ception of what motivated many white Progressives and other whites to support the cause of the Negro, then much of what has been written about them stands in need of critical examination. For example, monograph after monograph states categorically that those whites who called for the full enforcement of the Negroes' constitutional rights also supported full equality for them. On the contrary, their interest was in making *progress* toward this goal (full equality) rather than in any radical departure from past Negro-white relations. The Progressives were no more racial egali-tarians than the nineteenth-century reformers, but they did seem inter-ested in implementing justice and democracy.[17]

The white Progressives, though they lacked a real commitment to equal-ity now, did have a sense of responsibility to the poor, and therefore supported material equality and egalitarian goals. In contrast, the Negro Progressives and racial reformers had a real commitment to winning equal-

Table 9. Negro Population Engaged in Specified (nonprofessional) Occupations, 1890 and 1900[a]

Occupations	1890	1900	Percent Change
Agricultural workers	1,106,728	1,344,125	+ 21.5
Servants and waiters	401,215	465,734	+ 16.0
Draymen, hackmen, teamsters, etc.	43,548	67,583	+ 55.7
Porters and helpers (in stores, etc.)	11,694	28,977	+147.8
Masons (brick and stone)	9,760	14,386	+ 47.4
Miners and quarrymen	19,007	36,561	+ 92.4
Janitors and sextons	5,945	11,536	+ 94.0
Carpenters and joiners	22,581	21,267	− 6.5
Hostlers	10,500	14,496	+ 38.1
Iron and steel workers	6,579	12,327	+ 87.4

[a]Data extracted from *Special Reports, Supplementary Analysis and Derivative Tables, Twelfth Census of the United States, 1900* (Washington: Government Printing Office, 1906), Table 63, p. 231. Data relate to population 10 years of age or older.

Note: +Increase; −Decrease

ity for themselves and the Negro masses, and this distinguished them from whites who backed racial advancement.

Yet the white Progressives did make outstanding contributions to at least one body of knowledge—sociology. The sociologists studied the problems of housing, employment, recreation, race, and the like. They also challenged the assumption that the traits of self-reliance, independence, and rugged individualism were found primarily among rural Americans. The sociologists rejected the notion that poverty was due to a character defect. Instead they blamed modern society for the large numbers of urban poor. And they argued that care for the poor was a responsibility of the state and should not be left to churches and political machines.

The advent of the Progressive Era led to changes in perceptions about the causes of poverty. The urban reformers and Progressives argued that the city problem was not a personal but rather an economic one.[18] They pointed out that urban ills stemmed mainly from the fact that over the decades false economic relationships had resulted in two distinct classes— the privileged as opposed to the unorganized, misled, and undisciplined masses. The Progressives and urban racial reformers' solutions to urban problems were: that trained social scientists work among the undisciplined masses; that the social sciences and the sciences were tools for reshaping urban life; that the powers of big business must be curbed by government intervention; that local government must be taken from corrupt politicians; and that harmony in urban America required the creation of meaningful bonds between the native Americans, the immigrants, the migrants, and Negroes already acculturated to urban life. With the exception of the Anglo-Saxons, the other groups were, as perceived by some Progressives, Americans in the making.

The Progressives offered refreshing views of the modern American city. As a group, they placed self-interest above race and class, two emotional issues that tended to divide people. Some Progressives reasoned that "the city provides an opportunity for varied and humanizing social relationships."[19] Many Progressives also concluded that the modern industrial city tended to downgrade allegiance to clan and racial traditions. They believed that urban life resulted in individuals being judged on an impersonal basis, and by an advanced type of competition. This advanced type of competition would lead to cooperation and coexistence among the different racial, ethnic, and religious groups who lived in cities. Many Progressives believed too that the educational institutions of urban America had the capacity to unite the various groups into an American nationality.

Many urban Progressives thought that after the family the school system was the nation's premier socializing agency. A school system properly administered would indeed raise the various urban ethnic, racial, and religious groups to the Anglo-Saxon standard. The school system would teach all children self-respect and love of country. These attitudes and devotions, as the Progressives viewed them, foreshadowed the brotherhood of man, justice, and right.[20] Urban school systems were expected to assist migrants, immigrants, and native Americans in shedding their unique parochialisms. As a group, the Negro intellectuals endorsed and shared these views with the Progressives.

Negro leaders, North and South, bestrode the times—the Progressive Era—and, criticized or praised, worked for a middle way. Most Negro leaders embraced integration and eschewed separatism and segregation. They were wise enough to see very early that Progressivism, the strongly pulsed movement that it was, had to consider at least some of the needs of the rural and urban Negroes. These needs were unattainable without at least some integration.

Urban Negro leaders generally saw positive good coming from the reforms associated with the urban Progressives. Although urban Negroes were less than 25 percent (22.7%) of the total Negro population as of 1900, they faced many problems that were not addressed by Negro leaders of a rural orientation. These problems in the Northern cities included employment and housing discrimination that were not mandated by law, juvenile delinquency, overcrowded and unsanitary living conditions, *de facto* segregation in public education, and a denial of services by institutions that served the other segments of the city.

Table 10. Total Population of Selected Northern Cities, Number of Negro
Residents, and Negroes as a Percentage of Total Population, 1900[a]

City	Total Population	Persons of Negro Descent	Negroes as a Percentage of Total Population
Jersey City, N.J.	206,433	3,704	1.8
Boston, Mass.	560,892	11,591	2.1
Columbus, Ohio	125,560	8,201	6.6
Pittsburgh, Pa.	321,616	17,040	5.3
Philadelphia, Pa.	1,293,697	62,613	4.8
New York City	3,437,202	60,613	1.8
Chicago, Ill.	1,698,575	30,150	1.8
Detroit, Mich.	285,704	4,111	1.4
New Haven, Conn.	108,027	2,887	2.7
Cincinnati, Ohio	325,902	14,482	4.4
Cleveland, Ohio	381,768	5,988	1.6
Newark, N.J.	346,070	6,694	1.9
Providence, R.I.	175,597	4,817	2.7

[a]Data extracted from *Twelfth Census of the United States, Part 1* (Washington: U.S. Census Office, 1901), Table 59, p. cxxii.

The urban problems of Negroes in the Northern cities stemmed from two sources. First, white Northern society demanded segregation, but the legal system made no room for it. Second, the slow yet steady migration patterns dictated that some efforts be directed to solving the problems of the unskilled and the poor, as was being done for the Central and Eastern European immigrants.

Despite an absence of European immigrants in most Southern cities, urban Southern and Northern Negroes shared many concerns. In the cities of the South, Negroes were experiencing overcrowding, inadequate education, unsanitary living conditions, and strained relations with their white neighbors. The process of urbanization as it related to Negroes had a longer history in the South than in the North, particularly if the percentage of Negroes as a total of the population of the Southern cities is taken into account. Tables 10 and 11 show the numbers of persons of African descent in the nation's major cities as of 1900.

One historian wrote what is indeed true: the belief that Negroes lived and thrived only in the rural areas of the nation in general and in the rural South in particular until the Great Migration of 1916 persists in the minds of whites.[21] Large numbers of Negroes had lived in the Southern cities for generations. The most prominent forces sparking the movement of Negroes to the cities were social, cultural, recreational, and vocational.[22] This is not to say that the political climate of the rural South had no effect on

Table 11. Total Population of Selected Southern Cities, Number of Negro Residents, and Negroes as a Percentage of Total Population, 1900[a]

City	Total Population	Persons of Negro Descent	Negroes as a Percentage of Total Population
Nashville, Tenn.	80,865	30,044	37.2
Jacksonville, Fla.	28,429	16,236	57.1
Montgomery, Ala.	30,346	17,229	56.8
Charleston, S.C.	55,807	31,522	56.5
Savannah, Ga.	52,244	28,090	51.8
Mobile, Ala.	38,469	17,045	44.3
Birmingham, Ala.	38,415	16,575	43.1
Atlanta, Ga.	89,872	35,727	39.8
Washington, D.C.	278,718	86,702	31.1
Baltimore, Md.	508,957	79,258	15.6
Norfolk, Va.	46,624	20,230	43.4
Richmond, Va.	85,050	32,230	37.9

[a]Data extracted from *Twelfth Census of the United States, Population, Part 1* (Washington: U.S. Census Office, 1901), Table 59, p. cxxii. By 1900 there were 56 cities in the United States that listed 2,500 or more Negroes among their populations.

migration. But the movement of Negroes from rural to urban and Southern to Northern America was for reasons other than racial tensions and political problems.

Urban life was attractive to Negroes. Despite the racism in urban America, Negroes lived in the midst of prejudice and even received some stimulation from it. The stimulation of urban life also caused urban Negroes to reject the racial ideologies of rural-oriented Negro leaders. Urban as used here not only means a geographical location but also a state of mind in which individuals compete with each other without regard to race or color. Urban and urbane Negro leaders believed that people should not merely undergo parallel experiences, but that they must also undergo them together. And they argued persuasively that justice was broader "than political rights or than civil privileges, for it includes economic and social justice."[23]

Economic and social justice for Negroes was not to be found in the North or in the South in 1900. But urban Negro leaders did not despair, because of the presence of white occupational elites on public boards, in commercial organizations, private philanthropic agencies, and religious organizations. The public boards generally directed their aid to the wards of the state, a majority of whom were not Negro. Commercial organizations promoted citizenship, public health agencies, and sanitary living conditions; they underwrote public parks, playgrounds, art galleries, educationally sound public schools, and vocational training for youth. The churches that engaged in work among the poor, in addition to giving alms, stressed the brotherhood of man, the fatherhood of God, and the solidarity of human society.[24] Meanwhile the private and philanthropic agencies offered preventive and constructive assistance to the poor, in the hope of alleviating the misery found among thousands of urban residents.

The philanthropic agencies that engaged in social work seemed to be the Negroes' best hope. Unlike the other agencies that toiled among the urban poor, the private philanthropic agencies were headed and staffed by individuals who were fired by a hatred of injustice rather than by individuals who were moved to action by pity for the poor.[25]

The whites and Negroes who gave of their time and effort to the work undertaken by the private philanthropies were the urban occupational elites. They were among the best trained and most educated members of urban society—lawyers, doctors, social workers, professors, teachers, and the like. One historian referred to them as individuals whose educational training made them a part of a small but steadily expanding urban upper class.[26] Another source concluded that the urban occupational elites took an active interest in the problems of Negroes because they subscribed to a value system that "diluted the significance of all ethnic distinctions."[27] Despite their less than firm commitment to full equality for the Negroes (social equality), the occupational elites viewed color as an irrational and needless barrier in the industrial world. In the final analysis, an urban experience had a profound impact on the thinking of white elites, leading to the emergence of men and women (both Negro and white) "who were determined to secure a fairer deal for urban blacks."[28]

The occupational elites took a special interest in the social and economic problems of urban Negroes. They seemed most intent upon achieving some semblance of justice in urban America, endeavoring to improve the overall living conditions of the poor. The occupational elites generally rejected sociological studies that attributed many of the urban ills to the pathology of the urban poor. Instead they sided with the psychologists who insisted that social environment, rather than racial characteristics, was the basic factor in the development of personality and habitual conduct.[29]

The occupational elites, as a group, can be characterized as classical nineteenth-century liberals. They welcomed free and open competition, subscribed to Social Darwinism, and believed that the Anglo-Saxon was indeed the most perfect of individuals in terms of conduct, character, intellect, and love of freedom. They sympathized with the Southern Anglo-Saxon who had to deal with the Negro masses. Perhaps William D. Witt Hyde, president of Bowdoin College (Maine) best explained the duality of the occupational elites' handling of the race question, writing that:

Today, where large masses of both races in all stages of development are thrown together, we acquiesce in social segregation and the postponement of political privileges until intelligence and responsibility shall earn the right to it.[30]

The occupational elites of the Northern cities did not object to the Northern Negro voting because in 1900 they were so few in numbers that their vote was insignificant. But in the Southern states where the Negro vote was large, even the Northern whites feared the consequences of a largely undisciplined voting bloc. Rather than meddle in the political affairs of the South, the Northern occupational elites resolved to elevate the Negroes to the standards of the Anglo-Saxon, and, as well as possible, to integrate them psychologically into American society. What some historians call social control was an example of how the elites sought to integrate the underprivileged into the mainstream of American life.

IV

The organizations founded by Negroes, like those of an interracial character that promoted racial advancement, were authentic products of the Progressive Era. Yet the racial ideologies that undergirded the all-Negro and the interracial organizations were not identical. The all-Negro organizations were founded for the purpose of overturning racial segregation and discrimination. The interracial organizations were guided by the belief that while racial qualities were more or less quiescent, patriotic instincts were tools to unite the disparate groups of the society.[31] Many whites expected few changes in interracial relations because race prejudice was so ineradicably stamped into the character of America. They believed that the only hope of winning a fairer deal for Negroes was a union of civic-minded white and Negro occupational elites. The other ideologies undergirding interracial organizations were that white occupational elites would support some form of racial advancement because of their belief that "if America could not make her dream of democracy come true for all her [citizens] there could be no democracy for anyone";[32] and that a coalition of civic-minded whites and Negroes, rather than all-Negro organizations, was the most logical and desirable way of attacking racism in American society.

The reasons why scores of white occupational elites supported racial advancement were anything but altruistic. Any increased migration of Negroes to the North added to the problems already causing considerable concern among the urban reformers and Progressives. Class conflicts and antagonisms, industrial unrest, inadequate housing, and other problems haunted the urban privileged classes.[33] With their numbers steadily increasing, the Negroes' presence in the North gave the urban problem a color dimension. This factor alone created alarm among the urban occupational elites who saw a class and racial revolution in the making. Their way of lessening the probability of a racial or class revolution was to make certain that the underprivileged shared in the varied opportunities offered by the cities. It is a fact that the Negro migrants, like the European immigrants, had been pushed from their native land and pulled to the cities by similar, if not identical, forces.

The underlying causes that prompted Negroes to leave the South and migrate to the North contributed immensely to shaping their attitudes and expectations. Moreover, the cultural traditions accompanying the Negro migrants in no small way gave form to the communities in which they settled, and were decisive in determining their social, economic, and political behavior for generations afterwards. It was in recognition of these factors that Negro and white occupational elites created organizations to assist the migrants in acculturating to urban lifestyles and to rid them of types of behavior incompatible with urban life—tardiness, ignorance, poor personal and sanitary habits, and the like. Such personal improvement became a prime objective of the larger Progressive Movement.

The occupational elites had the good sight to recognize quickly that these problems were not unique to the Negro migrants. And they also recognized that there "was no one Negro problem and consequently no one solution."[34] At the same time, however, the occupational elites who showed a concern for the urban Negro had little faith in the capacity of the organizations already in existence and working among the urban poor to address the special needs of the Negro migrants.

The organizations created by Negroes and whites after 1900 to promote racial advancement assisted the Negro migrants in a number of ways. They embarked upon training programs, engaged in scientific social work—analysis, fact finding, and observation—and offered welfare assistance. Mrs. Celia Parker Wooley, a graduate of the Coldwater Female Seminary, established the Frederick Douglass Center in Chicago during 1904.[35] This Center ran a clubroom and workshop for boys, held classes in manual training for adults and teen-agers, and operated a school to instruct men and women in the arts of domestic service.[36] Richard R. Wright, Jr., a graduate of the Georgia State College, the University of Pennsylvania, and the University of Chicago, founded the Trinity Mission in Chicago after 1900.[37] Its clientele were working females who were recent arrivals from the South. Wright, like others interested in the plight of migrants, sought to instill in the young women moral uplift and sobriety, as well as to steer them to various types of occupations—domestic work and skilled jobs. Saint Mark's Episcopal Church (New York City), pastored by Dr. William H. Brooks, a founding member of the National Association for the Advancement of Colored People (NAACP), and the National Urban League (NUL), established social service missions in Harlem, the Bronx, and

Brooklyn.* This church also operated schools in the South to train youth, and funded orphan and child day nurseries in New York.[38] William L. Bulkley, New York City's only Negro high school principal and a charter member of both the NAACP and the NUL, used his school Number 80 (located in Manhattan) as a community social and educational center. The classes held at the school during the evening enabled adults to receive instruction in millinery, dressmaking, carpentry, cabinet-making, mechanical drawing, English, and stenography.[39]

Similar programs could be found in other cities with a large Negro population. By 1905 some sixty-four agencies in New York City and Philadelphia alone aided individuals in adjusting to urban life. Despite these valiant efforts on the part of Negroes and whites, the agencies were ineffective because their efforts lacked coordination and focused primarily on immediate needs without any real concern for long-term goals. Accordingly, the urban Negro and white occupational elites expressed alarm over the fact that so little had been done to raise the Negroes' economic status and to integrate them into the industrial world.

Ideas about how to integrate Negroes into the industrial world and to resolve urban problems grew and changed. The creation of the National League for the Protection of Colored Women (NLPCW), founded in 1905, was a part of this evolutionary process. Much of the credit for the founding of the NLPCW should be given to Frances A. Kellor, General Director on the Intermunicipal Committee on House Research. The NLPCW undertook scientific studies to determine what should be done to assist the women migrants from the South to acculturate into urban life. Its findings were alarming. Females often were employed for immoral purposes; work contracts were drawn up improperly, often robbing the women of most of their weekly salaries; and suitable housing for the women migrants was severely lacking. All told, urban life had a detrimental effect on many of the women who had come North in search of a better life than found in the South.

Several individuals shared Kellor's concerns about the migrant women. One of these was Ruth S. Baldwin, the wife of William H. Baldwin, Jr., a railroad executive and one of New York City's most active social reformers. The NLPCW also received strong support from other social activists and occupational elites. No stranger to reform, humanitarian, and educational advancement movements, William J. Schieffelin was born in New York City on May 4, 1866. He received the Ph.D. degree from the University of Munich (Germany) and was a drug merchant.[40] Eugene P. Roberts, a Negro physician who graduated from Lincoln University (Penn-

---

*The NAACP was founded in 1909, emerging as the political arm of Negro protest activities. The NUL's founding date was 1910. Principally involved in social and economic issues at the outset, the NUL has evolved as Negro America's foremost social service agency.

sylvania) and the New York Medical College, was a member of the New York City Board of Education.[41] And finally, Fred R. Moore, editor of the *New York Age,* a Negro newspaper, and later a member of the Board of Aldermen, expressed a profound interest in the work begun by Kellor.[42] Together they charted a course for the NLPCW, a course which was, however, too narrow in scope to deal effectively with a whole range of problems that confronted the migrants—men and women. In the final analysis, the NLPCW reflected a larger concern, the evil influences of the city on women, addressed by many persons during the Progressive Era.[43]

The problem of industrial discrimination, of course, affected both men and women. Founded in 1906, the Committee for Improving the Industrial Conditions for Negroes in New York (CIICN) investigated the rising incidents of discrimination in plants and businesses in New York City. The CIICN also studied housing discrimination, which confined Negroes to well-defined neighborhoods in the city, and became concerned with the political, economic, and social conditions that faced Negroes in New York City.

William L. Bulkley was the CIICN's chief architect.[44] The Committee began formal operation on June 19, 1906. Its first priority was to open craft unions and skilled occupations to Negroes on an integrated basis.[45] With Bulkley as its secretary (Schieffelin was the permanent chairman), the CIICN pressed various industries and businesses in New York City to hire qualified Negroes.

A product of a liberal education, Bulkley completed his undergraduate studies at Claflin University (a church-related Negro college in South Carolina), enrolled in the graduate program at Wesleyan University (Connecticut), and earned the Ph.D. degree in ancient and foreign literature from Syracuse University.[46] Bulkley, like many other Negro intellectuals, including Du Bois, called for complete political and economic equality for Negroes. Accordingly, the CIICN's program thrust mirrored the ideology of Bulkley and other Negro intellectuals who supported racial advancement in the urban centers.

The activities of the CIICN advanced integration. It monitored the activities of the New York Legislature and those of unions, when incidents of racial discrimination in housing and employment were obvious. The CIICN organized skilled Negro artisans and sought jobs for them in industry. Its efforts led to the opening of vocational schools for Negroes in Harlem and Brooklyn. Because of its persistence, the Manhattan Trade Schools for Girls altered its policy and admitted qualified Negro applicants. The CIICN received a pledge from the City and Suburban Homes Company, a construction firm, that Negro mechanics, bricklayers, and carpenters would be hired on all its work sites.[47] The CIICN had considerable impact in New York. Its achievements testified to its founders' power of persuasion and to individual efforts.

The individuals contributing to the success of the CIICN were occupational elites, professionals, and civic-minded Negroes and whites. These individuals were neither in the Du Bois nor Washington camps, but were firm believers in the right of individuals to compete with each other without regard to race or color. Oswald Garrison Villard, in addition to his work with the Committee, was a charter member of the NAACP. He raised, according to Washington, the amount of $150,000 in honor of Tuskegee Institute's Twenty-Fifth Anniversary.[48] Others contributing to the work of the CIICN included J. Elgas, superintendent of the New York City Evening School Division, and Charles R. Richards, department head, Manual Training, Columbia University.

Several of the CIICN's founders were charter members of the NAACP, and they also assisted in the work being done at Tuskegee. The two most prominent Negroes in the CIICN, other than Bulkley, were the Reverend Reverdy Ransom, a charter member of the Niagara Movement and the NAACP, and Samuel R. Scottron, a shoe manufacturer and a former member of the Brooklyn (New York) Board of Education. It should also be noted that Du Bois actively participated in the discussions leading to the founding of the CIICN, although he did not hold formal membership in it.[49]

The CIICN's work among Negro New Yorkers was unsatisfactory to a number of Negroes and whites. Some believed that more could be done in assisting the newly arrived migrants to acculturate to urban life. A study of New York City's Negro population, undertaken by George E. Haynes, provided the stimulus for yet another racial advancement organization in New York City.[50]

A Southerner by birth, Haynes was graduated from Fisk University and received an M.A. degree from the Yale University Divinity School; Columbia University conferred upon him the Ph.D. degree in 1910.[51] The organization founded in the wake of Haynes's study was The Committee on Urban Conditions Among Negroes in New York (CU-CANNY). The initial meeting was on September 29, 1910, with Ruth S. Baldwin presiding. This gathering, like the ones responsible for the founding of the NLPCW and the CIICN, represented the occupational elites, professionals, and civic-minded Negroes and whites. What set the CUCANNY apart from its prototypes was the fact that the people in attendance saw a need to coordinate all of the social service and philanthropic work then being undertaken among New York City's Negro residents. This belief planted the seed for coordinating not only the work being done among New York City's Negro population, but that being done in other cities as well.

Initially the CUCANNY's founders outlined programs and objectives that directly touched the lives of the Negroes in New York. These programs and objectives included: the coordination of existing social service activities of the NLPCW, the CIICN, and those of the CUCANNY; reliance upon the educational system as an instrument for influencing public opinion as regards equal opportunity in employment for Negroes; the establishment of a registry of all existing agencies that carried out social service programs in Negro New York; and an evaluation of their performance and effectiveness.[52] Above all else, the CUCANNY's founders believed that the migrants required sustained assistance in acculturating to urban lifestyles, and that integrating Negroes into the industrial world would advance their social and economic status.

The task of formulating a specific program was largely left to Haynes, the CUCANNY's Director of Work.[53] One of Haynes's first acts was to devise a curriculum for training Negro social workers. A former Urban League Executive Director said of Haynes:

> George Edmund Haynes, the colored professional, was a brilliant young sociologist and the first Negro to earn a degree at the New York School of Social Work. He developed the basic Urban League plan for concentrating on the Negro's urban problems and helping him overcome the hostility and unfamiliarity of modern, impersonal city life.[54]

Haynes believed that trained Negro social workers were necessary to help Negro migrants make the adjustment to an urban industrial environment.

Negroes were particularly lacking in social work training in 1910, and white colleges' curricula were inadequate for those Negroes who wished to engage in a new science "whose scope and limitations remained to be clearly defined."[55] Therefore Haynes, with the concurrence of the CUCANNY's founders, set about the task of establishing a social work program at a Negro college and directing the CUCANNY's work among Negroes in New York City.

Fisk University, Haynes's alma mater, was chosen as the site for the social work department. Haynes spent most of the 1910–11 academic year in residence at Fisk University, where he launched a social work program that reflected his views. First, Haynes believed that people in the cities should think of the problems of other groups as affecting the entire city. Second, the promotion of friendship among city residents, rather than racial isolation, would make for a wholesome environment for the various groups inhabiting the cities. Third, Haynes and others who wished to advance the Negro cause argued persuasively that the one qualification Negro social workers—but not white social workers—possessed was an abiding faith in the ultimate destiny of Negroes.[56] According to one source, many whites, who themselves were free from prejudice, seemed unable to comprehend its effects on Negroes. Thus they either insisted that their standards of family and social life were the norm and that all others were an aberration, or they reasoned that their Negro clients could not have much in the way of standards.[57] Haynes and other advocates of Negro advancement reasoned that Negro social workers, in conjunction with those from the larger society, would assist in "the building up of a natural federation among all [of the] different groups, preserving all that is valuable in their traditions."[58] Like Haynes, scores of Progressives, urban occupational elites, racial reformers, and civic-minded Negroes and whites were hopeful that social work would build a federation among the different racial groups in the cities, preserve in a reasonable degree all that was valuable in the heredity and traditions of each type, and link "all types together in a universal yet incoherent and distinctively American nationality."[59] Haynes and other Negroes and whites concerned with the modern American city, its physical, social, economic, and racial problems, were interested in fashioning a pluralistic society. But they did not necessarily subscribe to what is now called the melting pot thesis.

Haynes's belief in a pluralistic society did not cause him to lose sight of the Negroes' own problems and the solutions for them. Like many of the Negro intellectuals of the Progressive Era, Haynes too knew that the "capacity of the few must be developed and brought to the service of the many."[60] He also maintained that the "opportunities of life for the capacity of the many can be met by a system of education which will prepare them for the most intelligent labor."[61] But it can be argued forcefully that Haynes, like other Negro intellectuals of the Progressive Era, objected to any program that pinned down the Negro people either to industrial education or to higher education. Haynes was correct in pointing out that other groups in America pursued both industrial-vocational and higher education, and that Negroes should be accorded the same options. Haynes and scores of Negro intellectuals also reasoned correctly that racial advancement required leaders of action and thought rather than leaders who promoted industrial education as the panacea of the Negroes' social, political, and economic problems.[62]

Haynes and other Negro intellectuals as a group did not reserve all of their criticism for the Tuskegee program; nor did they entirely withdraw their support from the program. Perhaps it was T. Thomas Fortune who best summed up the Negro intellectuals' ambivalence toward industrial education as represented at Tuskegee Institute. Fortune said:

> I have always considered, in the main, that the Tuskegee idea was correct; but the principle is wrong that a man should first learn to work and then develop his head. My idea is you have got to educate the head before the hand. The more intelligent the head, the more intelligent the hand.[63]

Haynes's ideas on racial advancement encompassed all types of education for Negroes. But most important was his belief that any work among the urban Negroes, to be successful, had to be led by leaders of action and thought, whether they were Negroes or whites.

It is abundantly clear that the urban Negroes, North and South, had developed a racial ideology to their own liking by the 1890s. Not that they entirely disapproved of Washington's rural and Southern strategy, but urban Negroes and urban Negro leaders knew full well that there was no one Negro problem and therefore no one solution.

During the 1890s, urban Negroes sought solutions to their problems. But they and the Negro leaders of the first decade of the twentieth century had different ideas about whom to include in the agencies. Most of the racial advancement organizations founded during the 1890s were all-Negro. Those founded between 1906 and 1909 were more often than not interracial in character. The Negroes contributing to the formation of racial advancement organizations, beginning in 1905, were guided by beliefs such as these: Most white people are basically decent and a few basically vicious; the decent whites, like the few vicious ones, may be ignorant or shortsighted or fearful of Negroes and therefore respond to them in ways that violate the basic principles of democracy; there are three kinds of efforts at social reform—thinking, protesting, and doing (the NLPCW, the CIICN, and the CUCANNY used the research of thinkers, benefited from the efforts of protesters, and put both to good use in getting things done); and it was both expedient and desirable for Negro leaders to put their unreserved trust in whites who objected to legally enforced racial discrimination and racial segregation. In retrospect, it may have been unwise for the urban Negro masses to unreservedly trust either the white occupational elites or the Negro professionals. Yet entrusting the Negroes' future to those groups was the ideology underlying both the prototypes of the Urban League and the Urban League itself.

The Founding of the National Urban League: Scientific Social Work and Community Organization

By 1909 the urban white occupational elites and Negro professionals were in agreement that national interracial organizations seemed the best hope of protecting and expanding Negroes' political rights and advancing their economic and social status. The founding of the NAACP in 1909 was testimony to this belief, as was the creation of the National League on Urban Conditions Among Negroes (NLUCAN) in 1911. Both the Negro and white founders of the NAACP and NLUCAN believed that democracy was doomed if Negroes could not share equally in its benefits and were denied the same chances of self-realization that whites had.

Such chances, and equality of opportunity for Negroes in every facet of life, were negated by the racism that permeated the Progressive Era. Furthermore, most whites involved in racial advancement lacked any real commitment to full equality for every American citizen. Nonetheless, many whites among the occupational elites devoted considerable time and effort to raising the Negroes' social, political, and economic status. The founding of the NLUCAN marked a new stage of constructive social work among Northern and Southern urban Negroes.

Chapter 3 discusses the reasons why the NLUCAN was founded. It presents the conflicting interpretations of historians, social scientists, and others on the NLUCAN'S ideological roots. It then examines the influence of separatist ideology on the NUL and the NAACP during the Progressive Era, and the sharp cleavages that separatism created between the Negro professional classes and the urban Negro masses. This chapter also looks at the contributions made by the white occupational elites and

Negro professionals to racial advancement and to the creation of the NLUCAN. It dispels a number of the prevailing myths surrounding the NUL and the Urban League Movement (ULM) such as: the Urban League and the Urban Leaguers did not involve themselves in politics; Northern Negro lawyers joined the NAACP but not the NUL; and between 1911 and 1940 sharp ideological differences arose that provoked acrimony between NUL and NAACP officials.

I

The year 1911 was momentous for the history of racial advancement organizations. On October 16, 1911, the CUCANNY merged with the NLPCW and the CIICN to form the National League on Urban Conditions Among Negroes.[1] The merger came only after intensive study and serious dialogue among the white occupational elites and Negro professionals about how to address the needs of urban Negroes. The founding of the NLUCAN laid the groundwork for a national effort in which the problems of the Negro, city by city, could be systematically studied and dealt with.

There was both agreement and disagreement between the NLUCAN's Negro and white founders on the Negro problem. Its founders believed that Negroes in the Northern cities should have the same access to economic and political privileges that whites had.[2] But there was divided opinion on social equality among some of the NUL's Negro and white founders. A majority of the Negro founders believed in social equality, but they did not press the issue as did Du Bois. Whites in the NUL generally disavowed the concept of social equality between the races, concluding that it was a private matter and therefore was not subject to legislation and court decisions. Uniting the Negro and white NUL founders was the belief that the problems spawned by industrial and social unrest and by class conflicts and class enmities affected the society as a whole. Unless these problems were resolved, the NUL founders concluded, America in general, and urban America in particular, faced a dire and uncertain future.[3] They agreed that social work among the urban masses and educational programs directed at the whole society were valuable instruments to treat the serious problems of the society.

Urban racial reformers turned to social work, the social sciences, and education, using them in the hope of creating a new and radically different urban community, as will be shown. In 1911 the views of the urban occupational elites, Negro professionals, and the racial reformers were not readily accepted by either the white masses or the urban Negro masses. Most whites opposed integration, and many urban Negroes were nearing the point of realizing that integration was an unattainable goal for the immediate future.

The racial attitudes of many whites hardened during the Progressive Era, a time when Northern urban centers were witnessing a large influx of Southern Negro migrants. On the one hand, white attitudes paved the way for segregation and racial discrimination to be embraced by the federal government. On the other hand, white opposition to equality and justice contributed to the emergence of Black Nationalism in the cities. Black Nationalism was less of a problem in 1911 than was white racism. Before 1918, no single individual had appeared in urban Negro America who was able to articulate the tensions that seemed to be driving Negroes toward an acceptance of Black Nationalism as a strategy of racial advancement. But the warning signals were present. Street corner speakers in Harlem and other cities were urging Negroes to reject integration and to embrace Black Nationalism, or even separatism.

The Negroes in the NUL and the NAACP knew that some urban Negroes had already accepted Black Nationalism. They countered separatism with integrationist ideology. And they endeavored to enlist as much white support as possible, because little change was forthcoming without white cooperation. The fact that the NUL favored interracialism meant that most whites would not support its programs and efforts to reduce racial tensions in urban communities.

The white support that the NUL could count on came mainly from the white upper classes. Their economic and educational status exempted most from having to compete with Negroes for jobs and housing. Hence the white upper classes did not have to construct artificial barriers around their jobs and neighborhoods. And they did not object to the creation of organizations that sought to remove artificially created barriers around jobs and neighborhoods. In fact, they welcomed the creation of the NLUCAN (later known as the NUL).

The formation of the NLUCAN and its scientific approach to urban and racial problems received favorable reviews. *Survey* magazine referred to the merger as "a new stage in constructive social work among Negroes."[4] The *Pittsburgh Courier,* a Negro newspaper, resolutely stated that the NLUCAN was a new chapter in social uplift.[5] The *New York Times* predicted that the NLUCAN would scientifically and objectively study urban social ills, and would assist Negroes in meeting the demands of a modern industrial society.[6]

The NLUCAN was the nation's first Negro national social service agency. Within a few years of its founding, the NLUCAN became one of several platforms from which Negroes aired their views on what constituted justice in the industrial world. The NLUCAN refrained from tackling political equality directly (1911–1940), because the NAACP had preempted that issue.

The executive director and the NLUCAN's Board of Directors agreed that the agency's initial role in the search for equality was:

> To carry on constructive and preventive social work among Negroes, for improving their social and economic conditions in urban centers; to bring about co-ordination and co-operation between existing agencies working in the interest of Negroes, and to develop other agencies where necessary; to secure and train Negro social workers; to make studies in cities as may be required for carrying out the objects of the League.[7]

As chief executive officer, the job of translating the goals established by the NLUCAN's founders rested with Haynes.

Haynes's role in shaping the underlying ideology of NUL (NLUCAN) was anything but omnipotent. The same can be said of his influence on NUL strategies and programs of racial advancement. Haynes had to operate between a group of white occupational elites who, like the white abolitionists, were not totally devoid of paternalistic instincts, and a set of less than definitive goals written into the NUL constitution. The NUL's constitution charged its officers and members with the responsibility of encouraging, assisting, and engaging in any and all kinds of work for improving the industrial, economic, social, and spiritual conditions among Negroes.[8] On the one hand, Haynes interpreted the NUL constitution in the strictest sense, so as not to raise the ire of several powerful white Board members. On the other hand, he allowed himself wide latitude in planning programs to assist the Negro migrants in acculturating to urban life.

Haynes's interest in training Negro social workers was widely applauded by the whites in the NUL. But his interest in the social work program at Fisk University limited the time that he could spend on the administrative aspects of the NUL. Haynes was neither an able administrator nor an astute politician in the strictest sense, factors that ultimately brought him into conflict with the Negro and white NUL board members. But during his reign as the NUL chief executive officer, Haynes, with considerable support from the Board, fashioned a general program for the NUL to embark upon. A publication characterized the NUL's general program this way:

> It concentrated on social work and community organization rather than on reform of existing governmental structures. The Urban League [from 1911 to about 1948] did not . . . involve itself directly in legal cases. Political action and litigation [were] left to organizations such as the NAACP. Instead, the League [during its infancy] functioned as a community planning agency and [pressed] its demands through quiet negotiations with employers or governmental officials.[9]

How long the Urban League operated within the limitations imposed on itself, often at the urging of the white Board members, depended on factors such as these: Urban Negroes' acceptance of the League as their advocate of economic and social advancement; the personnel changes in the executive staff and the NUL Board; and the degree of white coopera- tion in the search for equality. In general the NUL, like several of the local affiliates, adhered to the course of action established by the founders for the duration of the Progressive Era.

The whites in the NUL had a large role to play in steering the League along the path established in 1911, sometimes without the full concur- rence of the Negro leaders and Board members. Among the whites who exercised direct influence on the NUL programs and policies was L. Hol- lingsworth Wood, a Quaker with an outstanding reputation as a racial reformer (the Quaker influence in the NUL and in several of the affiliates was enormous). Wood graduated from Haverford College (Pennsylvania) and earned the LL.B. degree from Columbia University. His involvement in both the New York Colored Mission and its Central Bureau was testi- mony to his dedication to racial advancement. The Colored Mission and the Central Bureau operated child care centers, employment bureaus, clubs for boys, temporary lodging facilities for the migrants from the South, and industrial training programs. Wood ultimately became the League's president, occupying this position until the 1940s.

Among other whites in the NUL were Paul Cravath, whose father was president of Fisk University, a Negro liberal arts college; Edwin R.A. Seligman, who was one of Haynes's professors at Columbia University; and Felix Adler, the founder of the Ethical Culture Society of New York. Adler organized lectures and discussion groups that acquainted employers with the immediate conditions that their employees were forced to live under.[10] He let it be known that private philanthropy of necessity had to step into the breach caused by the inability of municipal and state institu- tions to "cover the needs of the deserving."[11] One writer recorded that Adler and the "New York Society [Ethical Culture] must be given credit for starting the settlement work in the cities of this country."[12]

Other whites who assisted in the founding of the NLUCAN also deserve mention. Algeron S. Frissell, chairman of the Board, Fifth Avenue Bank, was a member of the New York City Board of Education (1901–05), and held the post of treasurer of the Civil Service Reform Association. In addition, Frissell was a member of the Hampton Association, a fund-raising agency of Hampton Institute. Frissell supported Hampton Institute because his brother Hollis was president of the industrial school.[13] A graduate of Wellesley College in Massachusetts who earned the Ph.D. degree from the University of Chicago, Sophonisba P. Breckinridge actively participated in both the NLUCAN (the name was changed to the National Urban League in 1917) and the NAACP. Breckinridge officiated as secretary of the Immi- grant's Protective League, was president of the Chicago Woman's City

Club, and was vice president of the National American Women's Association. The daughter of a U.S. Congressman, Florence Kelley earned the B. Litt. degree from Cornell University and the LL.B. degree from Northwestern University. She had been secretary of the National Consumer's League, and Chief Inspector of Factories, New York State; and she exhibited a profound dedication to the activities undertaken by Hull House in Chicago and the Henry Street Settlement House in New York City.

Some of the white founders of NLUCAN were known for their political views. John Haynes Holmes was a founder of both the NAACP and the NLUCAN, and was pastor of the Unitarian Church of the Messiah in New York.[14] Charles F. Kellogg noted that Holmes was a "Socialist with keen interest in social questions. He was an ardent supporter of the rights of labor, equality for women and social justice."[15] As an indication of his socialist leanings, Holmes predicted that industrial conditions in America would deteriorate to the point that Negro and white workers, of necessity, would organize "into one impenetrable phalanx against the greed and exploitation of the capitalistic class."[16] Moreover, he believed that a new social consciousness had resulted in a new conception of the city, but held that the city's problems were compounded by a decaying family structure. He called on the social worker to seize control of the cities from politicians and businessmen.[17] The views of Elizabeth Walton and Jane Addams were the basis for their support of social justice. Both women supported racial advancement and racial equality. Mary White Ovington, who was dedicated to the work of the NAACP and the NLUCAN, confessed to John Haynes Holmes that she was a profound Communist, adding, however, that a "communist state would destroy the basis of the civilization under which [she] lived and under which [she] had enjoyed an unusually happy life."[18]

Negroes who contributed to the formation of the National Urban League, like its white founders, also were at the top of the professional world. Kelly Miller, an academic dean at Howard University, belonged to both the NAACP and the NUL. He believed that Negroes and whites relied too much upon "education to accomplish results which lie outside of the circle of its aims."[19] Rather than repudiate its effectiveness as a racial uplift instrument, Miller underscored the need for Negroes to develop education that would provide for wise and competent self-direction. He reasoned that both classical and industrial education had a decided role to play in the development of opportunities and training for the Negro population.[20] George Cleveland Hall, a physician, organized the Civic League of Chicago in 1897, which sought economic, social, and political uplift.[21] Serving on the National Boards of both the NAACP and the NUL, Mary Church Terrell was the first Negro woman to sit on a Board of Education (Washington, D.C.).[22]

Fred R. Moore, according to William H. Baldwin, III, was elected to the

NUL Board as Booker T. Washington's unofficial contact.[23] But his loyalty to the Tuskegee founder has been questioned. Moore also was a close friend of the Reverend Reverdy C. Ransom, who was a critic of Washington and a charter member of the Niagara Movement (1905). Moore "boomed Ransom for a bishopric in the AME Church at the very time Washington was trying to head off the effort."[24] Therefore it appears that Moore's links to Washington were nebulous. Adam Clayton Powell, Sr., was a board member of the NAACP and the NUL, and was an active and astute politician in New York City. Elected seven times as president of the Afro-American Council, Bishop Alexander Walters swung the organization out of the Washington orbit. He was a member of the NAACP, and president of the AME Zion Church's Industrial and Development Corporation in New York City.[25]

The Negro and white elites who founded the NUL were a diverse group. Their ideological bent and proposed solutions for the Negro condition spread across the political spectrum. A number of them had no formal ties with Tuskegee Institute and Booker T. Washington. Others claimed no loyalty to Du Bois and the politically oriented NAACP. But they shared a common goal, which was to improve the health, living, educational, recreational, and social conditions of the urban masses. Toward this end, they both challenged and operated within the political system, and consistently worked for and with the poor to improve life chances in an increasingly complex and hostile society.

The urban reformers in the NAACP and the NUL supported both political and economic equality for Negroes. Thus there was and is a discernible overlapping of ideology and membership in the two organizations. The NAACP and the NUL of course recruited their leaders and members from the same group—from people with the same or nearly identical backgrounds in education, class, and dedication to racial reform and racial advancement. Social workers and teachers, for example, held membership in the NAACP, and Northern Negro lawyers joined the NUL.[26] Receiving the LL.B. degree from Ohio Northern University, Lawrence O. Payne was a member of the Cleveland Urban League.[27] Matthew Washington Bullock, who earned the LL.B. degree from Harvard University, was appointed the executive secretary of the Boston Urban League.[28] A graduate of the University of Chicago Law School, Earl B. Dickerson was vice president of the Chicago Urban League.[29] Sadie T. Mossell Alexander served on the boards of the NAACP and the NUL; her LL.B. degree was earned at the University of Pennsylvania School of Law.[30] Serving as the Chicago Urban League's director of research for a number of years, Milton J. Sampson was a graduate of the Chicago Kent School of Law.[31] The number of Northern Negro lawyers who worked in the Urban League Movement is too exhaustive to list here.

Historians, social scientists, and others offer conflicting interpretations on the Urban League. The most important of these deals with the Urban League's ideological orientation. Three historians insist that the ideological roots of the Urban League are traceable to the influence of Booker T. Washington.[32] But not all scholars agree that Washington's racial ideology was central to the NUL. One has said that both the NAACP and the NUL

> were manifestations of the break from the old leadership of Booker T. Washington and his virtues of rural life, of salvation through lowly labor well and willingly done, of cultivation of decency, sobriety, and manual skills so as to win the acceptance of the white world, of gradualism by such small steps that it seemed blacks could never reach social or political equality. The new organizations showed the ascendancy of Du Bois's leadership, of a whole new school of blacks who taught self-respect and insisted on equal rights and opportunities in education, labor and every other field of life.[33]

Other scholarly publications also echo the view that Washington's racial ideology was not the basis for the Urban League. A political scientist wrote:

> The history of protest in the twentieth century may be viewed as an accumulation of the effective strategies, beginning with the basically educational approach which the NAACP and the Urban League followed upon their founding in 1909 and 1910, respectively, adding the turn to the effective legal means of the NAACP during the 1930s.[34]

In characterizing the NUL, two political scientists asserted that both the NUL and the NAACP "reacted against Booker T. Washington's acceptance of the inferior status of the Negro, and both [have] worked closely with white liberals."[35] The NUL, wrote one student of Negro history, took "its place beside the NAACP as one of the two major betterment and protest organizations in the country."[36]

Not only is there scholarly disagreement on the NUL's ideological basis but also on the NUL's position on Negro migration. Did the NUL's prototypes believe, like Washington, that Negroes should remain in the South?[37] A careful examination of the literature shows that between 1905 and 1910, the social service organizations working in Negro New York cautioned migrants against moving to Northern cities unless "provisions had been made for a job in advance."[38] As for the NUL's position on Negro migration, two policy statements were issued between 1919 and 1925 on the issue. In 1919 the NUL reaffirmed the right of Negroes "to seek more promising opportunities and a fairer measure of justice wherever [they] believed they can be found."[39] In 1925 the Urban League claimed that it did not "encourage Negroes as a group to leave the South or stay in the South. It gives attention to making conditions better for Negroes wherever they go."[40] In the final analysis, the NUL's prototypes and the NUL itself did not encourage Negroes to remain in the rural South, as did Washington.

The assertion that acrimony existed between NUL and NAACP officials from 1911 to 1940 looms as large as that which ties the NUL's migration policy to Washington's racial ideology.[41] But the correspondence between NUL and NAACP officials between 1911 and 1940 does not show that the two civil rights organizations and their leaders were at war with each other. In 1915 Eugene K. Jones invited officials of the NAACP to attend a meeting, at which time the residents of Harlem were informed "of opportunities for improvement in conditions afforded by public and private welfare organizations having offices or branches in the district."[42] At the height of the migration during World War I, NAACP and NUL officials undertook a study from which a policy statement was formulated. The policy statement underscored the determination of both organizations to work jointly in an effort to address the "problems arising out of the influx of southern colored labor into northern industrial centers."[43] A thorough examination of archival collections did not uncover any data to indicate that there was acrimony between the NUL and the NAACP between 1911 and 1940.

The NUL was an authentic product of the Progressive Era. This does not suggest that Washington's racial ideology was totally meaningless in urban America, or that the NUL founders were either Washington's friends or enemies. But the fact that the NUL, from the outset, called for an end to segregation and racial discrimination in industry meant that its and Washington's views of the Negroes' place in America were not identical.

The creation of the NUL and the NAACP represented a major break with the nineteenth-century Southern and rural ideologies and tactics that delimited the Negroes' immediate place and status in American society. Both organizations looked to the "talented tenth" of the race to lead the search for equality. The Negroes in the NUL and the NAACP demanded nothing less than equality and equal justice. They rejected the notion that Negroes' alleged inferiority was the source of their problems. Their belief was that the Negro problem stemmed from past and present treatment at the hands of the larger society. The Negro intellectuals and the white Progressives both agreed that problems such as ignorance and poverty were the result of inherent weaknesses in the society. But the Negro and white founders of the NUL realized that positive changes in the society would not be forthcoming until the powerful institutions and the pillars of society agreed that change was needed. Moreover, they understood that full equality for Negroes was unachievable overnight. Hence their strategy of change was to use the institutions of society to convince people of a need for change, and to impart to the urban masses middle-class values. They saw in those values a means of uniting the disparate groups of society. Achieving that unity in urban America became a challenge for both the urban Negro and white reformers of the Progressive Era.

II

Psychologists, social workers, and urban racial reformers used the cities to test their theories on how to improve relations between different people. Indeed the problems of the cities cut across racial, ethnic, and religious lines. The social workers who were interested in the problems of city life compared the problems of Negroes and the European immigrants. Trained observers traced the historical development of the debilitating conditions that were unique to urban life, and they theorized on probable future trends should they not be resolved. The rise of sociology was in response to social conditions that were ever present in American cities. People of various backgrounds, cultures, classes, religions, and value systems had been thrown together without any consideration of these differences. The NUL's founders viewed scientific social work as a tool for downgrading racial and class differences, and an instrument for finding solutions to the problems of unstable family life, poverty, illiteracy, and the like.

The development of sociology and the training of social workers expedited observation, research, and comparison. Sociology and scientific social work were in their infancy at the birth of the Progressive Era. Du Bois referred to sociology and scientific social work as being "always wearisome, often aimless, without well-settled principles and guiding lines, and subject ever to pertinent criticism."[44] But sociology and scientific social work had advanced by 1911 to the point at which the Urban League's Negro and white founders could conclude with a high degree of certainty that the Negro problem in the cities could be viewed as a relationship between conditions and actions. Hence the NUL launched studies of the Negro condition in New York and other urban centers.

The NLUCAN's staff continued the sociological studies of urban Negro populations that were initiated by the NLPCW, the CIICN, and the CUCANNY. Most of their efforts were directed at identifying the problems arising out of urbanization, inequality, and economic discrimination. In the wake of these studies, the NUL staff formulated programs to improve Negro workers' relationship with labor unions in order to negate prohibitory legislation and traditional sentiments that barred Negroes from participation in labor unions, and to treat ills that were associated with city life.[45] In sum, the NUL leaders and the Board concluded that the Negro problem demanded "study and investigation rather than passion and obscurantism."[46]

Haynes's responsibilities as architect of the social work program at Fisk University kept him away from the National Office. Therefore the search began for a competent Negro to supervise the day-to-day operation and the organizational work of the NUL. This search led to Eugene K. Jones, who in 1911 was named the NUL's Field Secretary. Born on July 30, 1885, in Richmond, Virginia, Jones was a graduate of Virginia Union University (a Negro private college in Richmond) and Cornell University. A social worker by training, as was required by the NUL's guidelines for staffing the Urban Leagues, Jones also assumed the post of chairman of the Flushing, New York, Education Committee.[47] He had been an instructor of vocational education at the Central High School, Louisville, Kentucky, before accepting the job of Field Secretary with the NUL.

Jones proceeded with caution, realizing that Haynes was the NUL's chief executive officer. One of the points that Haynes and Jones did agree upon was that the Urban League was in need of financial support. They turned to the nation's industrialists for funds to underwrite the Urban League's activities, because contributions from the Community Chests and individuals were not enough to support the Urban League. A former NUL executive secretary recalled that only a few of America's philanthropic foundations and wealthy families and individuals made sizeable contributions to the Urban League between 1911 and 1940. They were the Rockefeller Foundation, the Spelman Fund, the Davidson Fund, the Carnegie Corporation, and the Rockefeller brothers. The Rockefellers contributed about $2,000 annually; donations from the Carnegie Corporation ranged from $5,000 to $15,000 annually. It was not until 1941, according to Lester B. Granger, the League's second executive director, that the Rosemore Fund included the organization on its list of gift receivers.[48] Obviously the NUL's formative years were lean ones in terms of finances. In 1915, for example, the expenditures of the National Office amounted to a mere $24,953. By 1920 it spent $27,713.[49] Big business was not financially generous to the NUL from 1911 to 1941.

The creation of Urban League affiliates and their membership in Community Chests broadened the NUL's financial base. The affiliates first had to qualify for membership in the Chests. Hence the National Board of Directors bided its time, not anxious to establish branches until a trained social worker was available to head each local, and until adequate funding was a certainty.

Affiliation with the NUL required the following: (1) the creation of a provisional committee comprised of Negroes and whites; (2) the election of a chairman; (3) the selection of a nominating committee that submitted names from which to choose a permanent local board; (4) a constitution committee to draft a set of by-laws, subject to the approval of the NUL's National Board; (5) a budget committee; (6) the selection of a permanent executive, chosen from a list of candidates supplied by the NUL (the executive director generally was a trained social worker); (7) a formal review of the proposed affiliate's application by the NUL National Board; (8) and, finally, a fund-raising drive under the direction of the permanent local Board.[50]

Affiliates were required to secure operating funds for two consecutive years prior to submitting a formal application for membership in a Community Chest. But membership in a Chest was not automatic. First, the affiliate had to convince the citywide philanthropic agency's Board that it was indeed a legitimate social service agency. Private philanthropic agencies in the cities of the North had a long history of meeting the needs of the poor, and the earliest affiliates, which were in the North, encountered little difficulty in gaining membership in a Chest.

The reverse was true in the South. That the Southern affiliates, in contrast to the Northern Urban Leagues, were not well received by Community Chests is easily explained. As the NUL's integrationist thrust won wide currency, Southern white supporters of League activities endeavored to disassociate themselves from the work of the National Office. In New Orleans the Community Chest's Board delayed the creation of an NUL affiliate by supporting denominational activities, and by refusing to fund nonsectarian work among poor Negroes.[51] In Jacksonville, Florida, whites friendly to the local Urban League insisted that it be named the Negro Welfare League. They were fearful of intimidation by the Ku Klux Klan if it was revealed that the local social service agency was an affiliate of the NUL.[52] The NUL's officials referred to the problems encountered by the Southern affiliates, when it was revealed that they were a part of the Urban League Movement, as "Northern Negro Hysteria."[53] At the same time, however, officials in the National Office could not ignore the fact that public acknowledgment of affiliation with the NUL was a potentially explosive issue in some Southern cities. Hence it was not unusual for NUL officials to make studies in Southern cities under the guise of representatives of Tuskegee Institute.[54] The National Board rarely objected to this arrangement. The important thing was that the Southern whites did not equate the NUL with Washington's program of racial advancement. And neither did the NUL officials.

Local affiliates' Boards, in contrast to local NAACP chapters, determined the course of action for their prospective agencies. They were semiautonomous bodies. The NUL Board could terminate a local's affiliate status for two reasons: (1) If high social work standards were not followed; and (2) if there was reason to believe that a local would discredit the work of the NUL. Indeed the NUL's affiliates were at liberty to disagree with policies emanating from the National Office. A few affiliates' executive directors and Boards have been more vocal than others. Traditionally, affiliates in New York City and Chicago have been the most autonomous of the group.[55] The fact that locals received most of their funding from Community Chests and local donors made them responsive to local racial attitudes. The National Office's power to terminate affiliation was not a particular concern of the locals.

The National Urban League addressed national questions, and the affiliates concerned themselves with local issues. Often it was the executive directors who decided which problems required extensive study and analysis. The Boards, however, were not rubber stamps for the programs and policies desired or formulated by the executive directors. Therefore it is an exercise in futility, according to one person long involved in the Urban League Movement, for any historian to compare the powers held by the Boards (national and local) with those exercised by the executive directors.[56] The executive directors ran the Urban Leagues. They, rather than the Boards, set the agenda for Board meetings, provided their nominal superiors with most of the pertinent information available to them, made policy recommendations, and carried out or refused to carry out policy directives adopted by the Boards.[57] The Boards either approved or disapproved of the policies and programs developed by the executive directors and therefore prevented a consolidation of power in the offices of the Urban League executive directors.

The Urban League Boards held veto power over the executive secretaries' decisions, programs, and policies. Because the Boards were generally comprised of a white majority, scores of urban Negroes questioned the work of the Urban League Movement. Urban Negroes—intellectuals, the middle classes, and the masses—who did not join the Urban League Movement were often its harshest critics. They objected to the fact that the Negro Urban Leaguers entrusted the destiny of Negro America to the white occupational elites. They were quick to point out the programs and strategies of the Urban League Movement would neither meet the needs of an expanding urban Negro population nor assist it in realizing its aspirations. Indeed the Negroes' rising expectations were the result of their migration to the Southern and Northern urban centers.

III

The mass migration of Negroes into the Northern industrial centers, commencing about 1914, placed stresses and strains on the NUL and its affiliates. Some one million or more Negroes crossed state lines between 1914 and 1925. Urban League affiliates, rather than the NUL, shouldered the burden of addressing the needs of the migrant population. They sponsored day nurseries, clubs for boys, girls, and mothers, ran courses for training school janitors, domestics, and people seeking employment in clerical positions, trades, and the like. Some of the problems facing the Negro migrants from the South reflected "what happens to a people who have been systematically oppressed and denied access to skills and opportunity."[58]

National Urban League officials were forced to rethink their programs in light of rising migration, and in response to additional work-force needs arising during the World War I era. Jones's meteoric rise in the League as a coequal of George Haynes in some ways complicated matters as regards policies and new directions. Haynes steadfastly believed that social work among Negroes was the NUL's primary task. Jones argued that social work among Negroes could be strengthened by vocational guidance. Moreover, he was of the opinion that the NUL and its affiliates had a decided role to play in the cultivating of urban black leaders.[59] Jones's views prevailed, and in 1917 he was given the title of executive director, an administrative change initiated by the Board, which irked Haynes. Vocational guidance increasingly became one of the NUL's major program interests.

The National Urban League's eventual emphasis on vocational guidance has been mistakenly equated with industrial training, a type of education associated with the Tuskegee Movement. One NUL official wrote that "with many the two are synonymous. Proper vocational guidance should be as useful in directing inclinations for architectural drawing and medicine as well as for blacksmithing and cabinetmaking."[60]

Vocational guidance conformed to the NUL's new direction as the war industries, heretofore the domain of white workers, employed blacks for the first time. As Robert R. Moton, Washington's successor at Tuskegee, recorded, "a great many unexpected results came out of the war [;] one of the earliest and most encouraging was the opening of industrial opportunities for Negroes in the North."[61] But these employment chances were only temporary. Craft unions, with few exceptions, would not admit Negroes, and therefore they were not a permanent part of the wartime prosperity. Some 500,000 Negroes worked in war industries but only about 85,000 carried union cards in 1920.

The war's end led to a large-scale dismissal of Negro American industrial workers. The single bright spot was that in mining, auto manufacturing, steel, and meat packing they were not subjected to wholesale dismissals. The NUL of course did not accept the return to prewar employment policies. In 1918 it created committees to lobby for the Negro American's industrial rights. One committee endeavored to persuade the American Federation of Labor (AFL) executive council to abolish racial discrimination within its ranks. The other committee sought out those with influence in the Labor Department, urging that the federal government underwrite its programs so that both the NUL and the local Urban Leagues could continue their industrial programs among the urban Negro population.[62]

The two NUL committees, as it turned out, had little to show for their efforts. Yet Fred Moore, a member of the special committee that appeared before the AFL to argue the Negroes' case, informed his fellow Board members that "various problems had been sifted out, and that effective co-operation had been obtained."[63] Moore's optimism was based on these promises from AFL officials: AFL leaders would refuse to be banqueted in Southern towns whenever Negroes had been barred from union functions; and Samuel Gompers, the AFL president, had assured NUL officials that Negro workers' opinions would be sought in advance of any policy statement issued by the AFL that clarified "the attitude of labor organizations toward Negro labor."[64]

It is unclear whether or not either AFL promise to NUL officials was carried out to the letter. Even if they were lived up to, Negro laborers received few benefits from them, because most Negroes in 1918 remained in the South. The AFL did not challenge the South's racial policies to any degree. In the South, as in the North, the racial issue was indeed explosive and firmly entrenched in the minds of a large segment of the working population. While the NUL's task was to improve racial relations both in the North and in the South, it could accomplish little without the cooperation of the unions. Yet in 1919 the NUL developed the machinery for addressing the labor problems found in the Southern cities. Jesse O. Thomas was named to the post of Southern Field Organizer, National Urban League, to undertake projects that would open employment opportunities for Negroes residing in the cities of the South.

Thomas was born at Summit, Mississippi, and was graduated from Tuskegee Institute. Following graduation, he served as field agent for Tuskegee, resigning the position after holding it for four years to accept the principalship of Voorhees Normal and Industrial School in South Carolina.[65] During the Great War, Thomas served as Examiner of Negro Labor for the U.S. Government, Labor Department, in New York City. His training made him well qualified to be the Southern organizer of the NUL, and his views on the Negroes' place in society mirrored those of Jones and other NUL officials.

Thomas was uncompromising on the rights of Negro laborers. His views often irked his immediate supervisor, George Haynes. At one point Haynes informed Thomas that while his political ideas and convictions were his own, his connection with the Department of Labor did not give him a license to further "any kind of political activity and propaganda."[66]

Thomas's work in the Division of Negro Economics enabled him to view the Negro's industrial problems objectively and scientifically. Employment opportunities for the expanding Northern Negro population, according to Thomas, were unsatisfactory. In 1919 employment managers in Long Island City, New York, declined to hire colored men on the ground that their introduction in factories would lead to disturbances.[67]

The only company in the city that employed a Negro was the National Casket Company, and he was a coal passer. Women in Long Island City and in other Northern cities faced similar experiences.

A return to the status quo sparked anger among Negroes. The Red Summer of 1919 resulted from racial polarization in America.[68] On the one hand, urban Negroes would not countenance any policy that did not respect their rights as Americans. On the other hand, the white population did not share the view that equality in every respect should be accorded the Negro population.

League officials of course viewed the racial riots with concern. They conflicted with the organization's scheme of orderly and constructive change. Hence the National Board proposed programs that, as it turned out, were only palliatives. Roger N. Baldwin, a Board member, president of the American Civil Liberties Union and a racial activist, made these suggestions in the hope of calming racial tensions: (1) the NUL should consider sponsoring mass meetings, at which race relations experts would air their thoughts; and (2) the NUL should underwrite parades and pageants to combat the hysteria surrounding the riots.[69] Baldwin's proposals were not acted upon; the Board voted to poll the affiliate Urban Leagues before deciding on appropriate action to take in the wake of the urban riots. While the riots died of their own volition, the problems causing them remained. The racial violence that characterized the Red Summer of 1919, and the anti-Negro sentiments of union and nonunion whites as regards Negro employment, were not fitting ways to close the Progressive Era.

The year 1920 marked the NUL's tenth anniversary. What did the NUL have to show for its ten years of existence? A former NUL executive secretary said this of the NUL's first ten years:

> For the wartime shut-off of immigration from abroad gave American farm labor in the South a chance at better paid industrial work. The Urban League promptly called industry-management's attention to the ability and availability of Negro workers. It is true that this first big Urban League success was largely cancelled out by the end of the war. Pressures by the new Ku Klux Klan, trade union opposition to Negro employment and willingness of management to go along with this opposition—these sent a majority of the new Negro industrial workers back to the ranks of casual and menial employment. It was then that the bitter saying originated—"The Negro worker, last to be hired and first to be fired."[70]

Between 1917 and 1919, the urban Negro in the North, and to some degree in the South, briefly tasted the better wages that industrial concerns offered. Since they were quickly lost, it became the task of the Urban League Movement in general and the NUL in particular to formulate new programs and policies for waging a more effective war on unions and industry. These new policies and programs would be instituted, beginning in 1920 and continuing between the two world wars.

4

The Urban League Movement from Harding to Roosevelt, 1921–1940

The few hard-earned gains that Negroes had achieved upon entering the industrial world during the war years had been lost by 1921. This "Return to Normalcy" was indeed a bitter reality for Negroes. The officials of the NUL and the Urban League affiliates knew that the bitter reality would lead to increased racial tensions in America, particularly in the cities. Neither the NUL nor its affiliates, however, were to blame for the "Return to Normalcy." And they did not attempt to claim sole credit for the Negroes' limited and temporary gains that had been realized during the war.

The changes in the Negroes' occupational status had been realized because the war had halted the influx of Southern and Central European immigrants. As it turned out, the "Old Americans" opposed any resumption of the magnitude of the pre-World War I immigration. They feared that the arrival of masses of Central and Southern European immigrants would threaten Anglo-Saxon supremacy in America. Their fears ultimately were expressed in congressional legislation that placed quotas on the number of immigrants whose country was located in Southern and Central Europe.

By the 1920s both the "Old Americans" and the "New Americans" also feared the Southern Negro migrant. But the Congress lacked the authority to stem the flow of Southern Negroes to the Northern cities. Hence thousands of rural and urban Southern Negroes migrated northward in search of higher wages, improved living conditions, greater educational opportunities, and a fairer measure of justice than found in the rural South. In the wake of their arrival to the North, Negroes quickly learned that equality did not exist.

The injustices and the racial discrimination found in the Northern cities placed additional responsibilities on the Urban League Movement. It not only had to assist the migrants in acculturating to Northern and urban lifestyles, but it also had to bear the responsibility of finding employment for them. In 1921 the Urban League Movement was simply not equipped to handle most of the problems that confronted urban Negroes. When the NUL was founded in 1911, the magnitude of the migration of the Southern Negroes during the war could not have been anticipated. Its programs of course had been shaped in accordance with its founders' views of the needs of a slowly expanding urban Negro population. In the wake of the Great Migration and the "Return to Normalcy," the Urban League had to rethink and reshape its strategies accordingly.

Chapter 4 discusses the ways in which the political climate of the 1920s and 1930s was instrumental in altering the basic philosophical thrust of the Urban League Movement. It examines the factors that led Negroes to shift allegiance from the Republican Party to the Democratic Party. This chapter shows how the Urban League broke new ground during the 1920s and 1930s by attempting to reform existing governmental structures. It also examines attempts by the Urban League to wage war on industry, labor, and management, in an effort to end the discriminatory hiring practices against Negroes. And finally, it looks at the Urban League's assaults on the New Deal, and the extent to which some Urban League officials were willing to cooperate with and eventually to join the Roosevelt team.

I

Between 1921 and 1940 the NUL and the Urban League affiliates bore the task of popularizing the need for equality of opportunity in housing and employment, and in resolving explosive racial tensions in urban America. As a manifestation of its new direction, the NUL and the affiliates undertook lobbying efforts in an attempt to reform existing governmental structures. The Urban League also repeatedly tried to convince AFL unions to drop their bars against membership for Negroes, and pressed employers to hire qualified Negroes.

This change of direction can be seen in five resolutions that were passed by the delegates in attendance at the 1920 NUL national conference. First, attention was called to labor's failure to accept Negro workers into the skilled unions. Second, League officials were directed to seek assurances from the AFL that it would promote Negro membership in labor unions. Third, the NUL Board was instructed to seek AFL cooperation in the promotion of a campaign that would educate all workers to the fact that discrimination by race, creed, or color was alien to and disruptive of the workers' goals. And finally, NUL officials were encouraged to meet regularly with AFL officials, in the hope of resolving longstanding differences;

and they were urged to monitor the enforcement of antidiscriminatory laws in several of the Northern states.[1]

The 1920 NUL resolutions, like the hard work undertaken by Urban League officials, did not resolve the problems facing the Negro workers. Hence the NUL sought the assistance of the federal government in opening employment opportunities to Negroes and in assuring equality of opportunity in American life. Board members of the NUL attempted to convince the Congress that the life of the Department of Negro Economics should be extended. The Congress was reminded that it had been the Department that had placed Negroes in jobs heretofore closed to them, and that this noble deed should continue. Urban League officials' pleas did not convince enough Congressmen to vote in the affirmative on the Department, and it expired. Jones then sent out feelers to President Warren G. Harding, testing his views on racial equality.[2] Because the Urban League Movement lacked the power to force the President to at least consider its views on racial equality, Harding did not have to act.

There were eleven persons on the NUL's payroll when Harding was sworn in as the nation's chief executive in 1921. The combined expenditures of the NUL and the twenty Urban League affiliates amounted to $117,393, and their salaried employees numbered only seventy-seven persons. Considering the budget of the NUL and the League affiliates and their personnel, the job of protecting and expanding Negroes' economic opportunities obviously required external support. Harding seemed the logical person to whom the NUL should turn.

Harding did not join the NUL in urging equality for Negroes. He avoided the issue of racial equality. Addressing a crowd in Birmingham, Alabama, in 1921, President Harding called for equal educational opportunities for all Americans, economic justice, and the franchise for everyone who met the accepted qualifications. Harding eschewed social equality between the races, insisting that racial ambitions and pride, in and of themselves, would prompt natural segregation.

Urban League officials were dismayed by Harding's speech, which was nothing more than a capitulation to racism. Negroes had been and would continue to be denied equal opportunity, because whites argued that segregation was the only way to prevent social equality between the races. Negroes rejected the view that social equality and equality of opportunity were inextricably linked, and exhorted Harding to place the federal government behind the drive for equal justice. Harding's brief and tragic tenure in the White House relieved him of additional Urban League pressures.

Harding's replacement, Calvin Coolidge, received numerous requests from NUL officials to take positive actions on the Negro condition. In particular, he was asked to refer to Negro migration and the problems of employment in his initial State of the Union address to the Congress.[3] Coolidge made a fleeting reference to Negro migration, but he, like Harding, refrained from speaking boldly on equality and equal justice. Not discouraged, Robert R. Moton, an NUL board member, informed the Board that he would meet with Coolidge and discuss the problems of migration and racial discrimination. The President seemed receptive to Moton's idea that a presidential commission should be established to study migration, but he did not follow through on implementing it. The NUL officials were left with the correct view that they and the Negro population at large did not have a friend in the White House.

Coolidge's failure to embrace equality of opportunity and equal justice forced the NUL to continue in its efforts to win union and labor officials' support for improving Negroes' industrial conditions. As during World War I, but more forcefully, NUL officials endeavored to expand Negroes' industrial opportunities. They did not remain hopeful, however, of placing Negroes in unions and industry *en masse.* But if even one Negro was either admitted into an AFL union or placed in industry, NUL officials believed, it would dispel a widespread opinion found among union members and employers alike that "Negroes [were] incapable of doing those jobs requiring a high degree of skill."[4] It was primarily for this reason that NUL officials incorporated vocational training and guidance into the program thrust of the NUL, a ploy that Jones should be credited with popularizing.

Jones's interest in vocational guidance and education has already been documented. But it is unclear whether it was Jones's idea to establish a national office of industrial relations; several of the League affiliates had industrial relations secretaries as early as 1917. In any event, Jones made public the plans to create a national department of industrial relations in 1921. John D. Rockefeller, Jr., offered aid in support of the national industrial department, pledging $4,500 a year for three years.[5] Jones projected the amount of $9,000 as a reasonable annual figure for operating the new department.

In 1925 the NUL announced the creation of the Department of Industrial Relations. T. Arnold Hill was named director. Born on August 23, 1888, in Richmond, Virginia, and a graduate of Virginia Union University in Richmond, Hill also studied sociology and economics at New York University. He was executive secretary of the "Chicago Urban League during the Chicago Riots of 1919 and took part in restoring peace."[6]

Under Hill's guidance, the Industrial Relations Department sought to improve relations with the AFL, and set for itself other tasks as well. It standardized the local affiliates' employment agencies in the hope of providing employers with a more efficient group of minority employees. Hill and his staff scientifically studied the job market in order to steer workers to vocations in which they were needed. The Industrial Relations Department also worked directly with large industrial plants in cities with and without a local affiliate in an attempt to procure greater opportunity for work and advancement on the job. Finally, the National Industrial Relations secretary sought to distribute Negro labor so as to prevent the congestion and suffering that resulted from unsatisfactory housing conditions.

The program of the NUL's Industrial Relations Department could not be implemented without the cooperation of the AFL. Thus in 1925 Hill asked for and received an invitation to consult with officials of the national craft unions. One conference, held in Kansas City, Missouri, took up discrimination and segregation in the constitution of the Brotherhood of Railway and Steamship Clerks, Freight Handlers, Express and Station Employees Union. The AFL in this instance insisted that removing the "white-only" clause from the union's constitution would reduce racial tensions. However, the AFL officials did not order the local to remove the white-only clause from its constitution. Therefore nothing concrete came out of the Kansas City discussions.

Hill did not break off discussions with AFL leaders in the wake of the Kansas City fiasco. He traveled to Washington, D.C., for a meeting with representatives of the various craft unions. He explained to them the desirability of organizing separate unions where state laws called for segregation, and integrated unions in those states with statutes that forbade discrimination based on race, color, or religion. Although the AFL officials listened attentively to Hill, they stopped short of responding positively to NUL overtures. Nonetheless, Hill reported to his superiors that future conferences with AFL officials would improve relations between Negro workers and the craft unions.

Subsequent meetings with Hugh Frayne, an AFL representative, did not improve Negro-AFL relations. Throughout the 1920s, Hill's contacts with union officials sharpened his perspective on the obstacles to Negroes' acceptance in craft unions. Under no circumstances were white workers and AFL local union leaders willing to drop the color bars. White laborers viewed Negroes as competitors and believed that their admission into unions would destroy the security that unions offered white workers. Despite these attitudes, William A. Green, president of the AFL, argued that the policy of the AFL for forty years had been that of equality within labor's ranks.

The AFL president and executive council's declaration that they did not bar the admission of Negroes in the craft unions was of little comfort to NUL officials. Nor was the AFL's pledge that it would support the creation of separate unions for Negroes. Hill repeatedly reminded AFL leaders that the NUL was not concerned with the placement of Negroes as Negroes, but rather "the removal of traditional restrictions against Negroes as workers."[7] The NUL's attack on organized labor's hiring policies was two-pronged. It sought to remove traditional restrictions against Negro workers by calling for integration in cities outside the South, and it also maintained the hope of removing the lingering vestiges of a slave psychology from the minds of the Negro migrants. In the final analysis, NUL officials resolved that white racism coupled with a residual slave psychology had chained Negro Americans "to certain occupations on the lower levels and therefore [inhibited] their industrial advancement."[8]

The NUL experienced little success in challenging white racism and removing from the minds of the Negro migrants a residual slave psychology during the years 1921 to 1940. It would take years of residence in urban America for both the Negroes and whites to change their attitudes about race. Realizing that altering Negroes' and whites' attitudes required time and patience, the NUL expanded its vocational training and guidance programs. But continued white resistance to the ideals of justice and equality forced more and more Urban League officials to rethink and revamp their programs of racial advancement. During the 1920s, for example, The Armstrong Association of Philadelphia and the Akron (Ohio) Association for Colored Community, two Urban League affiliates, discontinued the placement of Negroes as domestic workers altogether. The Armstrong Association reported in 1929 that it had found jobs for some 1,030 Negroes in the basic industries of the city, and the Akron Urban League (Association for Colored Community) had placed 634 Negroes in permanent jobs, 95 percent of whom were in industry.[9]

Not all of the Urban League affiliates had such glowing success to show in placing Negroes in industry. Indeed the inability of the Urban League Movement to alter dramatically the industrial picture placed it in disfavor with many urban Negroes. Their view of the Urban League Movement was that it had failed miserably in communicating to the urban masses that it saw their problems in economic terms.

Negro leaders who effectively communicated to the urban Negro masses that they saw their problems in economic terms subscribed either to Black Nationalism or to socialism. Spearheading the attacks on the integration programs of the NUL and the NAACP were A. Philip Randolph, Chandler Owen, and Marcus Garvey. Randolph and Owen were socialists; Garvey was a Black Nationalist. Randolph received his undergraduate training at Cookman Institute in Jacksonville, Florida, and attended night school at the City College of New York. Owen had studied law and was an instructor of economics and sociology at the Rand School of Social Science in New York (later named the New School for Social Research). He was also president of the National Association for the Promotion of Labor Unionism Among Negroes, a socialist-oriented labor organization. In addition to organizing street meetings and holding political discussions for groups of Negro college students, Randolph and Owen also founded the monthly socialist magazine, *The Messenger,* and attempted to radicalize urban Negro workers. They also promoted the solidarity of labor across racial lines. In this regard, the ideology of the NUL was in total agreement with that of Randolph and Owen. The two Negro social-ists, however, repeatedly assailed urban social and economic programs, particularly the political program of the NAACP and Du Bois's racial ideology. Owen and Randolph alleged that Du Bois was the only "world" leader who attempted to lead an oppressed people, and at the same time condemned revolution.[10]

Randolph's and Owen's vitriolic attacks on the programs of racial ad-vancement bodies in general and the NAACP and Du Bois in particular did not take hold among the urban masses. However, Garvey's caustic remarks about the NUL and the NAACP gained wide currency in urban centers. Born during August of 1887 in Jamaica, British West Indies, Garvey came to the United States in 1916, traveling extensively up and down the East Coast. Establishing headquarters in the Black Metropolis of New York City (Harlem), Garvey's program of racial uplift, racial solidar-ity, separatism, and Pan-Africanism attracted considerable attention for nearly a decade.

Garvey believed that the program of the Universal Negro Improvement Association (UNIA) was a viable alternative to those of the NUL and the NAACP. He portrayed the NUL and NAACP as a haven for bourgeois Negro Americans, and their leaders as "weak-kneed and cringing . . . syco-phants to the white man."[11] Whatever the truths of his indictments of the NAACP and the NUL, Garvey's rise to prominence reflected a new mood among persons of African descent who also were urban residents. Submis-sion to white supremacy was unacceptable to the "New Negro." The rise of the Garvey Movement not only articulated Negroes' rejection of white supremacy but also signaled a growing disenchantment on the part of urban Negroes: separatism seemed an easier goal to achieve than did integration. Hence Garvey symbolized some Negroes' hopes of a better tomorrow and their disgust with the present.

The Garvey Movement took into account the Negroes' past, and their hopes of a better tomorrow. But the extent to which the urban masses agreed with Garvey that their status in America was linked directly to European colonialism in Africa is unclear.[12] It is, however, clear that they saw little chance of winning full equality and equal justice in a society that countenanced inequality and racial discrimination. Hence, among the ur-ban Negro masses, Black Nationalism was an acceptable alternative to integration.

The city, wrote Guy B. Johnson, "has been the birthplace of intense racial consciousness and of nationalism."[13] Racial consciousness can be expressed in many forms. Black Nationalism, for example, manifested itself well before the Civil War, as shown in Chapter 1; it also was present during the post-Civil War years. There is considerable truth in the statement:

> But history teaches us that the subordinate race, having tasted half-freedom and having sipped of the higher culture of the "superior" race, but finding the barriers set up against complete equality, turns to nationalism as a means of achieving its aspirations.[14]

In sum, the Garvey Movement was one of several manifestations of a racial consciousness nurtured in urban America, each of which had its good and bad points.

The growth of nationalism among urban Negroes was an outgrowth of increasing racial consciousness, and of the tensions existing between Negroes and whites.[15] Largely because of those tensions, the Garvey Movement afforded an asylum for individuals "who were dissatisfied with life for many reasons, which could in this case be attributed to their status as Negroes."[16]

Millions of Negroes of course were dissatisfied with their status. Yet not all of them were attracted to the Garvey Movement. Some directed their energies through the church, through secret organizations, through organizations for the betterment of conditions; others pressed for better educational facilities, for civil improvement, "for economic development and for greater participation in politics."[17] Still others, who were artistically talented, expressed their newfound racial consciousness through art, literature, and history. All were intent upon improving their own status and that of the Negro masses.

In one degree or another, the adherents of racial advancement subscribed to the basic value systems of the larger society. A quick look at Garvey, Randolph, and Owen seems to bear this out. Garvey seemingly admired the Protestant work ethic, and also created institutions in the UNIA that paralleled those found in the larger society. Randolph and Owen advised Negroes to reject capitalism and its institutions, but they hoped for the growth of "democracy" and its extension to Negroes. The three men, however, were viewed as radicals, illustrating the many uses of the term.

Garvey insisted that radical is a label assigned to people "who are endeavoring to get freedom."[18] Such a definition of a radical perhaps explains its application to Jones. A report on Negro radicalism, compiled by an unidentified Department of Justice investigator, questioned Jones's loyalty to America and its institutions. When the report was released to the public, League officials had little doubt that the executive director's name would be cleared. Board Member Julius Rosenwald publicly went to Jones's defense, disavowing the assertion that he was a subversive, or that the NUL was a communist organization.[19] Despite the Board's unreserved support of the

NUL and Jones, those in positions of responsibility in the NUL did not take the charges lightly. The Red Scare had created what seemed at the time a new and perhaps a permanent dimension of intolerance in America.

The collective incidents of racial, ethnic, religious, and political intolerance that characterized the Red Scare era and the 1920s were as much responses to past attitudes as they were hasty reactions to ill-conceived notions about Communists and radicals. Many Americans believed that unless the federal government crushed the Communists and radicals, America's democratic institutions would be destroyed. Particularly distressing to Negro leaders was the fact that there seemed to be a resurgence of hostility to all who were not Anglo-Saxon or white Protestant. Solutions to Negroes' problems in general and those unique to urban Negroes in particular, NUL officials presumably concluded, stood little chance of being realized in such an atmosphere as that associated with the Red Scare era and the decade of the 1920s. Despite this belief, NUL officials endeavored to keep Negroes' problems before the public. But the coverage given the work of the NUL and the ULM by newspapers and magazines was inadequate.

Perhaps it was during the 1920s that the NUL and the ULM first gave proper recognition to the value of publicity in the search for equality, with the creation of its own publication, *Opportunity*. Begun in 1923 under the editorship of Charles S. Johnson, a sociologist, *Opportunity* gave the work of the NUL and the ULM among urban Negroes wide exposure, and became an outlet for Negro writers, poets, and playwrights. But the emphasis given the fact that *Opportunity* served as an outlet for Negro writers seems to suggest that it was founded primarily for this purpose. Not so. Executive Director Jones perhaps best put the founding of *Opportunity* in a balanced perspective:

> The League feels that the very generous space which has been given it by the newspapers and magazines has been of great help. But the League should not and could not command as much space to express its ideals as the importance of its mission justifies. The reports on its investigations and research work alone call for considerable space if only the practical parts of its findings are presented. The League therefore has launched on a new venture which should have the wholehearted support and encouragement of all white and colored people who are interested in the scientific treatment of the "problem" and who wish to see more "cooperation" between the races.[20]

The launching of *Opportunity* was another manifestation of the NUL's new thrust. The magazine became a platform for both Negroes and whites for accepting or rejecting "American" values. *Opportunity* ultimately became the medium through which NUL officials gave wide publicity to their aims and ideals. No less important, *Opportunity* was used by NUL officials to create among the white population a positive attitude toward Negroes; to present objectively facts of Negro life; and "to make possible through an emphasis on frank and unbiased presentation of facts and views at least a dependable guide to action."[21] Between 1921 and 1940, the NUL's slogan, "Not Alms, but Opportunity," was a signal to businessmen, governmental officials, labor leaders, and organized and unorganized white laborers that Negroes expected their just share of America's riches.

II

During the 1920s, NUL officials sought the cooperation of the nation's major businesses in opening employment opportunities to Negro workers. Among the major industrial and white-collar businesses contacted were Standard Oil and the Metropolitan Life Insurance Company. NUL officials urged Standard Oil to consider hiring Negroes as salesmen, filling station managers, and demonstrators. In addition to offering its services in the identification of qualified persons to fill these positions, the NUL also reminded Standard Oil officials that a significant number of Negroes owned cars, heated their homes with oil, and purchased its products. Standard Oil's senior officials took the NUL's request under advisement, but they did not establish a national hiring policy. Rather they cooperated with the Urban League affiliates only when white opposition to Negroes working as salesmen, filling station managers, and demonstrators did not materialize. The only promise that Standard Oil made to the NUL was that it would review its hiring policies. Standard Oil ultimately disclosed that there were Negroes on its payroll, although it would not say what positions they held. Repeated attempts by the NUL to gain access to Standard Oil's personnel files were futile.[22]

The NUL's contacts with the Metropolitan Life Insurance Company's officers paralleled those with Standard Oil. Rumor had it that Metropolitan Life planned to scrap its policy of limiting Negro employment to janitorial positions. The League of course sought immediate clarification. A reply from Metropolitan Life informed NUL officers that it had no intention of scrapping its employment policies, and that Negroes would continue to be employed as janitors.[23]

Standard Oil's and Metropolitan Life's intransigence on the question of hiring Negroes further underscored NUL officials' belief that the Northern Negroes had to involve themselves in the political process if radical changes in the society were to be realized. Some changes had already been realized as a result of the growing Negro vote in the North. Jones, for example, pointed to changes in the North:

> With the great influx to the North, more Negroes have received the ballot. As a result Negroes have been elected to the State Assemblies of Ohio, Pennsylvania, New York, Illinois and New Jersey, and City Councils or Boards of Aldermen of New York, Chicago, Philadelphia, Morrisville, Pennsylvania, and other cities.[24]

Indeed, as the data show, Negroes in a number of Northern cities had elected representatives to various levels of government in order to protect and defend their interests.

The gains that Northern Negroes had made in public education employment had been realized through political participation. A record number of 200 Negroes were teaching in the New York City school system. Integrated teaching faculties also existed in the public schools of Cleveland, Buffalo, Detroit, Boston, and Chicago. If political pressure had led to the hiring of Negro teachers, it could also lead to Negroes being employed in other occupations, several NUL officials believed.

The urban Northern Negroes increasingly turned to political pressure to advance their status. Urbanization, North and South, had made it increasingly difficult for whites to keep Negroes in their "place." City living had resulted in a more sophisticated Negro than found in the rural South. In the cities "movements" among Negroes had emerged that fiercely resisted second-class status. Rural Negroes, unlike those of an urban orientation, were "not subjected to mass suggestion except at the camp meeting and revival."[25]

Though the NUL has subjected Negroes to mass suggestion, it has generally not been a mass movement organization. Local Urban Leagues have on occasion spoken on behalf of the urban Negro masses. The Urban League secretaries have spoken for the masses either because whites have viewed them as the Negroes' spokesmen or because their involvement in nonpartisan, and sometimes even partisan, politics have made them spokesmen.

The Urban League Movement's officials have often been portrayed as not politically oriented. While it is true that NUL representatives did not endorse partisan political candidates, they did involve themselves in the political process. Jones, for example, was actively involved in the affairs of the Republican Party, but as a private citizen. John C. Dancy, the Detroit Urban League executive secretary, served on the advisory council of both the Detroit Citizens League and the Wolverine Republican Club of Detroit, two highly political bodies.[26] Urban League officials engaged in political activities because of their own personal commitment to fulfilling their responsibilities as citizens, and because of their endeavors, commencing about 1920, to reforming existing governmental structures.

The Urban League's growing interest in reforming the existing political structures gave the 1928 presidential election an added importance. Alfred E. Smith, an urban politician, knew that the Northern Negroes' growing political strength had to be taken into account. Moreover, the cities for the most part were controlled by Democratic machines. The urban political machines courted the Negro vote, and most of the gains Negroes had achieved were through the urban Democratic machines. Herbert Hoover, the Republican candidate, did not alter his party's pro-big-business posture to any large degree. Unlike Smith, Hoover was unconcerned about the urban Negro vote; his political strategy was to capture the support of big business and to court the Anglo-Saxon, Protestant vote. The fact that Smith was a Catholic and a product of urban America meant that Hoover was free to capitalize on the anti-Catholic and antiurban sentiments of a sizeable segment of the American electorate.

The Negro leaders in the NUL were not concerned about the candidates' religious affiliation. Their concern was how to extract meaningful promises—promises that were not made to garner votes—from the two candidates. Since the NUL did not endorse political candidates, it refrained from telling Negroes how to vote, but did urge them to exercise intelligence and independence in the election of a President and a Congress.

The Urban League reached a wide audience of potential voters by opening the pages of *Opportunity* to candidates and to partisan writers. Clarence Darrow, one of America's distinguished trial lawyers, advised Negroes to vote independently, noting that neither party had their interest at heart.[27] Norman Thomas, the Socialist Party's presidential candidate, accused Democrats and Republicans alike of condoning racial bigotry, but reserved his harshest criticisms for Smith, the Democratic Party's candidate. Thomas bitterly attacked Smith's decision to remain silent in the wake of the Texas Democratic Party's decision to bar Negroes from voting in the state's primary.

Thomas's views did not damage Smith's image among Negro voters, at least among Negro voters in New York City. A record number voted the Democratic ticket, both at the national and local level, in the 1928 elections.[28] Whatever Smith's shortcomings as a national candidate, his record as a politician who believed in racial advancement was firmly fixed in the minds of New York City's Negro population. But more important, the 1928 presidential and local election returns signaled a shift in the urban Negroes' allegiance from the Republican to the Democratic Party. Beginning in 1928, the strategy of the Northern Negro politicians was to seek racial advancement through local and state political machines, in the hope that some impact would be made at the national level as well. The Great Depression of 1929 and its devastating impact on Negroes not only limited their influence on local politics but also forced them to bypass local politicians and seek much-needed help from the national government; at least some Negro leaders felt that this was their most effective strategy for the duration of the Great Depression.

III

While it is problematical whether the Republicans had triggered the Great Depression of 1929, it is clear that the economic crisis had a significant impact on reshaping party alignments, as millions of Americans voted to end Republican rule in Washington. More important for this study are Negro leaders' perceptions and criticisms of the Republican Presidents.

Some of the criticisms raised against the Republican Presidents were warranted. In 1927, for example, reports reached the NUL that Red Cross officials were dispensing aid to the flood victims in the Mississippi Valley in accordance with their race. The NUL and other Negro organizations pressured the President (Coolidge) to create an advisory commission for the purpose of ending racial discrimination in the dispensing of flood relief. This was a clear example of the NUL's new strategy of reforming "existing institutional" structures.

There are conflicting views on the reasons why Negro leaders called for the creation of an advisory commission to the Red Cross. One account is that Negro leaders were incensed over reports alleging that Negroes were being held in peonage in several of the refuge camps established in the wake of the flood.[29] Another account argues that the NUL called for the establishment of an advisory committee to ensure equal treatment of Negroes in receiving Red Cross assistance. It has been established that Jones of the NUL remained in contact with the White House until Coolidge agreed to appoint Negro advisors to the Red Cross and to dispatch Negro relief workers to the flood area.[30] The final version, written by Robert R. Moton, who served on the advisory commission, along with Jesse O. Thomas, an NUL official, noted that there were complaints of peonage and discrimination in the granting of relief to the flood victims.[31] Whatever the truth, the Negroes' treatment at the hands of Republican Presidents irked NUL officials.

The NUL expected the national government to consider the special needs of the urban and rural Negro population. Its officials, for example, compiled numerous reports, documenting the high unemployment rate among urban Negroes. From 1929 to 1931, the unemployment rate among urban Negroes climbed to astronomical heights. In Cincinnati, the number rose from 85 to 800; in New York City it increased 300 percent in one year; and in Chicago the Negro population, which was 4 percent of the total, constituted 25 percent of the city's relief roll.[32]

Hoover refused to consider the special needs of the Negro. Rather, he bided his time as the Depression crisis grew worse. Additional NUL reports detailing the unemployment among Negroes reached the President's desk. In 1931 a report written by Ira De A. Reid, an NUL official, "The Negro in the Industrial Depression," further documented the plight of the Negro. Thirty-one percent of Baltimore's Negro population was receiving relief assistance. In Charleston, South Carolina, 70 percent of the Negroes were on relief. Pittsburgh's Negro population was only 8 percent of the total, but Negroes constituted 38 percent of the unemployed.[33]

The high rate of Negro unemployment did not move Hoover to action.

Hence the NUL and other Negro organizations expanded their attacks on the national government to include the manner in which federal monies were distributed in the Southern schools. Officials of the NUL informed Hoover that Negro schools in the Southern states had received only 37 percent of the money that was due them in federal grants for vocational and home economics programs. Hoover also was chastised for not inviting Negroes to participate in the White House Conference on Child Health and Protection.

Hoover and his cabinet were stung by the criticisms. While some attention was given to equalizing the federal grants to the Southern schools, the unemployment among Negroes was largely ignored. Indeed unemployment among Negroes had reached a crisis stage, as shown in Table 12. In the final analysis, the Negro population in general and NUL officials in particular broke with the Republican Party, in part because "Hoover had veiled but thinly his contempt of the race."[34]

The break with the Republican Party was most notable among urban Negroes. Why they turned to the Democratic Party is understandable. The Northern cities were under the control of Democratic machines, and these machines at least showed a greater concern for the Negro problem than did the National Republican Party. What few political triumphs urban Negroes had experienced had been realized through Democratic urban political machines. And a majority of the Negroes who had been elected to public office were backed by local Democratic political machines.

Residence in urban centers that were controlled by Democratic political machines had been instructive to Negro leaders and the middle classes alike. Urban Negro leaders had realized the value of working both inside the normal channels of the body politic and independently too. The demonstrations headed by Negro leaders in Harlem during the 1920s had opened employment opportunities that had before been closed to Negroes. In Boston the local Urban League was successful in placing several Negro interns and nurses in the city's hospitals. The St. Louis Urban League (Missouri) had led a successful boycott against a white-owned grocery store in a Negro neighborhood, leading to the employment of Negroes in the store.[35] The "Don't Buy Where You Can't Work Campaign," often under the direction of a local Urban League, had won important victories against employment discrimination. As it turned out, a growing number of urban Negro leaders, including Urban League officials, concluded during the 1920s that agitation, boycotts, pressure group tactics, direct action, confrontation, and the like were the correct strategies to reform existing institutional structures.

Officials of the NUL devoted a considerable amount of their time to reforming existing governmental agencies. But the Urban League Movement, between 1929 and 1940, did not lose sight of the fact that it was a

Table 12. Employment and Unemployment in Cincinnati, Ohio, by Race, 1933 to 1940[a]

| May | Percentage of Whites | | Percentage of Blacks | |
	Employed Full Time	Unemployed	Employed Full Time	Unemployed
1933	53.97	28.04	32.83	54.32
1934	65.89	21.19	32.75	53.40
1935	69.80	17.80	37.90	51.00
1936	75.91	17.52	44.49	49.45
1937	87.09	8.00	55.69	35.97
1938	70.00	16.35	36.42	52.69
1939	80.16	12.79	47.81	45.25
1940	81.34	10.69	56.24	35.05

[a]Data extracted from "Unemployment in Cincinnati, May 1940," *Monthly Labor Review*, 51 (December 1940), pp. 1367–69. As can be seen the percentage of unemployed Negro workers in May 1940 was higher than the percentage of unemployed white workers at the depth of the Depression.

social work agency rather than a mass movement organization. By retaining its basically social work orientation, the Urban League Movement was able to receive Community Chest funds. The extent to which the Urban Leagues adhered to a basically social service orientation or made new departures can be ascertained by examining their relations with the New Deal administrations.

Americans anxiously awaited the 1932 presidential election. Franklin D. Roosevelt became the nation's chief executive at a time when talk of socialism was strong in intellectual circles. Most Americans cared little about democracy or socialism, but they were troubled by the economic crisis, and they voted Hoover out of office. Hoover's defeat at the polls in 1932 did not mean that Roosevelt was a popular and appealing candidate, but that most Americans had little confidence in Hoover to lead the nation.

Contrary to popular belief, the philosophies of Hoover and Roosevelt were not as radically different as the partisans of both tried to fix in the public mind.[36] Both men were convinced that massive assistance to big business was required of the federal government in order for the nation to escape the grip of the Depression. Their differences can be seen in their appeals to the "common man." Hoover steadfastly refused to examine the impact of the Depression on most Americans, but argued that federal aid to big business was a must. Roosevelt decided early to place the federal government behind the right of labor to organize and bargain collectively, and to convince the "common man" that his administration would provide monies to help the less fortunate for the duration of the Depression.

Roosevelt's concern for the laborer, big business, and the "common man" became known as the New Deal.

President Roosevelt's call for a New Deal for the American people was certainly refreshing to Negroes. Many of Roosevelt's Negro supporters viewed the election of twentieth-century America's second Democratic President as the start of a revolution in racial matters. In some ways the election of Roosevelt did spark a racial revolution. The extent to which Roosevelt brought Negroes into the national government signaled a new direction for the Democratic Party. In other ways, however, Roosevelt's election did not promise racial revolution. He did practically nothing to eliminate two grave injustices—segregation and discrimination—from American society.

Most of the criticisms that were hurled at the New Deal administrations stemmed from Roosevelt's repeated failures to address openly and forthrightly segregation and discrimination in American life. But some NUL officials may have disliked Roosevelt because of their Republican loyalties as well as for his refusal to denounce segregation and racial discrimination. It should be noted that most white Republicans and Democrats were not in favor of dismantling racial segregation in America. What troubled several NUL officials was the fact that the privileged position given Southern Democrats in the Roosevelt administration blocked any chances of civil rights legislation being enacted. Moreover, the fact that American white ethnics flocked to the Democratic Party meant that Negroes had to compete with them for the party's scarce political resources. These were factors that influenced several NUL officials' opinions of Roosevelt.

Some Urban League officials remained loyal to the Republican Party, despite their repudiation of Republican Party policies as orchestrated by Hoover. Jones was a Republican, as was James H. Hubert, an Urban League executive secretary, and Albert Bailey George, a municipal judge in the District of Columbia. They and scores of other Negro Republicans believed that the Democratic Party held little hope for most Negroes.[37] Hence New Deal programs came under Urban League fire in the aftermath of Roosevelt and the Congress's first 100 days. (The NUL's relations with the Roosevelt administration after 1940 will be dealt with in the next chapter.)

Criticisms of New Deal programs came from NUL officials who were Republicans, from those who joined the Roosevelt team, and from those who were Democrats but who did not accept appointments in the New Deal agencies. Several NUL staff members received and accepted invitations to work in Washington because, as one NUL Board member put it, they felt duty bound to seize "the opportunity to promote the League's programs through Washington."[38] Supposedly there was a belief within the NUL that cooperation from Roosevelt was possible either through political pressure or by being on the Washington scene to monitor New Deal programs. Jones, who joined the Commerce Department in 1933 as an advisor on Negro affairs, was not overly critical of Roosevelt and the New Deal. And neither was Mary McLeod Bethune, a Board member who served Roosevelt as director of Negro affairs on the National Youth Administration (NYA). But T. Arnold Hill, who accepted a job in the Works Progress Administration and in the NYA as a consultant in 1939, indicted Roosevelt and the New Deal for fostering segregation and discrimination.[39]

Roosevelt did not respond to the charges. The reasons are many. Throughout the 1930s, the President believed that his policies had made America a better place in which to live for the average man and woman. Moreover, as has been suggested, he wanted some semblance of justice for Negroes, but realized that the prejudices that had been fostered for more than two hundred years could not be "done away with overnight."[40] His wife, Eleanor Roosevelt, disclaimed this view, arguing that while the New Deal was not always fair to Negro Americans, "it is not the intention of those at the top."[41] Roosevelt at no time felt his job to be that of tampering with or overturning established racial patterns. Therefore his actions convinced a number of NUL officials and Board members that they, in the future, would have to weigh the political consequences associated with working as a government employee.

The political consequences that NUL officials, Board members, and other Negroes had to weigh before accepting or rejecting New Deal appointments were many. First, the Negroes' growing allegiance to the Democratic Party had contributed to the creation of a New Majority. The question was: How could Negroes benefit from their partnership in the New Majority? Second, Roosevelt's support of labor's right to organize and bargain collectively seemed to hold out new possibilities to urban Negroes. Could labor continue to ignore Negroes? Third, the New Deal had the potential of fostering a revolution in rural Southern America, as thousands of Negroes "availed themselves of adult education classes of the WPA,"[42] and new buildings financed by WPA funds were erected on Negro college campuses (state-operated Negro colleges). Visiting health clinics, health education, and nursery schools funded by the New Deal were found in scores of Negro Southern communities. Traveling libraries, made possible by WPA money, took books to Negroes in areas where libraries were either off-limits to them or were not provided by local government. These were the plusses and minuses that Negroes invited to join the New Deal agencies had to ponder.

The extent of Roosevelt's commitment to racial advancement was unclear throughout his terms in office. Therefore Negroes had to decide whether their presence in Washington gave them an opportunity to express Negro opposition to legally enforced segregation and discrimination.

Another important question was whether or not Roosevelt had the political courage to defend Negroes' constitutional rights, and to call for legislation that made lynching a federal crime.

Roosevelt was timid in addressing the issues of segregation, racial discrimination, and lynching. His refusal to speak out against segregation and discrimination and to back antilynching legislation irked NUL officials. T. Arnold Hill lashed out at Roosevelt, condemning him for not supporting the efforts of those national legislators who called for antilynching legislation. Jones denounced Roosevelt for not supporting civil rights, advising the Urban League affiliates' executive secretaries to forward letters and telegrams to Senators who had voted against the antilynching legislation.[43]

Officials of the NUL not only prodded Roosevelt to eschew racial segregation but also to back equality of opportunity. They remained hopeful that Roosevelt's prolabor stance would benefit Negro workers, only to find that the reverse was true. But they did not despair, opting for another strategy. During September of 1934, L. Hollingsworth Wood, NUL President, announced the creation of Workers' Councils within the Department of Industrial Relations. Lester B. Granger was appointed as head of the Councils.

Granger was the son of Dr. and Mrs. William Granger (his father was a physician), and was born in Newport News, Virginia. Granger, unlike his five brothers, did not pursue a medical career. Following graduation from Dartmouth College, Granger enlisted in the United States Army (World War I), eventually receiving assignment to the all-Negro 92nd Division which was stationed in France. Upon receiving an honorable discharge from the Army, Granger served as industrial relations secretary with the Negro League of Newark (New Jersey). It was then that Granger realized he needed additional training to be an effective social worker, and consequently enrolled in the graduate program at the New School for Social Work in New York City. Following his graduate program, Granger was employed (1922–30 and 1931–33) by the Bordentown, New Jersey, Manual Training School for Colored Boys. In 1930 he organized an Urban League affiliate in Los Angeles, and he also was on the staff of *Opportunity* magazine before being named director of activities of the Workers' Councils.[44]

To some, Granger was a radical. He had supported a number of "liberal" causes, and his name frequently appeared on the House Committee on Un-American Activities. For example, he was cited by the Committee for membership in the American Committee for Peace and Democracy, among other "questionable" groups.[45] It is problematical whether Granger was ever a subversive. But one Urban Leaguer informed me that several individuals, whose association with Granger spanned the years, referred to him as a "weekend Communist."[46] Granger vehemently denied that he was ever a Communist.[47] It is safe to say, however, that Granger's political views were left of center.

It is no small wonder, then, that with Granger at the helm, the Workers' Councils' activities among Negroes were also left of center. They were, according to one League supporter, a "radical approach at the time to promote the economic interests of Negroes."[48] The Council promoted both worker solidarity across racial lines and separate unions when Negroes were barred from white unions. But more important, the Councils not only called for self-determination of Negro workers, but also declared their intention to break down the discriminatory barriers that prevented Negroes from joining AFL unions and gaining meaningful employment in industries.[49] The Councils warned the AFL that it would encourage Negro workers to join a rival union if their needs were not met.[50] The rival union was the Congress of Industrial Organizations (CIO), which theoretically eschewed discrimination. The CIO unions accepted Negro members not so much because white members welcomed them into the ranks of organized labor, but because in the industry-wide unions hundreds of unskilled jobs went begging if Negroes did not fill them. Another important factor is that a number of the CIO unions were controlled by socialists until the 1940s. The socialist labor leaders believed in worker solidarity across racial lines. In the final analysis, the NUL's warning that it would encourage Negroes to join a rival union reflected the urban Negroes' growing impatience with the stand-pat AFL.

A split in labor ranks created a situation in which Negro workers had an opportunity to join a rival union. One piece of legislation enacted by the Congress during Roosevelt's first hundred days in office, the National Industrial Recovery Act (NIRA), Section 7 (a), and a similar provision of the National Labor Relations Act (NLRA), protected workers' rights to organize and bargain collectively. John L. Lewis of the United Mine Workers of America, among other CIO union leaders, objected to the fact that the skilled workers in CIO-organized industries were not allowed to hold membership in a CIO union. Lewis viewed this as an attempt on the part of AFL unions to curb the powers of the CIO unions, and he disregarded AFL directives and organized the men in CIO unions.[51] Lewis and other CIO union leaders' defiance of AFL directives resulted in a labor war.

The NUL officials had not anticipated the magnitude of the labor war. They did not, as they had earlier threatened to do, urge Negro workers to break with the AFL and join the CIO unions. Neither did NUL officers turn their backs on the rebel CIO unions. As the AFL-CIO struggle intensified, the NUL and several Urban League affiliates reaffirmed their belief in labor's right to organize, and urged the cooperation of the white labor movement in opening opportunities for Negro workers.

A strike in 1934 gave the NUL the opportunity to test the federal government's position on Negro labor's right to organize, and the extent of the AFL's commitment to racial solidarity across racial lines. The Wehr Steel Foundry, located in Milwaukee, was an open shop before the 1934 strike. Following the strike an AFL union was formed, and Negroes in the plant were barred from joining it. Subsequently the local union sought formal recognition from the AFL's Executive Council, and demanded that all Negroes be expelled from the industry (Wehr Steel Foundry). In the ensuing weeks, rumors circulated that the sole purpose of the strike had been to drive the Negro workers from the plant.

The NUL's Department of Industrial Relations investigated the rumors, finding them to be essentially correct.[52] Thereupon Hill forwarded the data to the National Labor Relations Board (NLRB). Its chairman, Lloyd K. Garrison, declined to intercede on behalf of the plant's Negro workers, stating that the NLRB's jurisdiction was "limited to particular controversies . . . burdening interstate commerce or which involve Section 7 (a) of the Recovery Act."[53]

Garrison was queried on his recollection of the facts surrounding the Wehr Foundry strike. He did not recall the event; but he did point out (in 1977) that the Attorney General of the United States "was reluctant to enforce the provisions of the NIRA if a racial question was involved."[54] Moreover, he exclaimed that the issue was not that of interference with the right of workers to organize. Had the Wehr Foundry owners, Garrison pointed out, interfered with the workers' attempts to organize a union, then the NLRB would have proceeded with an investigation and would have made a summary ruling.[55] The significance of the Wehr Foundry strike and the resultant events indicated to NUL officials that Section 7 (a) of the NIRA was of little benefit to Negro workers, and that the federal government would not protect the rights of Negro workers to organize and bargain collectively. Several NUL officials realized that Negro workers were in for a protracted struggle with the AFL and the federal government in regard to the right of all workers to be under the protection of organized labor.

IV

T. Arnold Hill was one of the NUL officials who had concluded that little cooperation was forthcoming from the AFL and the federal government in ending economic discrimination against minority workers. But Hill was not the NUL executive secretary and therefore could not change the course of the NUL. Jones's temporary departure from the NUL to work in a New Deal agency resulted in Hill being named the NUL's acting executive secretary. In 1935 Hill unveiled his plans on the NUL's future direction: "The course then, of the National Urban

League, is clear, unequivocal, direct actionable leadership in a program designed to organize Negroes for an intelligent, factual, concerted presentation of the grievances that beset them."[56] Among those grievances were Roosevelt's failures to denounce segregation and racial discrimination, the AFL unions' anti-Negro policies, and the high unemployment found among Negroes. The local Urban League executive secretaries gave Hill their unstinting cooperation in identifying those problems confronting Negroes.

Hill knew that Jones envied his relations with the locals. Jones did not trust Hill and therefore felt uncomfortable with Hill at the NUL's helm. In 1937 Jones returned to the NUL, which was a blow to Hill's ambitions and dreams. Several factors had prompted Jones to resume leadership of the NUL. He resented the fact that the Urban League local executive secretaries turned to Hill for advice and guidance before Hill became the acting executive secretary.[57] Hill had worked in the field; his relations with the local executive secretaries was firmer than Jones's; and most of the local executive secretaries believed that Hill's perspective of the Urban League Movement was broader than Jones's. A growing number of the local Urban League executive secretaries concluded that Jones's ideology and his approach to urban problems reflected the view of "Old Urban Leaguers," which was that the NUL would work itself out of business.[58] They agreed with Hill that the role of the Urban League must be that of reforming existing governmental structures and launching a war on both labor and industry. In the final analysis, Hill's popularity with the local executive secretaries, rather than his racial ideology, was what had troubled Jones the most.

Jones and Hill kept their feelings toward each other hidden from the public between 1937 and 1940, and they also did not reveal their true feelings to the NUL Board. The Board learned of the "feud" when Hill forwarded a letter to Jones tendering his resignation "as director of the Industrial Relations Department, effective June 1, 1940."[59] The Steering Committee, NUL Board, sought from Jones an explanation about the conversation that Hill mentioned in his letter of resignation.

Jones acceded to the request. He recounted that on the night of March 12, 1940, Hill had visited his home, at which time he told of his plans to resign from the NUL executive staff. Toward the end of the conversation Hill had remarked that his decision to resign had brought him contentment "for the first time for a long period."[60] Hill also remarked, according to Jones, that his decision to tender his resignation was not intended to win any concessions.[61]

Jones's account of the conversation did not satisfy the Steering Committee members. Again they asked of Jones why Hill had resigned. Rather than elaborate any further, Jones urged that the Committee accept Hill's letter of resignation. Before the Steering Committee acted on Hill's letter, word reached the Urban League executive secretaries that Hill had resigned. The Steering Committee received letters from the local executive secretaries, urging it not to accept Hill's letter of resignation. The Steering Committee accepted the letter only after Hill informed its members that he would not withdraw it.

Hill's resignation assured Jones's preeminence in the NUL. For the moment there was no one in the NUL whom the local Leagues' executive secretaries spoke of as Jones's replacement. Jones was not a young man, and his declining health made it apparent to the Board that a search for his successor had to commence. Jones momentarily refused to relinquish the title of Executive Secretary, because he intended to play a key role in the selection of the future executive director.

Jones announced on November 14, 1940, that effective October 1, 1940, Lester B. Granger had been named "Assistant Executive Secretary in charge of Industrial Relations."[62] Naming Granger as the assistant secretary came as a complete shock to more than one Urban Leaguer. But in retrospect, Jones's choice should have been expected. Granger, unlike Hill, did not view the NUL's future role in the search for equality to be that of a mass movement organization. Granger's belief was that the NUL would continue to build relations with the power structure, and to seek a better understanding of the white power structure.[63] In short, Granger's ideas were more consistent with Jones's than Hill's were. Jones felt that with Granger at the helm he could leave the post of NUL executive secretary with the assurance that Granger would not forget that the NUL's commitment to the search for equality was not so much that of a Negro organization, but that of a professional social work agency.[64] It remained to be seen whether or not Granger's social work techniques could win equal opportunity for Negroes. But it was certain that with Granger at the helm the NUL's interest in reforming existing structures (governmental and nongovernmental) would continue unabated.

The very fact that the NUL survived the Great Depression, and the fact that several of its officials came to the realization that a change in course was needed, constitute the most striking accomplishments of the Urban League Movement between 1921 and 1940. And the NUL's change of course during the 1920s, which led to attempts to reform existing governmental structures, was also significant. Its officials had generally reminded white America of its failure to live up to its ideals of equality and equal justice. A former Urban League executive secretary summed up the accomplishments of the NUL from about 1929 to 1940. He wrote:

If the Urban League ever proved its worth, it was during the days when every-thing we had was invested in a crash program to pull unemployed Negro Amer-ica out of the dumps. Reporters called us "briefcase boys" as we hustled across cities and states and to Washington with our bags bulging with briefs on Negro needs and affidavits of racial discrimination. We pounded away at lax, corrupt or hostile officials and demanded a larger degree of the "Negro's share." We adver-tised lists of examinations to be held. We trained classes of prospective appli-cants. We multiplied many times the number of Negro civil service employees throughout the country.[65]

The Urban League Movement, between 1921 and 1940, did not eliminate from American society segregation and racial discrimination. But during the years 1921 to 1940, it grew in size to equal the proportions of the job it was faced with—continued hostility from a large segment of white America and sustained opposition to racial equality from the various levels of government.

5

Making the Dream of Democracy a Reality, 1941–1945: Lester B. Granger at the NUL's Helm

Eugene K. Jones was still the NUL executive secretary when the war clouds hanging over Europe drifted across the Atlantic Ocean, reaching the shores of the United States. But it was only a matter of time before he would hand over the reins of leadership to Lester B. Granger. A change of executive director did not mean an overhaul of the NUL's major programs nor its transformation into a mass movement organization. Since its founding, the NUL had endeavored to relate every problem with which it dealt to the overall interest of the American community and to the personal and family interest of people of whatever race. Stated in another way, the NUL's prime objective since its founding was that of ending racial discrimination—in jobs, housing, public services, and neighborhood relationships—in every area of civic life.

Granger's primary task as the new NUL executive director was to end racial discrimination in every area of civic life. Neither he nor Jones believed that the NUL should represent the man in the street. Both Granger and Jones were wedded to the belief that the Urban League represented "men and women and children in their homes, workers on their jobs and citizens of both races in their positions of civil responsibility."[1]

Granger's and Jones's definitions of what constituted civil responsibility differed markedly. This meant that whatever new departures the NUL embarked upon with Granger at the helm were the result of how the two men defined civic responsibility. Jones believed that the NUL's job was to prepare Negroes for the time when changed attitudes and expanded industry would create vast new job opportunities for those who had the qualifications. Jones's view of the Negro rested squarely in the Progressive tradition, because of his belief in the inevitability of an expanding industrial democracy. Granger urged constitutional guarantees for his fellow Negroes, and was less patient than Jones with such stabilizing factors as law and order, and a gradualist type of democracy. Indeed Granger believed that unless Negroes were quickly and permanently integrated into the mainstream of modern urban living, they would be left behind socially, culturally, and economically.

Chapter 5 discusses Granger's impact on the Urban League and the Urban League Movement. It also shows how Granger steered the NUL into the civil rights arena, abandoning a 1913 agreement hammered out between NUL and NAACP officials to the effect that the organizations would not duplicate each other's efforts. This chapter points to the reasons why the NUL and the NAACP remained uncooperative with each other for some twenty years, and shows how A. Philip Randolph was able to mediate some of the disputes that marred NUL-NAACP relations. It also examines the ways in which the NUL, under Granger's leadership, sought to reform existing governmental structures, and studies the impact of NUL recommendations on governmental officials in the wake of urban riots of the World War II era. The role of the NUL and the Urban League affiliates in challenging housing and employment discrimination is also documented. Finally, this chapter continues its examination of NUL's relations with the Roosevelt administration, specifically, why Granger and other Urban Leaguers were sometimes hostile to Roosevelt and the New Deal.

I

Although President Roosevelt's New Deal programs had salvaged capitalism as an economic system, those programs appeared incapable of solving America's economic crisis permanently. A close examination of New Deal programs shows that they had little impact on unemployment among Negroes. Moreover, Roosevelt left unchanged a system of segregation and discrimination that limited Negroes' chances of winning parity with the white population. Hence during the 1930s Negro leaders chastised the New Deal President, reminding him that millions of Americans clearly perceived that the American dream for Negroes remained largely a dream.

Negro leaders articulated what the American dream was to them—equal justice under the law, the franchise for millions of Southern Negroes who were denied this right, an end to segregation in the military, and expanded employment and improved housing for millions of rural and urban Negroes. Roosevelt did not deny that Negroes had every right to call for changes in American society that would advance their status, but he would not risk implementing these changes called for by Negro leaders. He feared alienating white American ethnics, Southern whites, and the labor bloc.

The expansionist policies of the Third Reich and America's decision to become the supplier of armaments for the beleaguered European nations gave Negro leaders new hopes of forcing change. By 1939 the NUL, along with other organizations, found itself confronting new problems relating to wartime demands and population shifts, while the old ones—inequality in the industrial and political world—still remained unresolved. Realizing that little could be done in 1939 to overturn racial discrimination and legally enforced segregation in America, the NUL turned its attention to the plight of the Negro worker in the North and in the Southern urban centers.

The concern of the NUL and the NAACP with the labor problem began as early as 1939.[2] Prodding the federal government and the governments of the Northern states to embrace equality of opportunity did not set well with whites. As Du Bois concluded, "theoretically and historically, whites in the North had stood up for equality, but their economic interests were on the side of discrimination."[3] Roosevelt knew that Northern whites supported the limiting of Negroes' industrial opportunities and therefore did not give serious thought to placing the power of the federal government behind equality of opportunity. Yet NUL officials, along with other Negro leaders, prodded Roosevelt to take the lead in erecting safeguards to prohibit discrimination in wartime employment and training. They called for this action because, as Table 13 demonstrates, Negro males were concentrated in unskilled and low-paying jobs. The one factor that caused Negroes to challenge discrimination and segregation was the manner in which America and other democracies denounced the racism of Nazi Germany. Roosevelt did not need to be reminded of the fact that no other group in America had more reason to broaden and expand, and not merely defend, democracy than did Negroes.

Negro leaders, just as during the World War I era, let it be known that the Negro was prepared to defend democracy. From 1940 to the end of 1941, the collaborative efforts between officials of the NAACP and the NUL were outstanding. Walter White directed his efforts toward protecting Negroes' constitutional rights (preventing unlawful discriminatory practices from occurring), and Granger sought solutions to the economic and industrial problems facing Negroes. But NUL-NAACP relations deteriorated after Jones retired. The reasons for this deterioration will be discussed at a later point in this chapter. It can be said that the intensity with which Jones and White pursued economic and political equality for Negroes not only set the stage for later NUL-NAACP confrontations, but also caused the NAACP to address economic and social issues and the NUL to address political issues.

Table 13. Negro Male Employed Workers (except Those in Public Emergency Jobs), by Social-Economic Groups, and by Geographic Divisions, 1940[a]

	Total	Professional Persons	Clerks and Kindred Workers	Skilled Workers, Foremen	Semi-skilled Workers	Unskilled Workers
United States	2,936,795	49,485	75,738	128,762	344,228	1,675,345
Geographic Divisions:						
Middle Atlantic	233,015	6,321	19,642	17,440	49,691	133,238
South Atlantic	1,125,790	16,007	20,952	44,418	126,578	698,954
East North Central	199,354	5,288	12,631	18,690	41,873	112,973
New England	20,275	588	1,064	1,064	1,664	11,899
Pacific	28,323	1,035	1,718	1,871	4,433	11,899
West South Central	572,128	9,339	9,140	17,707	48,867	313,937

[a]Data extracted from *Sixteenth Census of the United States: 1940, Comparative Occupational Statistics for the United States, 1870–1940, Population* (Washington: U.S. Government Printing Office, 1943), Table 35, p. 200. Statistical data on employed Negro females can be mined from Table 36, p. 201. All divisions of the United States are not included in this table. Neither are all general occupation headings included in the table. Hence, the numbers given will not equal the total employed in the general occupations summed by regions.

Urging the federal government to protect and expand Negroes' economic and political rights not only set the NUL and the NAACP on a collision course but also caused tensions between the NUL and the federal government. Roosevelt and his advisors refrained from coordinating their "equal opportunity" programs with the NUL. The 1940 National Defense Advisory Commission's (NDAC) first directive was a case in point. Jones, Granger, and other NUL officials were furious that the directive did not mention that it was they who had urged the federal government to ban discrimination in all industries awarded defense contracts. The most infuriating thing to them, however, was that the directive merely suggested that those industries awarded government contracts desist from engaging in discriminatory hiring practices.[4]

Few industries abided by the directive. The NDAC could not end discrimination in defense industries because it lacked enforcement powers. Not pleased with the 1940 NDAC directive, Channing Tobias, an educator, White, Granger, and Mary McLeod Bethune, an educator and NUL Board member, met on May 20, 1940, with Sidney Hillman, Roosevelt's choice to head the Office of Production Management (OPM). The OPM was the agency that supervised the industrial war effort. During the meeting they discussed with Hillman the possibility of an executive order prohibiting discrimination in defense industries.[5] Hillman told them flatly that no such directive would be forthcoming from the President, but that he would do his best to eliminate discrimination. This was an empty promise, inasmuch as Hillman did not support full employment opportunities for Negroes.

Hillman was an unusual individual, to say the least. He had immigrated to the United States from Lithuania at the age of twenty. He was president of the Amalgamated Clothing Workers Union, a CIO union with a considerable Negro membership, and had served the New Deal administration in the capacity of member of the board of the National Recovery Administration (NRA), the National Youth Administration (NYA), and the Fair Labor Standard Division (FLSD). Hillman's appointment as director of the Office of Production Management (OPM) was in recognition of his standing in the labor movement, and was one way that Roosevelt chose to settle a debt to the Democratic Party's Left.

Hillman's record as head of OPM and his real commitment to equality of opportunity are open to debate. Although Will W. Alexander joined the OPM at Hillman's invitation, he and several other New Dealers questioned Roosevelt's decision to name Hillman as head of the OPM. Born in Polk County, Missouri, on July 15, 1884, Alexander rose to the position of one of the South's most respected white liberals. He was executive director of the Committee on Interracial Cooperation, 1919–30; was acting president of Dillard University, a Negro private college, from 1931 to

1935; and was a member of the Commission on Minority Groups in Economic Recovery from 1934 to 1935. Indeed it seemed a logical choice on the part of Hillman to invite Alexander to work in the OPM offices.

Alexander insisted that Hillman was very timid about the race question, adding that Hillman was a "Jewish boy from Eastern Europe."[6] Alexander accepted the part-time job in the OPM with the understanding that a Negro would be hired to look after the Negro problem. Robert C. Weaver, a Harvard-trained Ph.D. in economics and a Negro, was Alexander's choice. Hillman acquiesced to Alexander's wishes, but opposed giving Weaver anything but a fancy title. Hillman was, according to Alexander, of the opinion that a Negro was not the right person to discuss equality of opportunity in employment with the presidents of major corporations, and insisted that a white assume the responsibility. Moreover, Alexander related that Hillman opposed placing nondiscriminatory clauses in federal contracts. Alexander was not sure whether Roosevelt knew of Hillman's position on nondiscriminatory clauses and Negroes meeting with presidents of major corporations. But he knew that Hillman met frequently with Roosevelt, misleading the President into believing that there was solid agreement within the agency on how best to proceed with the Negro problem.[7]

The extent to which Hillman influenced Roosevelt's views on equality of opportunity is unclear. But it can be argued that Roosevelt was misinformed about Negro leaders' unhappiness over continued limited employment opportunities and segregation. A meeting of leaders of the Brotherhood of Sleeping Car Porters, held during September 1940 at the Harlem YMCA, spelled trouble for the Roosevelt administration. Not only did they chastise Roosevelt for not ordering nondiscriminatory clauses in government contracts, but they also called on Roosevelt, the Congress, and the heads of federal agencies "to see to it that no discrimination is practiced against American citizens entering all departments of the Army, Navy and Air Corps on account of race or color."[8] Mrs. Roosevelt was present when the resolutions were passed, and no doubt informed the President of them.

Roosevelt's views of what had transpired at the Brotherhood of Sleeping Car Porters' meeting are not known. Perhaps he treated the passage of the resolutions in the same manner that he had in an earlier request of Negro leaders for a White House meeting. Two days after Mrs. Roosevelt had attended the meeting at the Harlem YMCA, she telephoned Steven Early, secretary to the President, informing him of her meeting with the President and that he (Early) was to arrange a meeting of Negro leaders at the White House. Those attending the meeting were the President; the Undersecretary of War, Robert Patterson; Walter White of the NAACP: Secretary of the Navy Frank Knox; and T. Arnold Hill, formerly of the NUL.

The White House meeting convened on September 27, 1941. The Negro leaders did not raise the subject of employment discrimination, but submitted a memorandum urging federal officials to end segregation in the armed forces of the United States. The Negro leaders left the meeting believing that progress had been made. But on October 9, 1941, a statement from the White House and a press conference of Stephen Early both gave the impression that the armed forces would remain segregated because the Negroes at the White House and the governmental officials in attendance had agreed that it should.

Randolph was furious upon seeing the press release, as were the Negroes present at the meeting. White demanded that the President fire Early. On January 15, 1941, Randolph issued a statement to the news media, stating that Negro America had to bring its power and pressure to bear upon the agencies and representatives of the federal government to exact their rights in national defense employment and the armed forces of the country. Moreover, in his press release Randolph suggested that ten thousand Negroes march on Washington, D.C. It should be remembered that Randolph was an avowed socialist and therefore opposed racial separatism. But the urgency of the situation required that the Negro masses be organized to impress upon Roosevelt the seriousness of Negroes' demands for justice and equality.

The Randolph press release of January 15, 1941, gave birth to the 1941 March on Washington Movement. Negroes by the thousands heeded the call. By the end of May 1941, Randolph raised the ante, calling for 100,000 Negroes to march on Washington. By the end of May, white politicians realized that the March was not an idle threat on the part of Randolph. The fact that organizations such as the NAACP and the NUL supported Randolph made white officials take notice of Randolph's influence within Negro America.

At first Roosevelt and his supporters made little effort to comply with the demands of the 1941 March on Washington Movement, but instead sought to stop it. Both Roosevelt and Hillman sent circulars to industries, urging but not instructing them to employ more Negroes. A bill was introduced in the Congress by Senator W. Warren Barbour, of New Jersey, which, if enacted, would have established a committee to investigate complaints of discrimination in national defense.[9] Neither of these ploys seemed capable of heading off the March.

Roosevelt turned to Anna M. Rosenberg, a political confidante, and New York City Mayor Fiorello La Guardia for guidance when all else had failed. Why the President turned to them for their assistance in heading off the March is intriguing. La Guardia was on good terms with most of New York's Negro leaders and Roosevelt knew this. At first La Guardia did not wish to become involved in the March on Washington controversy because he was up for reelection. If the March did not achieve what Randolph hoped that it would, La Guardia's involvement stood to cost him votes. If he did not involve himself in the controversy and Randolph did achieve some of his objectives, La Guardia also stood to lose the Negro vote. Weighing both sides of the controversy, La Guardia's advice to Roosevelt was to convene a White House meeting at which the issue could be debated. Roosevelt accepted La Guardia's advice, announcing that he would see White and Randolph, members of the military, and his executive staff.

The White House meeting convened on June 18, 1941, and both White and Randolph were present. Another notable person in attendance was Aubrey Williams of the National Youth Administration, who as a Southern white was a fighter for Negro equality. Roosevelt remained in constant touch with Anna Rosenberg before the meeting, as she was the President's link to La Guardia. The evidence suggests that it was La Guardia who informed the President of what Negro leaders wanted. Will W. Alexander claimed that Rosenberg became a leading figure in the attempts to head off the March on Washington because she falsely told the President of her meetings with John L. Lewis, one of Roosevelt's nemeses during the New Deal and World War II eras.[10] Whatever the reasons, the outcome of the June 18 meeting was that Roosevelt instructed Williams and Rosenberg to meet with La Guardia and Negro leaders and draft an order banning discrimination in defense industries. The order was to be a mandate, not a matter of policy.[11]

On June 25, 1941, Roosevelt issued Executive Order 8802, banning discrimination in the employment of workers in defense industries.[12] The March, set for July 1, 1941, was called off in the wake of the issuance of Executive Order 8802. The NUL's wavering support of the March on Washington Movement meant that it could not accept full credit for the gains made as a result of Randolph's plans to lead 100,000 Negroes to the nation's capital.

What was the source of the NUL's wavering relationship to the March? First, the NUL had consistently refused to be a party to mass demonstrations, but it would have been political suicide for its officials not to have supported Randolph. Second, one League official claimed that the NUL and its affiliates had introduced 150,000 "Negro workers into plants that had never before employed them—as this was before there was a President's FEPC [Fair Employment Practices Committee]."[13] Third, the March on Washington Movement was an overt political act, which was a strategy NUL officials, and notably Jones, had sought to avoid being a party to. Moreover, NUL officials worried that the employment gains arising out of FEPC were only temporary, and if so, the NUL would find itself facing an identical situation to that at the close of World War I. These seem to be the major reasons why the NUL reluctantly cooperated with the March on Washington Movement.

The officials of the NUL were not the only individuals who questioned what impact Executive Order 8802 would have on employers' hiring practices. George S. Schuyler believed that the Order did not "amount to a row of pins."[14] Will W. Alexander did not think that the situation "would have been very different if there [had not] ever been an FEPC."[15] Roy Wilkins of the NAACP claimed that Roosevelt ignored Negroes' economic and political rights between 1933 and 1945 because of their concentration in the South.[16] Granger charged that Roosevelt refrained from placing the power of his office behind equal opportunity because he was "actively anti-Negro."[17] Whatever the President's opinion of Negroes, it is certain that his issuance of the Executive Order was not intended to usher in a new era of racial relations; nor did the President have any intentions of fulfilling Negroes' calls for full and true equality during his tenure in the White House. Yet Executive Order 8802 was important, if for no other reason than it placed the federal government squarely behind Negro leaders' desires to ban discrimination in defense industries.

Not all of the NUL officials fully supported the Executive Order. But Jones and Wood praised the order in glowing terms. Even they, however, raised the issue that the Fair Employment Practices Committee, the agency established to monitor industries' compliance with the order, lacked any enforcement powers. At the same time, NUL officials realized that their traditional way of opening employment opportunities for Negroes—collecting facts, persuasion, and mediation—"would never break the impasse that had already begun to form for Negro labor."[18]

Unquestionably the breaking of that impasse became the NUL's number one objective. But there was little that the NUL could do in opening employment opportunities without the cooperation of the Roosevelt administration. Several Urban Leaguers found it very difficult to work with Democrats. Jones, however, did not allow his party affiliation (Republican) to stand in the way of his relationship with Roosevelt, as was the case with Granger. Granger's dislike of Democrats was no secret to anyone who knew him. He believed that little could be done to advance the Negro cause with a Democrat in the White House. In particular, he disliked Roosevelt because of his belief that Roosevelt had avoided racial questions for fear of alienating Southern Senators and members of the House of Representatives. And Granger questioned Roosevelt's choice of Mark Ethridge to chair the FEPC.

Mark Ethridge, a white Southerner, was a journalist, having served either as editor or assistant editor of the *Raleigh* (North Carolina) *Times* and the *Washington Post,* among others. Despite Granger's misgivings about Ethridge, representatives from the NUL, along with representatives from the NAACP, met with the FEPC on September 17, 1941, to discuss the various ways of enforcing the order. All agreed that the FEPC's initial hearing would commence on October 1, 1941, in Los Angeles. The NUL's agreement to cooperate fully with the FEPC was Jones's last official act as NUL executive secretary.

II

Ill health forced Jones, executive secretary since 1917, to retire at the end of 1941, and Granger was named to succeed him.[19] Jones's leadership as NUL executive director had won him praise from those closest to him. Granger declared that Jones had been the most dynamic force in the Urban League up to 1941.[20] Guichard Parris, the NUL's future publicity director, acknowledged that "Jones was the man who really built this agency from nothing."[21] Another Urban Leaguer recorded that the "Wood-Jones team set and maintained for thirty years a high-level operation."[22]

Granger wasted little time in establishing himself as the NUL's chief executive officer, as far as power was concerned and also in shaping the NUL's future direction. The NUL's future direction, of course, was in the reforming of existing governmental institutions and in addressing civil rights issues. As Granger explained it, besides helping to win the war, the NUL was also hopeful of building "the kind of United States in which we wish to live after the war is over."[23] Granger decided against relying upon Jones's "quiet" style in the search for equality. Between 1941 and 1961, Granger endeavored to give the NUL a highly visible role in making the American dream a reality for Negroes. Granger's actions and hopes not only meant that the NUL would pursue civil rights and social work activities, but also that it would challenge the NAACP, the nation's premier civil rights organization.

Granger realized that civil rights was an issue that no Negro-oriented organization could ignore. Moreover, he concluded that Executive Order 8802 was especially popular among urban Negroes. Granger decided to enlarge the executive staff in recognition of the growing importance of civil rights in the national political arena, and to be able to work more forcefully toward the NUL's aims. He created the posts of industrial relations field secretary, field secretary, and public relations director. The industrial relations field secretary's job was to remain in constant touch with the local Urban Leagues, union officials, Chambers of Commerce, and similar organizations. The field secretary's primary responsibility was to improve NUL relations with Community Chests, the Urban League affiliates, and the Council of Social Agencies. All publicity statements, NUL publications, and contacts with financial sources were handled through the public relations director's office.[24] Each of these positions, as Granger envisioned them, would enable him to keep abreast of events occurring throughout America, and to furnish him and the executive staff with the information required to analyze objectively the problems confronting urban and Northern Negroes.

Between 1911 and 1941, the NUL and the Urban League Movement had remained small operations. There were only nine salaried employees on the NUL staff, and its annual budget was a mere $52,000 when Granger assumed the NUL executive secretary's post in 1941. The Urban League Movement's budget in 1941 (there were thirty-seven local Urban Leagues) was $600,000.[25] Financial strictures, coupled with white opposition to equality of opportunity and equal justice, had stymied the work of the Urban League. Another factor that had prevented the Urban League from aggressively pursuing complete equality for Negroes was the style of both Jones and Wood. Jones steered clear of civil rights issues, abiding by the 1911 NUL-NAACP agreement not to duplicate each other's efforts. Moreover, Jones's philosophy was that in the field of race relations,

> You don't preach, you demonstrate—and in arguing for change you demonstrate that change pays off for the person who is making the change. In that way you're not running around trying to convert people. You hand people the facts and let them convert themselves.[26]

Jones was a patient man. He believed that both Negroes and whites had to be patient if past injustices were to be corrected to their satisfaction.

Granger's and Jones's views of the NUL *vis à vis* the federal government and civil rights organizations, and the role of the NUL in the search for equality, were not always identical. Granger, unlike Jones, fully committed the NUL to the task of reforming existing government structures. Granger also enlarged the NUL's programs to include civil rights issues. From 1941 to the end of the Granger years (1961), the NUL often refrained from cooperating with other civil rights organizations, because Granger believed that the NUL should go it alone rather than join in with the NAACP and similar organizations in civil rights issues. Granger and Jones believed that NUL objectives could be achieved by maintaining high standards of social work techniques. They also shared the belief that the NUL and Urban League affiliates' departments should be headed by individuals who were trained in social work, sociology, and race relations. And both Granger and Jones believed that the most serious problems facing the urban Negroes—hunger, poverty, ignorance, inadequate recreational facilities, health problems, and explosive racial tensions in the cities—were unresolvable as long as segregation and discrimination persisted. They hoped that the FEPC would end discrimination in employment.

Though Granger distrusted the FEPC, he maintained a wait-and-see attitude toward it. In some instances his expectations that the Committee would serve the cause of Negro America were realized. For example, in

1942 the Brooklyn Navy Yard discontinued classifying workers on the basis of color upon receiving a federal order authorizing the change. The New York Telephone Company, following an FEPC investigation of its hiring practices, placed Negro receptionists in its Harlem offices. Frank Fenton, the AFL representative on the FEPC, threatened to lift the charter of the local Chemical and Oil Workers Union of Bellville, New Jersey, if it "persisted in alleged discrimination against Negroes."[27] In other instances, Granger and other NUL officials expressed regret that similar changes were not occurring throughout the United States. They blamed the federal government's wavering relationship with the FEPC for the slowness with which discrimination in the defense industries had been eliminated.

NUL officials withheld public criticism for nearly a year. Only after the FEPC was placed under the jurisdiction of the War Manpower Commission (WMC) during July of 1942 did Granger and other NUL officials publicly voice their complaints. Granger's dislike of Roosevelt, among other factors, led him to conclude that the President had transferred the Committee from the War Production Board (WPB) to the WMC in order to end the Committee's independence, which it had enjoyed within the WPB. Granger would not accept Paul McNutt's promise not to interfere with the Committee's operations, probably because of his dislike of Roosevelt and the New Deal administration.

McNutt did not keep his promise. One of his first acts following the transfer to the WMC was to postpone a scheduled hearing of the FEPC, which was an investigation of alleged railroads' defiance of Executive Order 8802. Granger viewed McNutt's actions as a beginning "toward immobilization of the Committee's authority."[28] Neither McNutt nor Roosevelt responded directly to the charge. But it was a certainty that the FEPC hearings, scheduled for January 25–27, 1943, had been postponed indefinitely, and that McNutt would not disclose the reason. Granger was convinced that the postponement was McNutt's way of ending the independent status of the FEPC. His perception was incorrect. A source close to the scene disclosed that the President was searching for a competent replacement for the chairman of the FEPC, because he knew that the Committee was floundering under Ethridge's leadership.[29]

Granger was determined to have the hearings on the days that they had already been scheduled. He and other NUL officials took their case to John L. O'Brien, general counsel of the OPM, who ruled that "common carriers were defense industries and therefore were subject to Executive Order 8802."[30] Upon receipt of the ruling, NUL officials petitioned Roosevelt to order that the hearings be held as scheduled. Although he did not accede to their request, Roosevelt did arrange for Attorney General Francis Biddle to meet with NUL and NAACP officials. In retrospect,

Roosevelt used the meeting to buy time, and he was spared the embarrassment of having to inform NUL and NAACP officials of Ethridge's failure.

By the spring of 1943, Roosevelt had found a replacement for Ethridge. It was then that he issued Executive Order 9346, on May 27, 1943, which, among other things, restored the FEPC to its independent status. Roosevelt not only received warm praise from some Negroes for his issuance of the Order, but most Negro leaders also approved of the new FEPC chairman, Monsignor Haas.[31] Because he was elevated to the bishopric of Grand Rapids, Michigan, Haas occupied the chairmanship for a brief time. His successor was Malcolm Ross.

Ross had been the director of information for the National Labor Relations Board since 1942. Prior to that time, Ross had been a news reporter, having served on the staffs of the *New York Morning Herald* and the *Dallas News*. Ross was the FEPC's chairman when the railroad hearings resumed on September 15, 1943. He accepted full responsibility for the ruling, which decreed that the Brotherhood of Locomotive Firemen and the ten railroads cited in the complaint were in direct violation of Executive Order 9346.

Neither the union nor the railroads took kindly to the ruling. Representatives of both groups argued that the Railroad Labor Board, rather than the FEPC, was the proper agency for resolving the issue. Stung by earlier NUL criticism, Roosevelt withheld comment on the ruling. Roosevelt broke his silence only after Comptroller General Lindsay C. Warren questioned the FEPC's authority to investigate the unions and the railroads, declaring that the powers granted the FEPC were directory rather than mandatory. Roosevelt released a statement to the effect that Executive Orders 8802 and 9346 required contractors and unions not to follow discriminatory hiring practices on account of race, creed, color, or national origin.[32]

The President's statement did not alter the federal government's wavering relationship with the FEPC. Roosevelt's strategy of relating to the FEPC was comprised of two parts. He knew that an effective FEPC would antagonize labor, the Southern bloc, and European ethnic groups, all necessary for the Democratic Party's survival.[33] Roosevelt did not abandon the FEPC because he did not want it to appear that Executive Order 8802 had been forced on him. Roosevelt's handling of the FEPC was one reason why Granger disliked him so much, and why Granger also formed negative views of Democrats and the Democratic Party.

Roosevelt was not the only person whom Granger disliked and distrusted. He also disliked Roy Wilkins of the NAACP. Granger's dislike of Wilkins first surfaced in 1942, after Wilkins had issued a news release to the effect that representatives of the NAACP, but not those of the NUL, had supplied information to *Fortune* magazine, which was preparing a publication on the Negro.[34] In 1943 Granger sought the Board's "advice on present and future relations with the NAACP."[35] In this instance Granger was upset following a news release over Wilkins's signature. The news release told of Granger's refusal to sign a statement written by NAACP officials that castigated Lindsay Warren for ruling that the FEPC's powers were suggestive rather than mandatory. Granger did not deny that he had refused to sign the NAACP statement. But he did justify his action on the ground that NAACP officials had refused to sign an NUL statement protesting the National Housing Agency's segregationist policies.[36] The running feud between Granger and Wilkins, while annoying to several NUL Board members, was not the important issue. What was important was that Granger and Wilkins saw themselves as competitors in the civil rights and racial advancement arena. The era of NUL-NAACP cooperation had come to an end.

The individuals responsible for solid NUL-NAACP cooperation either were leaving or had already left the Urban League Movement. L. Hollingsworth Wood, the remaining link between the NUL's past and present, announced his retirement as president of the NUL at the height of the Granger-Wilkins feud (Wood had served as NUL president since 1916). William H. Baldwin, III, Wood's replacement, noted that Jones's tasks had been made easier by Wood's steadfast dedication to the work of the Urban League Movement. No other NUL president wielded the power and remained the NUL president as long as Wood did. The rapid succession of NUL presidents between 1941 and 1961 helped to strengthen the position of executive secretary. Perhaps Wood's successors had no desire to wield the power that he did. Baldwin characterized the NUL presidents between 1941 and 1961 as men "whose first interest was necessarily in making a living."[37] In the final analysis, a rapid succession of NUL presidents enabled Granger to establish himself as the dominant and often overpowering figure in the NUL. At least this was true between 1942 and 1956.

As the dominant figure in the NUL, Granger took full advantage of a succession of NUL presidents. William H. Baldwin, III, was the first of a series of NUL presidents. Born on September 17, 1891, in Saginaw, Michigan, to Ruth S. and William H. Baldwin, Jr., Baldwin's involvement in the Urban League commenced in 1916. He cited filial loyalty (his mother was one of the NUL founders) rather than concern over racial matters as what had attracted him to the work of the Urban League Movement.[38] Baldwin organized the Brooklyn Urban League in 1917, and served as its president from 1917 to 1927. He was also a trustee of Fisk University in Nashville.

Baldwin assumed the NUL presidency at the height of the Granger-Wilkins feud. He deplored the fact that the NUL and the NAACP leaders no longer were willing to lead the search for equality as partners. Therefore he endeavored to smooth relations between Granger and Wilkins. On December 14, 1943, Baldwin informed the Board that Walter White had agreed to an NAACP-NUL meeting "as soon as Mr. Granger determined the number of representatives and a date."[39] Granger's initial response to the impending NUL-NAACP meeting was favorable. Following an NAACP release implying that the League supported the creation of an all-Negro hospital (Syndenham) in Harlem, Granger called for a complete break with the NAACP. The Board rejected Granger's suggestion, but decided not to hold the meeting with NAACP officials, because Granger opposed it.[40] Baldwin met privately with Granger, explaining that it was folly to believe that any permanent solution could be found to the impasse. His advice to Granger was that NUL officials should ignore Wilkins's press releases.[41]

Baldwin's effort proved futile. Granger and Wilkins continued taking swipes at each other. As the NUL-NAACP struggle for leadership of the civil rights movement continued unabated, Randolph entered the picture. His skill as a mediator did not make Granger and Wilkins friends, but neither man could ignore the fact that Randolph's stature commanded the respect of all classes of Negroes. They could ill afford to have Randolph publicly state that their desire to lead the Negro struggle took precedent over the Negro condition. Therefore they continued to compete with each other, but not publicly.[42]

Randolph was able to achieve public cooperation from Granger and Wilkins on the railroad controversy. As with the drive to end racial discrimination in defense industries, Randolph was one of several Negro leaders who informed the public of the conditions confronting "colored firemen on various railroads in the South."[43] On February 18, 1941, a "nonpromotable contract" was entered into between the railroads and the Brotherhood of Locomotive Firemen and Enginemen. This contract not only ousted Negro firemen from their jobs, but it also denied them contractual rights of seniority, pension, and promotion.[44] Randolph formed a Citizens' Committee to Save Colored Locomotive Firemen's Jobs. In the wake of Randolph's activities, the NUL and the NAACP protested the actions of the railroads and the union, especially after McNutt had postponed the FEPC hearings that were to investigate the railroads and the unions.

The Committee to save Negro firemen's jobs garnered the support of several powerful Americans. Mrs. Roosevelt lent her name to the Committee as honorary chairman, with the understanding that her acceptance involved "no obligation or duties."[45] Mayor La Guardia assumed the permanent chairmanship.[46] With this backing, Randolph insisted upon a resumption of the scheduled railroad hearings; he argued that their resumption would "save the prestige and authority of the FEPC and of the Executive Order it implements."[47]

Despite Randolph's role in pressuring the federal government to resume the railroad hearings, Granger took full credit "for initiating [them], and also for securing an interpretation of the railroads as being defense industries."[48] Randolph did not mind the NUL taking credit for the positive outcome of the railroad hearings, inasmuch as he, unlike Granger and Wilkins, was not interested in publicity but in results.

Both Granger and Wilkins enjoyed the attention given them by the news media. Granger had hopes of rivaling the NAACP in the news media's coverage of the Negroes' growing demands for equality and equality of justice under the law. But neither could Wilkins claim prescience; his actions too had caused the NUL-NAACP dispute. Individuals close to Wilkins characterized him as having a fondness for combat with other Negro organizations, and an enjoyment of pushing people around unnecessarily. In the final analysis, the extent of Granger's and Wilkins's hostility toward each other prevented the formation of a united front for resolving the racial issues of the World War II and the post-World War II eras.

III

Granger's and Wilkins's petty bickering did not stand in the way of NUL assaults on the policies of federal agencies condoning housing discrimination, and did not soften its attacks on city officials' policies that created explosive situations in urban centers. The NUL's initial entry into the urban housing issue was at a time when the NUL and the NAACP were on friendly terms with each other. In 1911 the NLUCAN (NUL) convened a conference, at which its officials and those of NAACP discussed the "improper sanitary and moral conditions of Negroes' homes growing out of neglect by the City of New York Departments."[49] The outcome of the conference was the creation of a Housing Bureau within the NUL, headed by John T. Clark, a Negro lawyer. The Housing Bureau, from 1914 to 1940, did little more than conduct housing studies at the request of the Urban League affiliates, and during the 1930s it urged officials in the North to desegregate public housing.

The federal government's entry into the housing field during the 1930s was a factor that caused the NUL to begin attempts at reforming existing governmental structures. During the 1930s Urban League affiliates sought to place some of their staff members on agencies that directed publicly financed housing. In some instances they experienced success. By 1940 fourteen local Urban Leagues had representatives on rent control committees, advisory housing committees, and housing authorities.

The presence of Urban Leaguers on the various agencies did not end segregation in public housing in the Northern cities. Hence the NUL made Northern integrated housing (publicly financed housing) one of its main goals during World War II. In the fall of 1940 the NUL's staff asked Charles Palmer, the Federal Defense Housing Coordinator, to clarify the federal government's ambiguous housing policies in regard to urban Negroes.[50] Without replying directly to the request, Palmer forwarded a memorandum to the Defense Housing Staff, suggesting the adoption of a housing program that would not adversely affect the nation's total defense productivity. Officials of the NUL interpreted the memorandum to mean that defense housing in the North would be assigned on a nonracial basis. City officials, meanwhile, believed that the Palmer memorandum allowed public opinion to set the racial composition of defense housing.

Several tense situations arose out of the dubious Palmer memorandum. One was in Buffalo, New York. Disputes over the racial composition of public housing in that city had plagued the community since 1934. In that year the WPA announced the construction of a housing development in a Negro residential area, but the site was abandoned after option-grabbing drove land costs to prohibitive heights.[51] Meanwhile the erection of yet another federally funded housing development, the Kenfield project, an integrated housing unit in a predominantly white neighborhood, drew a storm of protest from the surrounding community, causing the development to be closed to Negro occupancy. Both the NUL and the Buffalo Urban League protested the decision, but to no avail.

After the above events, and with ruffled feelings on both sides, in May of 1941 the Division of Defense Housing announced plans to build an integrated housing development in North Buffalo. Mindful of the Kenfield incident, the NUL urged John M. Carmody, Federal Works Agency administrator, to assure the whites in the area that only a few Negro families would be allowed in the project. Carmody rejected the idea of a quota system, and whites in the area concluded that the development would eventually be for Negroes only.[52] Strong protests by whites led the federal government to abandon the North Buffalo site. A later announcement told of erecting housing for Negroes on land outside of the city limits. Nearby white inhabitants, upon learning of the statement, objected to the selection. This time those whites were joined by Polish-American (Roman Catholic) priests and local politicians in denouncing the federal government for attempting to integrate white neighborhoods; this site was also abandoned. The selection of yet another location, this time in South Buffalo, provoked a similar response. The mayor and other local politicians denounced this latest site, charging that white citizens had not been contacted prior to the announcement. They threatened to thwart any housing that was not built in neighborhoods that already were inhabited by Negroes.

By the summer of 1941, new housing for Buffalo's Negroes had become an emotional and potentially explosive issue. Local politicians, real estate brokers, business owners, the local citizenry, and even representatives of the Roman Catholic Church had joined forces to prevent the erection of new housing in any area that was not designated a Negro section. The NUL angrily demanded that the Federal Works Agency not capitulate to racist elements in the city, and carry "forward the housing project planned for Buffalo and too long delayed."[53] Federal officials responded favorably to the NUL's blast by announcing that an all-Negro housing project would be constructed in South Buffalo.

The whites residing in South Buffalo did not take kindly to the decision that housing for Negroes would be built in an adjoining neighborhood. These whites were organized by Catholic priests to oppose the housing development. The government, however, stood by its decision, and it informed the whites that the housing project would be all-Negro. The fact that the federal government had sanctioned segregated housing in Buffalo infuriated NUL officials no less than the involvement of the Catholic priests did. Moreover, the fact that the Reverend Charles Coughlin of Detroit supported the actions of the Buffalo priests became a source of irritation to NUL officials.

Granger wrote to the Most Reverend John A. Duffy, Bishop of the Diocese of Buffalo, charging the priests and Coughlin with contributing to a campaign of hate that was "directed against Negroes who are loyal Americans and *bona fide* citizens of Buffalo."[54] While the bishop did not vindicate the actions of the priests, an aide of the bishop did inform Granger that Father Charles Coughlin, who had made notorious inflammatory broadcasts during the 1930s, was "one of the best friends that the Negro has now in Buffalo or will ever have."[55] Albin Krebs of the *New York Times* concluded that the Reverend Coughlin was one of many fiery preachers who played upon the emotions of a distraught and fearful populace during the Great Depression of the 1930s. He began radio broadcasting in 1926 after the Ku Klux Klan burned a cross in the churchyard of the Shrine of the Little Flower in Detroit. Coughlin's early broadcasts were devoted to religious subjects, but during the fall of 1930 he began attacking the Communists, modern capitalism, and unionism, scapegoats that many Americans seemed to want. On the other hand, Coughlin's friendly references to Hitler and Mussolini and his increasingly anti-Semitic broadcasts and magazine articles led his followers to revere him and his opponents to loathe him. Ultimately, the Papacy ordered Coughlin not to make any further broadcasts, but this order did not immediately silence him.

The note that Granger received from an aide of the Buffalo bishop regarding Coughlin was unsatisfactory, as was the federal government's approval of segregated housing. Indeed it was a foregone conclusion that

Coughlin was not a friend of the Negro and that the federal government withheld its support of integrated housing whenever whites objected to it.

The manner in which the federal government handled a housing impasse in Detroit underscored the fact that white opinion influenced housing decisions. The background of the Detroit housing crisis, however, differed markedly from that in Buffalo. Whites in Detroit had for several decades resorted to violence and extralegal tactics to contain a burgeoning Negro population that had increased from 5,800 in 1910 to 198,000 by 1940. The federal government's plans to increase Negro housing in Detroit added fuel to an already tense situation. In 1941 the Federal Works Agency unveiled plans to erect an all-Negro housing project—The Sojourner Truth Development—named after the famous Negro conductor of the underground railroad during the slavery period. A coalition of priests, politicians, community business leaders, and individuals opposed the project. Bowing to pressure, the federal government announced that the development would be for white defense workers. The decision prompted Negro leaders, CIO officials, and others to demand an explanation from the federal government. A hurriedly arranged meeting between a delegation of white and Negro citizens, Baird Snyder, the acting administrator of the Federal Works Agency, and Charles Palmer, coordinator of defense housing, resulted in the project reverting to an all-Negro development. In the meantime Granger had wired Palmer and Snyder, castigating them and the federal government for not standing by the original decision, which had designated the development a Negro housing unit.[56] What troubled Granger the most, however, was the fact that the federal government neither had a coherent housing policy to accommodate the needs of defense workers nor one that would protect the interests of the Negro defense workers.

The decision to open the Sojourner Truth development heightened fears and created additional tensions between scores of whites and Negroes. In fact, some of Detroit's white citizens publicly announced that they would prevent Negroes from moving into the project. These were not idle threats. Waving the American flag and planting a burning cross in public view, nearly two hundred whites stood outside the project the night before Negroes were to move into the development. By the next morning, February 28, 1942, the crowd had swelled to a howling mob of nearly two thousand angry whites armed with knives, rifles, shotguns, and other deadly weapons. The arrival of moving vans, trucks, and cars loaded with furniture sent the mob into the streets, and not until mounted police arrived were the vehicles able to depart. Within a few hours of the initial clash, a second one erupted. A truck bearing fifteen Negro men armed with lead pipes precipitated a bloody clash. Quick action by the police kept the injured to fifteen persons.[57] The project remained closed as the federal government pondered its next move. Detroit's City Hall, however, acted swiftly.

Sizing up the situation, Mayor Edward J. Jeffries declared that the project would remain closed. He was of the opinion that three thousand police would be required to ensure the safety of the Negroes who had rented apartments in the project.[58] Meanwhile Detroit Police Commissioner Frank D. Eamen, who had opposed the project, publicly stated that the police would not provide protection if the Negroes attempted to occupy the project.[59]

The actions of Eamen, Jeffries, and other white officials were an embarrassment to Roosevelt. The proponents of the housing project charged that Eamen, Jeffries, the Ku Klux Klan, and other hate groups were responsible for the housing riot. Representatives from local civil rights organizations, the NUL, the Detroit Urban League, the United Auto Workers Union, and individual citizens traveled to Washington and conferred with Justice Department officials in the wake of the riot.[60] All sides agreed that the project would remain a housing development for Negro war workers. Yet NUL officials could not forgive the federal officials whose actions had given encouragement to whites opposing the housing development. As stated previously, Granger held the Democratic administration in Washington responsible, primarily because of its ties to labor, white ethnics, and the Southern bloc. He also regarded the urban Democratic machines as being unsympathetic to the aspirations of Negroes.

The manner in which Detroit's City Hall and the Democratic-controlled legal system handled the Sojourner Truth project confirmed Granger's suspicions. A grand jury investigation resulted in the indictment of the offices of two anti-Negro groups—the National Workers League, and the Seven Mile-Fenelon Improvement Association. The officers of both groups were charged with violating Negroes' civil rights and seditious conspiracy.[61] None of the indicted were ever brought to trial, however.

The indictments did lessen the white opposition to Negroes occupying the Sojourner Truth Housing Project. During May of 1942 Negroes moved into the project under the watchful eye of a thousand State Troopers and nearly one hundred city police. The federal government acted responsibly in the sense that it backed NUL officials on the need for public housing for Negro war workers. But the fact that the housing project was segregated indicated a reluctance on the part of the federal government to embrace integrated public housing as a national policy. The federal government's failure to embrace integrated housing and its reluctance to underwrite improved housing for Negro war workers set the stage for explosive racial tensions in a number of urban centers during World War II.

Between June and November of 1943, race riots occurred in places as diverse as Detroit, New York, and Los Angeles. Nearly every major city contained the elements that were conducive to racial clashes. The two most devastating racial riots in 1943, in terms of personal and property damage, erupted in Detroit and New York. Indeed the riots during the summer of 1943 signaled that the strategies of the NUL and the NAACP, and the ideologies underlying both organizations, were being reviewed by scores of urban Negroes.

As stated previously, both the NUL and the NAACP were authentic products of the Progressive Era. Their strategies to promote change in society precluded confrontation, direct action, and extralegal tactics. Ending segregation and racial discrimination, however, remained their number one priority. Both the NUL and the NAACP had long tried to end racial discrimination and other forms of injustices through elections, education, training, and other conventional channels. Urban racial violence generally indicates that "rioting is at once a cause and result of dissent; both a symptom and a political tactic."[62] The riots also made it quite clear that when urban Negro America found the conventional channels of protest and political activity obstructed, it would resort to other methods of action.[63]

In the most basic sense, the 1943 riots were attempts by some Negroes to bring the federal government into their disputes with City Hall as the third party. Whether or not the scores of Negro participants in the riots realized it, the federal government could ill afford to have the war industries shut down. Therefore the federal government had a direct stake in curbing the violence, in part because of the propaganda value that the riots offered America's adversaries. In the final analysis, the riots, as one political scientist has stated, served as a measurement of the extent to which relatively deprived groups may seek redress of legitimate grievances.[64]

The Detroit riot was an attempt on the part of segments of the Negro community to seek a redress of legitimate grievances. The riot had its origins in the strained racial relations that had marked Negro-white hostilities for several decades. The more immediate causes of the riot were linked to the 1942 Sojourner Truth Housing riot described above, as well as to the race strikes at the Packard Motor Car Company, the Dodge Truck Company, the Timken Detroit Axle Company, the U.S. Rubber Corporation, Vickers, and the Hudson Naval Arsenal.[65] Moreover, the presence in Detroit of practitioners of racial hatred, namely Gerald L. K. Smith and Father Charles Coughlin, added to the already tense atmosphere that engulfed the city.

On June 20, 1943, a clash between a white sailor and a Negro civilian, following several minor altercations on a bridge linking Belle Isle Park to the mainland, triggered a riot. The spread of wild rumors, particularly that a Negro woman and her child had been thrown into the river by whites, added fuel to the fire.[66] By nightfall the looting and wrecking of white-owned stores in Negro neighborhoods had commenced. Before the first night of rioting had ended, Negro gangs had set upon whites, and white gangs had sought out Negroes to administer beatings. By Tuesday morning, the day that the police and the United States Army had brought the riot under control, twenty-six persons were dead (twenty-three of whom were Negroes), more than one hundred had suffered serious injuries, and over fifteen hundred had been arrested.[67]

Detroit's politicians, police, city administrators, and most of the white population imputed the riots to agitation by "militants." The Urban League rejected this view and sent its own investigators to the scene of the riot. Its representatives concluded, upon weighing the evidence, that Negroes were unhappy over inadequate housing, frequent labor disturbances in the city, continued employment discrimination, police brutality, and the general patterns of segregation and discrimination that the white population had insisted upon.[68] In addition, the League called attention to inadequate recreational facilities in the Negro areas of Detroit, citing this as another factor that caused the rioting.[69] Officials of the NUL and the Detroit Urban League also stated that the Negro population resented the arbitrary action of the police in making arrests during the riot. Taken into police custody were more than twelve hundred Negroes and fewer than two hundred whites, although the evidence indicated that an equal number from both groups had participated in the three-day riot.[70] The most damaging evidence presented by League investigators was an incident in which four Negroes, entrusting their safety to white police, were handed over to a white mob.[71]

These disclosures disturbed Detroit's Negro and white citizens even more deeply. Detroit's white politicians had ascribed the rioting to a bunch of hoodlums who were attempting to thwart "law and order" in the city. But the rioting was more than that. As stated earlier, Negro participation in the rioting was a way of gaining access to the political process. The urban Negro population, at least a segment of it, abandoned the traditional ways of affecting the political process. Violence, rather than votes and politics, was a means of forcing the "white establishment" to recognize Negro demands. And more so than during "Red Summer" of 1919, the actions of urban Negroes during 1943 pointed to an increasing reliance upon violence to force the redistribution of scarce political and economic resources. By 1943 urban Negroes and those who had moved into urban centers during World War II were acutely aware of discrimination in American society. This perception had reduced their tolerance for injustice. The new opportunities made available to the urban Negro masses between 1941 and 1943 had also heightened aspirations. After it was abundantly clear that their aspirations were unrealizable, those masses manifested a distinct hostility toward the white power structure. In 1943 urban Negroes were also reevaluating the strategies of the NAACP and the NUL to end discrimination in American society. But the larger society was not cognizant of the changes that had been brought on by the urbanization of Negroes. Nor did it see a need to support changes that would prevent further rioting.

It was the Urban League Movement that bore the task of popularizing the means of curbing violence, and preventing its use as a way of participating in the political process. In a report presented to Detroit's City Hall by the NUL and the Urban League of Detroit, the Urban League Movement recommended the following: an increase of Negroes on the city's police force; more frequent garbage and rubbish removal in the densely populated residential areas; more and better housing for the city's Negro population; and the retention of federal troops in the city for at least ninety additional days. No less important, but in the tradition of the NUL's social work program, its officials called for educational courses in race and human relations for the entire city.[72]

Mayor Jeffries, Detroit's chief executive officer, and other city officials accepted the Urban League's recommendations on ways to resolve racial tensions in the riot-torn city of Detroit, but withheld final approval of any of them. Yet there was some activity on the part of Detroit's public officials to improve interracial relations. An interracial commission, appointed by the mayor, was charged with the responsibility of assembling information as may "be available to formulate such programs as it thought advisable, and to make such recommendations as the information and its experience may dictate."[73] Among the twelve members of the commission were: William J. Norton, Executive Vice-President of the Children's Fund of Michigan; Fred M. Butsel, a highly respected attorney; John F. Ballinger, Superintendent of Public Welfare of the State of Michigan; and Walter Hardin, a Negro who was also director of the Interracial Division, United Auto Workers Union (CIO).

Despite this distinguished group of individuals, the commission was not well received either by the Urban League or the Detroit community. The Urban League publicly attacked the Commission, charging it with failure to place the blame for the riot where it belonged—on the white citizenry of Detroit. Another committee formed in the wake of the June 1943 race riot was more favorably received. The Metropolitan Detroit Youth Council (MDYC) recommended, among other things, that the youth of Detroit establish an Exchange Meeting Program, and that interracial committees be formed in the city's schools and between schools as a way of defusing racial hostilities.[74] The MDYC's primary purpose was to increase interracial contacts among the youth of the city.

Both the NUL and the Detroit Urban League were quite receptive to the idea of increasing interracial contacts between Negro and white youth.

While other agencies were formed in the wake of the riot to ease tensions, the program of the MDYC had the most immediate and long-term effect on the Urban League Movement. One of the local Urban League's major thrusts, beginning in 1943, was to promote interracial contacts outside of the Urban League Movement. But for the immediate future, and in anticipation of racial troubles in other urban centers, NUL officials and officials of the local Urban Leagues urged city governments to begin taking the necessary steps to head off racial outbursts. In sum, the Urban League Movement called on city officials to begin institutionalizing racial commissions in political structures.

A race riot occurred in New York City before any remedial action could be instituted there. During the course of making a routine arrest, James Collins, a white policeman, was accused of handling a Negro woman too roughly. The arrest was made in the lobby of the Braddock Hotel, located at 125th Street and 8th Avenue in the heart of Harlem, a Negro community. Private Robert Bandy, a Negro soldier, took offense at the manner in which Collins arrested the Negro woman. Patrolman Collins, in turn, took the comments from Bandy as an affront to his authority and, reacting too quickly, shot Bandy. A rumor to the effect that a white policeman has shot and killed a Negro soldier who was protecting his mother against police brutality quickly spread throughout the Harlem community. One interesting sidelight to the rumor is the fact that the police insisted that the "mother" in question was a "lady of the evening" who used the lobby of the hotel as a point of solicitation. Whatever the truth of the matter, the Harlem community believed otherwise, and tempers flared. A riot of major proportions erupted in Harlem. Congregating in the vicinity of 125th Street and 8th Avenue, an unruly mob proceeded to smash store windows, loot white-owned stores, and "rush the hospital where the wounded soldier had been taken."[75] Repeated assurances from the hospital staff that the soldier was alive, and that the woman arrested by the white policeman was not the soldier's mother, failed to calm the aroused crowd. That night saw little calm in Harlem, as roving gangs of youths and adults destroyed property in the area of 125th Street.[76]

Prompt action by Mayor Fiorello La Guardia, the police, and most of Harlem's Negroes prevented the disturbance from escalating into a major race war. To ensure against continued trouble, eight thousand members of the New York State National Guard stood by in metropolitan armories. In addition, city officials recruited more than fifteen hundred civilian volunteers, most of whom were Negroes, to enter the area, to resolve the conflict, and to cool tempers.

When the riot ended, five lay dead, about five hundred were injured, some five hundred were arrested, and property damages amounted to about $5 million. While a minor incident had triggered the riot, it was poor housing, job discrimination, and other interrelated problems that caused the riot in the first place. The NUL and the Urban League of New York made the usual on-site inspection, and fixed the blame for rioting on continued segregation and discrimination.

In the weeks following the riots in New York, Detroit, and other cities, the federal government devoted little time to probing the conditions underlying the riots. While some people proposed governmental intervention on behalf of the Negroes, most white Americans insisted that Negroes were primarily responsible for their plight, and that they were receiving what was due them. Governmental officials sought to dodge the issues by proposing only palliatives. United States Attorney General Francis Biddle, for example, proposed limiting migration into defense centers, especially where there was already overcrowding.[77] It was unclear whether or not Biddle was referring only to the Negro migrants. Accordingly NUL officials, following a go-it-alone policy rather than seeking NAACP cooperation, implored the Attorney General to clarify his ambiguous proposal. After considerable prodding, Biddle stated that the federal government had no plans to control the flow of people into defense centers, racially or otherwise.[78] He would not, however, enter into discusisons with NUL officials on the federal government's role in eliminating housing and employment discrimination, and in ending Jim Crow in the South.

Biddle's reluctance to discuss housing and employment discrimination, as well as Jim Crow in the South, meant that Roosevelt did not see a reason to end these practices. Hence it was a foregone conclusion that the housing disturbances and the 1943 riots had not convinced Roosevelt, state and city political officials, and federal agency heads that segments of the urban Negro population would no longer subscribe to conventional methods of airing their grievances.

The housing disturbances and the 1943 urban riots also brought home a message to NUL officials. They were a repudiation of NUL strategies—fact-finding, negotiation, and mediation. The NUL's reports and recommendations in the wake of the housing disturbances and the riots were aimed at urban Negroes, city halls, federal agency heads, and Roosevelt, but to no avail. By 1943 Granger and other NUL officials realized that reforming existing governmental structures was a Herculean task.

Randolph's call for a massive and all-Negro March on Washington Movement had radically altered urban Negroes' search for equality. From 1909 to 1941, it was unthinkable for upper- and middle-class Negroes to demand their rights outside of an interracial structure. Randolph's proposed March on Washington clearly showed that mass power—Negro power—was capable of extracting from the President a pledge to end employment discrimination in the war industries. Randolph's strategy of dealing with a recalcitrant President was more in tune with the views of urban Negro America than were the more sedate strategies of the NUL and the NAACP. The head of the Sleeping Car Porters Union explained his decision to forge an all-Negro movement: "We shall not call upon our white friends to march with us. There are some things Negroes must do alone. This is our fight and we must see it through."[79] An all-Negro movement was necessary, as Randolph saw it, because the time had come to dispel the long-held myth that Negroes could not accomplish anything without white support.

It remained only a matter of time before several Negro Urban Leaguers, influenced by a growing belief in self-determination, would seek a diminution of white influence and a larger role for themselves in the NUL. Granger of course did not agree that white influence in the NUL should be diminished. Neither did Granger agree that the NUL and the NAACP should jointly head the search for equality, a position that not only angered several NUL Negro Board members but ultimately led to Granger's downfall. Granger's insistence on a wider NUL role in civil rights, however, was the prime reason that the NUL would continue its efforts to reform existing government structures.

6

The Urban League Faces a New Issue: Armed Forces Segregation

The NUL's interest in the armed forces' racial problems peaked at the time when Negroes were demanding an end to segregation, and not merely equality of opportunity in uniform. Chapter 6 discusses the process by which the NUL became involved in the controversy surrounding segregation in the armed forces. This chapter also shows how NUL executive secretary Lester B. Granger was drawn into the controversy, and how his approach to desegregating the armed forces differed from that of the NAACP leaders and A. Philip Randolph. Finally, this chapter shows how the NUL pursued civil rights issues without abandoning its social service orientation.

I

Segregation by race, or the total exclusion of Negroes from the U.S. military, dates back to the Militia Act of May 8, 1792. The Act, enacted by the Congress, declared that every able-bodied white male citizen between the ages of eighteen and forty-five would enroll in a military unit.[1] While the 1792 Act did not specifically bar Negroes from service in the militia, it did leave to the states the decision regarding the racial composition of the militias. In the absence of a federal law, between 1792 and 1820 several states barred Negroes from the militia.

In 1820 the War Department barred Negroes and mulattoes from service in the regular army.[2] The racial composition of the militia units was, as in the past, left to the states. While scores of Negroes served in militia units from 1820 to 1860, the U.S. regular army remained an all-white corps. In 1862 the Congress amended the Militia Act of 1792, enabling Negroes to wear the Union uniform.

Amending the 1792 Militia Act neither ended state control over the racial composition of their militia units nor made Negroes permanent members of the U.S. Army. A bill, approved on February 24, 1864, stated:

> But men of color, drafted or enlisted, or who may volunteer into the military service, while they shall be credited on the quotas of the several states, or subdivisions of states, wherein they are respectively drafted, enlisted, or shall volunteer, shall not be assigned as state troops, but shall be mustered into regiments or companies as United States Colored troops.[3]

This rescinded the 1820 War Department's memorandum barring Negroes from service in the regular army. It is problematical, however, whether the Act of 1864 was intended to give Negroes a permanent role in the Army.

Congressional passage of the Military Reorganization Act of July 28, 1866, and the enactment of a similar bill three years later enabled Negroes to serve in the regular army of the United States. This feat was accomplished by the creation of the 24th and 25th Infantry and the Ninth and Tenth Cavalry regiments, four units comprised of Negro noncommissioned personnel and white officers.[4]

From 1866 to about 1907, considerable debate revolved around these units. Because the Congress did not clarify its intent in the creation of the four Negro regiments, the Reorganization Acts were interpreted in several ways. Some War Department and Army officials interpreted the Acts as mandating segregation. Some members of the Congress believed that segregation in uniform was illegal, while others insisted that the Acts mandated segregation in uniform. A smaller group of national legislators debated whether or not Negroes were needed in the Army. The debate widened after Representative Henry B. Banning introduced House Resolution Number 1018, which, if enacted, would have removed all "restrictions now existing in regard to the enlistment of colored citizens in any arm of the United States Army."[5] This resolution was defeated, but not before Democrats in the House and the Senate, during 1876–77, introduced a series of bills to disband the colored regiments.[6] None of the Democratic-sponsored bills received the necessary votes for passage either.

The War Department, unlike the Congress, was not divided on the presence of Negroes in the regular army. There was, however, sharp disagreement within the War Department and the military establishment about which units Negroes could serve in. General William T. Sherman informed Secretary of War J.D. Cameron on February 21, 1877, of his willingness "to take black and white alike on equal terms."[7] Secretary Cameron wrote to General Benjamin F. Butler on February 5, 1877, that:

> I advise that the word black be obliterated from the Statute Book, that whites
> and blacks be enlisted, and distributed alike, as has been the usage in the Navy
> for a hundred years. Contact and usage would obliterate prejudice of race, and
> all regiments would be alike.[8]

Between 1866 and 1884, much of the discussion on the Negro soldier
pertained to disbanding the colored units and to establishing integrated
units.

The discussions of Negro military personnel changed radically about
1884, and attitudes hardened after a Negro attempted to enlist in the
Signal Corps, an arm of the Army created by the Congress on July 28,
1866.[9] The debate revolved around W. Hallet Greene, a graduate of the
City College of New York, who sought enlistment in the Signal Corps.
He was denied admission on the grounds that "the affirmative legislation
creating the four colored regiments has always been construed to exclude
colored enlisted men from the other portions of the Army."[10] Secretary of
War Robert Todd Lincoln annulled the decision barring Greene from the
Signal Corps, and informed W.B. Hazen, Brigadier and Brevet General,
that:

> The Signal Officer of the Army is hereby ordered to give such orders and
> instructions to the officers now or hereafter serving under him as recruiting
> officers for the Signal Corps of the Army as will prohibit the rejection as a
> recruit by any such recruiting officer of any applicant for enlistment in the
> Signal Corps on account of color, or on account of the African descent of such
> applicant.[11]

Hazen refused to execute Secretary Lincoln's order. His actions not only
denied Negroes equality of opportunity in uniform, but also promoted a
dual Army.

Despite a gradual acceptance of a segregated Army and the total exclusion of Negroes from certain arms of the Army, the debate over whether
or not the Reorganization Acts restricted Negroes to the four regiments
continued unabated. In 1904 the Army Adjutant General George B. Davis issued a ruling that the Congress had willed in 1866 that Negroes
would be confined to four regiments of the Army.[12] A War Department
memorandum of 1907 stated that "no law is known to exist prohibiting
the acceptance of colored men in white organizations."[13] In 1912 a ruling
by the Judge Advocate General concluded that Negroes were restricted to
service in the four regiments created in 1866 by the Congress and therefore were ineligible for service in the Coast Artillery.[14] However, another
ruling from the Office of the Judge Advocate General did not rule out the
placing of Negroes in white units. This ruling declared that "there is no
legislation which would prevent the enlistment of colored cooks in white
regiments of volunteers, and that such enlistment would be legal."[15] By

1921 both the War Department and senior Army officers argued for segregation, and a general acceptance of their arguments indeed limited Negroes' chances of equality of opportunity in uniform.[16]

The limiting of Negroes to the four regiments created by the Congress in 1866 was what led to attempts by Negroes to end segregation in the armed forces. Two issues separated Negro leaders and the War Department and senior military officials. The first was the War Department's firm "no" to Negroes wishing to enlist in the Air Corps.[17] The second was the decision of the War Department and senior Army officials to convert the four Negro regiments into service units so as to be able to expand the size of the Air Corps.[18] In the wake of these actions, Negro leaders called for an end to segregation.

The War Department's determination to bar Negroes from the Air Corps and to assign most Negroes in uniform to service jobs only did not escape the attention of NUL officials. Editorials appearing in the NUL's official organ *Opportunity* denounced armed forces segregation as vehemently as did the Negro newspapers and the *Crisis,* an NAACP publication. One editorial stated that the time had come to reverse the policies of limitation and exclusion from the various branches of the military and naval services.[19] A second pointed out that "nowhere is racial prejudice more entrenched than in the Army and the Navy of the United States."[20] A third declared that the bureaucrats in the War and Navy Departments "have the same conception of race relations as was commonly held about 1890."[21] Elmer Carter, editor of *Opportunity,* made the most caustic remarks about Navy and Army Department officials, charging that their policies were deliberate attempts "to humiliate the Negro citizen, and to stigmatize the Negro officers."[22] Carter called on the President to ban segregation in the enlisted ranks as well as in the Officer Corps.

There were only five Negro officers in the regular army in 1940, and three of them were chaplains.[23] In 1940 West Point listed only four Negro graduates since its founding.[24] The War Department insisted that it neither discriminated against Negroes who wished to become officers nor supported segregation. While it is arguable that the War Department was not to blame for the fact that so few Negroes were West Point graduates, it did, however, mandate segregation in the use of PX stores, recreational facilities, mess halls, training camps, and living quarters.

President Roosevelt and the War and Navy Department officials tried without success to convince Negro leaders that they neither promoted nor supported racism in the Army, Navy, Air Corps, and Marine Corps. The coverage given America's two armed services policies by the Negro and foreign press was a source of embarrassment to President Roosevelt.

The role played by the Negro news media in airing racial segregation, both in the civilian and military phases of the war effort, did not escape the President's attention. George Schuyler maintained that it was the *Pittsburgh Courier,* a Negro newspaper, which "took the lead in the reform of the Army."[25] Schuyler and other staff members of the paper won the ear of New York Congressman Hamilton Fish, who had commanded a Negro unit during World War I. Fish repeatedly introduced legislation forbidding segregation in the selection of men to serve in the Army. With few exceptions, Fish's colleagues in the House, and the Senate, rejected the legislation. Subsequently, and upon the advice of staff members of the *Pittsburgh Courier* and Negro leaders, Fish proposed legislation to create separate units in all arms of service, and to authorize the commissioning of Negroes in the Army.[26]

While Roosevelt had few objections to expanding opportunities for Negro enlisted men, he balked at the idea of integration and the commissioning of Negro officers, even though Negroes had correctly charged the War Department with perpetuating segregation. Roosevelt proceeded with caution. He first sought to gauge popular opinion among Negro leaders at a White House meeting on September 27, 1940. Attending this meeting, in addition to the President, were Navy Secretary Frank Knox, Assistant Secretary of War Robert Patterson, Walter F. White of the NAACP, T. Arnold Hill, Assistant Director of the National Youth Administration Division of Negro Affairs, and A. Philip Randolph, president of the Sleeping Car Porters Union. The Negro delegation explicitly informed Roosevelt and the War and Navy Department representatives that Negroes objected to Jim Crow in the armed services, and that anything short of equality of opportunity was unacceptable. Knox and Patterson argued that the full execution of the war, rather than the dismantling of the two-armed-services policy, was the pressing issue of the day. Roosevelt did not appear to be particularly opposed to either argument, enabling the meeting to end on a harmonious note. Considerable hostility arose, however, from within Negro America as the result of an Army directive of October 1940. The memorandum, issued with Roosevelt's solid approval, implied that the Negro leaders at the September 27, 1940, meeting had approved of segregation in the Army. The most infuriating part of the memorandum was the section that barred Negroes from officer rank in the regular army, and mandated that Negro American chaplains and physicians be assigned only to colored units.[27]

Officials from the NUL joined those from the NAACP in denouncing Roosevelt. The fact that neither Jones nor Granger had been invited to participate in the conference was viewed as a slap in the face. Presumably Roosevelt and War and Navy Department officials were unaware of the NUL's official position on segregation in the armed services.[28] Whatever the reason for the oversight, Jones, in a telegram to Roosevelt, informed the President that any enforcement of the Army directive of October

1940 was unacceptable to him and other NUL officials as well as to the Negro population.[29]

Public denunciations of the 1940 Army directive by the NUL, the NAACP, and other organizations and individuals did not go unanswered. In order to rectify what appeared to be a political blunder, the War Department, with Roosevelt's blessings, announced that Benjamin O. Davis, Sr., had been promoted to the rank of Brigadier General. Schuyler insisted that the promotion was prompted by political considerations, although he was quick to point out that Davis was well deserving of it.[30] The fact that Roosevelt revealed the promotion only weeks before the November presidential election gives credence to Schuyler's conclusion. As an added measure, and presumably to appease Negro voters, the War Department decided to assign Negro reserve officers to "colored units of the Army."[31] The decision to activate Negro officers, while welcomed, did not address the question of racial segregation in the Army.

Davis's promotion and the fact that he assumed command of the Ninth and Tenth Cavalry regiments, which were staffed by white officers, did not solve the segregation controversy either. The Negro press did, however, praise Roosevelt for promoting Davis and recognizing his contributions to the Army. At the same time, the Negro press reminded the War Department that its decision to place white officers in Davis's command was a violation of War Department regulations: the War Department decreed in 1940 that white officers would not serve under Negro officers.[32] At the moment it seemed that Roosevelt was more concerned with curbing Negro criticism than with his own violation of a War Department directive.[33] In the final analysis, the NUL received considerable publicity from the events surrounding the much-discredited War Department memorandum.

II

Lester B. Granger revealed that the coming of World War II "gave the headlines that the Urban League needed."[34] The press that the NUL received was largely the work of William Paley, president of the Columbia Broadcasting System.[35] In addition, the financial support given the NUL by the Taconic, Field, and William Paley Foundations enabled the NUL to expand its activities in America. It should be noted that these foundations supported the work of the NUL despite the fact that much of it was no longer social service in orientation.

By 1941 the NUL resorted to pressure group tactics in an effort to end the practice of both employment discrimination and of separating Negro and white armed forces personnel.[36] Segregation and other injustices had indeed contributed to racial tensions, as evidenced by the bloody racial clashes between Negroes and whites during World War II, one of which occurred in the fall of 1941 at Fort Bragg, North Carolina.[37] A second incident, at Alexandria, Louisiana, in January of 1942, was precipitated by the arrest of Negro soldiers by civilian police. Twenty-nine soldiers were shot as open warfare erupted with civilians.[38]

Negro leaders capitalized on these and other racial clashes, and called for a speedy end to the Army's antiquated racial policies. With the sudden increase of Negro personnel in the Army, racial clashes became more frequent, followed by increased calls for a desegregated Army. Yet the War Department created additional Negro regiments rather than integrate Negroes in those already formed. From rough estimates, there were approximately 13,000 Negroes in Army uniform in 1940; by 1944 there were 675,000. The fact that most of the training camps were located in the South contributed to additional racial tensions. Negro soldiers from the North objected not only to Southern racial customs and laws but also in a number of instances refused to abide by them. The War Department, however, insisted that local and regional laws and customs be strictly adhered to.

The federal government presumably did not see its policies as fostering racial unrest in the Army. Instead the federal government held the Negro press responsible for instigating racial tensions on military posts. For example, Archibald MacLeish, director of the Office of Facts and Figures (the predecessor of the Office of War Information), called an informal conference with Negro editors in an attempt to "counsel them on treatment of news."[39] They refused MacLeish's counsel, informing him that "unless the Negro was accorded his constitutional rights as a citizen they would not cease militant crusading."[40] In the aftermath of the informal conference, at least four Negro newspapers reported visits from the Federal Bureau of Investigation (FBI). The staff of the *Pittsburgh Courier,* one of the papers visited, told FBI agents to cease in their efforts to frighten Negroes into silence, and to begin investigating "those forces fostering Fascism in America."[41] Although the Justice Department was unable to muzzle the Negro press corps, the FBI and the various military intelligence units maintained a watchful eye over it throughout the war years. Political leaders of the Negro communities were also placed under FBI surveillance during the World War II era.

Negro leaders and the Negro press, while not abating in their attacks on segregation, made special efforts to support the fight against Nazism. Lester B. Granger, for example, stated that "no special racial objective is so important at this time as Victory for Democracy."[42] At the same time, he let it be known that "we continue even in the midst of war to fight for Negroes' right to work, live and die on the basis of American equality."[43]

The Army was reluctant to alter its racial policies, as traditions were not easily changed. Indeed, as one source stated, "the Army maintained that segregation was only a factor, that this was the way it always had been, always would be, and so on."[44] Roger N. Baldwin, a Board member of the NUL and a trustee of NAACP funds, declared that public agitation "became an effective tool to free the masses of folk from bondage."[45]

By 1943 public agitation and pressure group tactics had finally achieved limited results. The Army had ceased altogether relying on a quota system to limit the number of Negroes who could volunteer to serve their country in uniform, and some integration was permitted.[46] But the War Department would not as yet admit that segregation transgressed democratic principles. By 1943, however, someone in the War Department recommended that the Army must henceforth take into account the psychological needs of Negro soldiers. And there was also a detectable awareness on the part of some Army officers that segregation had contributed to racial tensions. A manual illustrating the manner in which Negro soldiers wished to be treated was given to all Army officers.[47] Presumably the contacts between NUL officials and senior Army officers had made the manual possible, inasmuch as the NUL had a profound interest in improving interracial relations.

These changes were indeed impressive, but anything short of desegregation could not silence those who called for an end to the two-army policy. Representatives of the NUL met with Undersecretary of War Patterson on April 2, 1944, in order to assess the Army's new direction, and to recommend further changes. From this meeting came an agreement to commission Negroes for service in the Industrial Personnel Division of the Army.[48] Other changes followed in the wake of the meeting between NUL officials and War Department representatives, although the NUL could not take sole responsibility for them.

On July 8, 1944, Major General James A. Ulio, the Army Adjutant General, directed that Army posts discontinue segregation in the use of recreational facilities.[49] The fact that the Army now supported "social" integration drew both praise and criticism. The NUL Board of Directors praised the Ulio memorandum. Representative John E. Rankin of Mississippi and Alabama Governor Chauncey Sparks wired President Roosevelt, denouncing the changes ordered by Major General Ulio. The War Department denied that it supported social integration, but argued that it was only fair to extend to Negro personnel "the same privileges for rest and relaxation."[50]

The Ulio memorandum, while a step in the right direction, did not end racial confrontations on Army posts. The callous manner in which some senior officers interpreted the memorandum did in fact heighten racial tensions. At Selfridge Field, Michigan, an Army Air Corps base, Negro officers were moved to Godman Field, Kentucky, after they had attempted to use a club reserved for white officers.[51] Upon arrival at Godman Field, Negro enlisted Air Corps personnel sat with white soldiers in the post theater at nearby Fort Knox. They were ordered out of the theater by military police and placed under arrest.[52] Such racial confrontations over the use of recreational facilities became commonplace in the Army and the Air Corps.

Colonel Frank D. Gore, Commanding Officer of Deming Army Air Force (AAF) Field, New Mexico, evaded the intent of the Ulio memorandum by allowing white enlisted personnel to decide if Negroes could attend all Non-Commissioned Clubs (NCC) on the field. After the Negroes learned of this plan, their spokesman, Sergeant William P. Baker, attempted to inform Gore that his decision violated the Ulio memorandum. Gore refused to listen to Baker, and ordered him not to speak any further, an order that Sergeant Baker disregarded. As a result, Baker was courtmartialed for insubordination and was demoted to the rank of private.[53] Similar incidents occurred at Freeman Field, Indiana; at Mather Field, California; and at Brookley Field, Alabama, among others.[54] These clashes subsided at the war's end.

III

The rapid demobilization of the armed forces following the end of World War II drastically reduced the number of Negroes in uniform, and also eliminated the conditions sparking racial confrontations. Yet the actions of the War Department and senior Army officials during the immediate postwar period showed their determination to perpetuate segregation. The "Report of Board of Officers on Utilization of Negro Manpower in the Post-War Army," better known as the Gillem Board Report (1945), officially sanctioned racial segregation. Specifically the report recommended: (1) a retention of the integrated units formed during the war; (2) segregated units, although not over the size of a regiment; and (3) the integration of specialists.[55]

Officials of the NUL viewed the Gillem report as a setback for the Negro soldier. Granger publicly condemned it, stating that the report left "unanswered certain questions of segregation."[56] His skepticism was justified in that there were no guarantees that the Army would follow through on its promise to integrate specialists. A circular, dated April 27, 1946, and credited to Patterson of the War Department, rescinded the Roosevelt-sponsored policy of October 1940, which "forbade intermingling of colored and white personnel in the same regimental organizations."[57] But a subsequent War Department memorandum, issued during August (1946), did indeed anger Negro Americans. Without any forewarning, they were barred from reenlisting in the Army, and notices of induction were cancelled. The one exception was that those with critical occupations were exempted from the ban. The Army justified the policy by pointing to that section of the Gillem Board's report which limited Negro entry in the Army to 10 percent of the total personnel.

An investigation of the Army's Negro policy by the Negro press corps uncovered a startling fact: Negro recruits were inducted only if they made a score of 99 on the Army General Classification Test (AGT), while whites had only to score 70. The Public Relations Department of the War Department justified the test score differential on the ground "that it would raise the standard of colored personnel in the Army to that of the colored civilian population."[58] This of course was an unconvincing explanation. In the midst of the sparring, Robert R. Kelly, a nineteen-year-old Negro, initiated a suit against Secretary Patterson and Selective Service Director Louis B. Hershey in order to test the legality of the decision that refused Negro volunteers, draftees, and those seeking reenlistment.[59] *Opportunity* magazine chastised the Army for its "restrictive quota on future enlistments."[60] The issue was finally resolved when President Harry S Truman rescinded the directive.

The War Department did little in the way of furthering the rights of Negro Army personnel between 1946 and 1948. Accordingly, Negro leadership in the persons of A. Philip Randolph and Grant Reynolds, a former World War II Army chaplain, formed the Committee Against Jim Crow in the Military Services and Training (CAJCMST). In testimony before the Senate Armed Services Committee in 1948, Randolph and Reynolds urged both Negro and white men of military age to refuse induction unless segregation was ended.[61]

Randolph's and Reynolds' testimony not only alarmed the Congress, but also caused the NUL Board to meet in special session. Because news media representatives knew of the NUL's position of armed forces segregation, they had an interest in learning of Granger's reactions to the Randolph and Reynolds testimony, and particularly about nonviolent protest.

In anticipation of queries from the news media, Board members of the NUL endeavored to draw up a statement for public release that would be acceptable to news reporters and Negro America alike. There was divided opinion within the NUL on how to respond to the Randolph-Reynolds view. Granger believed that the NUL had to respond to the news media's inquiries, but he cautioned against denouncing the testimony itself. Board member William H. Dean warned against any official mention of the civil disobedience proposition, although he urged his colleagues to speak out against Army segregation. William H. Baldwin, III, withheld comment, but the same cannot be said of his successor, Lloyd K. Garrison, the new NUL president. Garrison was the grandson of William L. Garrison, an antebellum abolitionist. Accounts of Lloyd K. Garrison published in the *New York Times* (February 20, 1946) and *Current Biography, Who's News and Why* (1947) noted that he was a graduate of Harvard College and the Harvard Law School.

Garrison, as the NUL president, let it be known that he and the Board were not required to provide "an answer for every individual argument or proposal of a controversial nature."[62] The Board members did not share this view, deciding, after extended discussion on the Randolph-Reynolds testimony, to wire the President and the Secretary of Defense. This wire urged the federal government to begin the necessary steps "to cope with the evils of segregation in the Army."[63]

Randolph's and Reynolds' call for civil disobedience went well beyond the tactics that NAACP and NUL officials had used to challenge Jim Crow in uniform. Senator Wayne Morse took offense to the Randolph-Reynolds testimony, and charged them with advising young men to be disrespectful of legally constituted laws.[64] President Truman and Defense Department Secretary James V. Forrestal withheld public comment, choosing instead to seek the counsel of Negro leaders as well as that of senior military personnel on how to proceed. It should be pointed out that Forrestal had sought Granger's advice before the Randolph-Reynolds testimony, and had also given thought to meeting with other Negro leaders.

Forrestal arranged a meeting between sixteen Negro leaders and Defense Department officials, to be held on April 26, 1948, in Washington, D.C., with Granger serving as their spokesman at the request of Secretary Forrestal. Granger had earlier served the Navy Department in the capacity of civilian aide, when Forrestal was its Secretary. Forrestal forewarned Granger before the meeting that he would not urge the issuance of an executive order to eliminate segregation in the armed forces.[65] Granger, in turn, informed Forrestal of his strong disapproval of the racial policies that had the support of the Defense Department.[66]

At the April 26, 1948, meeting, Granger, in a prepared statement, told Defense Department representatives that every sector of opinion among Negro America shared "the intense resentment and moral indignation which prompted the Randolph statement."[67] Forrestal reminded all present that the desegregation of the armed forces demanded "time and educational effort."[68] Beyond this, the Defense Department Secretary had little to say during the meeting. Truman, however, had to be more exact on the issue.

Truman, unlike Forrestal, had to concern himself with the fall presidential election. The emerging Dixiecrat revolt had split the solid South, long a mainstay of the Democratic Party. Despite the defection, Truman garnered a majority of the votes cast by the delegates to the Democratic National Convention, held in Philadelphia. Roy Wilkins of the NAACP pointed to the fact that one of Truman's first acts following the Democratic Convention was his issuance of the Army Desegregation Order on July 26, 1948.[69]

Executive Order 9981 was well received in Negro America. George Schuyler maintained that "Truman spoke out frankly on the issue of armed forces segregation. He [was not] as evasive and apparently indifferent as Roosevelt had been."[70] Granger did not comment on the order in his reminiscences. But the fact that Granger consented to serve on the committee to advise the President and the Defense Secretary on desegregation matters indicated his general acceptance of the intent of Executive Order 9981.

Granger accepted his appointment to the Committee on Equality of Treatment and Opportunity in the Armed Services (Fahy Committee) with the understanding that every vestige of racial segregation would be eliminated from the nation's fighting forces. But he and other members of the Fahy Committee lost an important and sympathetic ally with the resignation of Forrestal in early 1949. Granger believed that Truman had betrayed Forrestal shamefully. In 1948, according to the NUL executive secretary, Truman promised Forrestal that "he would have a job as long as he was President."[71] After Walter Winchell and Drew Pearson put out the word that Forrestal was not loyal to Truman, he was replaced. Granger blamed Truman for Forrestal's suicide.[72]

Louis B. Johnson, named by Truman as Forrestal's replacement, made every effort to delay the desegregation of the armed services. The Army took full advantage of Forrestal's untimely departure and in 1949 created its own advisory board. The Chamberlin Board subsequently released its report on February 9, 1950, and recommended: (1) continued segregation, and that Negro representation in the Army not exceed 10 percent of the total; and (2) that Negro soldiers be given greater "opportunities through the creation of new units in a greater variety of service branches."[73] Truman rejected the Chamberlin Board's recommendation, and instructed Army Secretary Gordon Gray to open the "army to qualified applicants without regard to race or color."[74]

The new policy took effect on April 1, 1950, and was a major victory for the Fahy Committee. But it was not until the Korean War that the Army proceeded to desegregate. It is ironical that after all the talk about the Negroes being inferior as combat personnel, the units in war-torn Korea were among the first to integrate, while those in Europe continued in the old Army tradition of separating Negro and white soldiers. Most important, however, was the speed with which the Air Force, a unit of the Army (Army Air Corps) before 1949, ushered in a new era of race relations on becoming an independent unit of the armed services.

IV

The United States Navy officially ordered the separation of Negro and white sailors during the presidency of Woodrow Wilson,[75] after which Negroes were either barred completely or were recruited only as stewards and messmen. During World War I white officers informed Negro volunteers that "they were wanted only for the mess department."[76] Negro enlistments in the Navy ceased altogether during the 1920s, as Filipinos and Guamanians were recruited as messmen and stewards.[77] It was not until 1934 that Negroes could again volunteer for duty in the U.S. Navy. Even then, they were assigned to shore duty, and by 1941 there were only 2,807 Negroes in the Navy. The Marine Corps, under the aegis of the Navy Department, had banned Negroes since its founding during the 1790s.[78]

Naval policies were altered in 1943: Negroes could enlist in the Marine Corps, and they could hold general service ratings (ratings other than messman and steward) in the Navy. By the end of 1943 more than 100,000 Negroes were in the Navy. The Navy Department had, however, established a separate boot camp—Camp Robert Small—to prevent integration. Although general ratings were open to Negro recruits by 1943, they were generally concentrated in ratings that were viewed as "heavy work" jobs. Negroes of course complained about the inequality of opportunity that existed in the Navy, and segregation, along with unforeseen events, led to explosive racial tensions.

On July 17, 1944, an explosion at Port Chicago, California, an ammunitions supply depot, claimed the lives of 323 sailors, 203 of whom were Negroes.[79] Following a week's furlough, the Negro sailors were reassigned to an ammunitions depot in the San Francisco area and ordered to resume loading ammunition. These men refused to handle any ammunition, disobeying the order. The Commandant of the Twelfth Naval District (West Coast) personally visited the base and ordered them to return to work. Thirty-four of the 300 refused to obey the direct order. A few weeks later it was learned that all 300 had been charged with insubordination, and 200 had been found guilty by a Summary Court Martial Board. The remaining 100 were ordered to stand trial before a General Court Martial Board.[80] Negro newspapers provided their readers with ample coverage of the event. They took the Navy to task for the swiftness with which it brought the men to trial, for the excessive fines levied against 200 of the men, and for holding 100 for trial before a General Court Martial Board. Racial frictions in the Pacific, however, soon replaced the Port Chicago "mutiny" on Negro newspapers' front pages.

On Christmas Eve of 1944, a disturbance of major proportions erupted on Guam, climaxing a series of racial confrontations on the Pacific island. A white Marine shot and killed a Negro sailor. In response, Negro sailors armed themselves, commandeered two trucks from the naval supply depot, and headed in the direction of the Marine camp for a showdown. They were apprehended by white Marines and were immediately charged with mutiny. During July of 1945, Major General Henry Larsen, the island Commander, confirmed rumors that thirty Negroes had received sentences ranging from four months to four years. None of the white Marines had charges lodged against them.

The NUL seized upon this and other racial conflicts to strengthen its case against the Navy. In the meantime, Navy Secretary Forrestal hinted that a Negro was being considered to advise him on matters relating to Negro naval personnel. When queried about the Port Chicago "mutiny," Forrestal would only say that he, like Negroes who wore the Navy uniform, supported a policy that guaranteed "equality of opportunity and the chance to work on the same basis as anyone else."[81]

Forrestal announced during February of 1945 that Granger was his choice to become the Navy's civilian Negro advisor. The fact that Granger was asked to serve showed the NUL's deep interest and involvement in armed forces segregation problems. Moreover, Forrestal was a member of the NUL, a $100 a year contributor.[82] Granger accepted the appointment, and met with Forrestal during March of 1945. The NUL's executive secretary urged the Navy Department to conduct a thorough investigation into conditions facing Negro personnel. In addition, he also emphatically asked Forrestal to consider assigning Negro nurses to all naval hospitals, to commission those qualified for officer rank, to open all ranks to Negroes, and to provide wider news coverage for those involved in naval combat.[83] In the final analysis, Granger left no doubt in Forrestal's mind that he and other Negro leaders were indeed unhappy that the Navy practiced segregation.

In July of 1945 Forrestal announced that Granger would embark upon a Pacific fact-finding tour for the Navy. The tour commenced during September of 1945, with visits to Pearl Harbor, the Philippines, and to seven other Pacific islands. Granger met with Admiral Chester W. Nimitz at Pearl Harbor and won his promise to back a program that would integrate Negroes into every phase of naval life.[84] Granger and his naval aide, Lieutenant Bob Roper, a young white Southerner, met with scores of Negro sailors in private, listened to their grievances, and recorded the pertinent information for inclusion in the final report to Forrestal.[85]

Granger submitted the report upon completion of his Pacific tour. In it he charged the Navy with "permitting downright discrimination against colored personnel in the Pacific."[86] A tour of the Atlantic naval bases also uncovered discriminatory practices. Forrestal studied both reports. While there were no immediate changes in naval policies, the Navy Secretary did correct two past wrongs: the mutiny charges against the men involved in the Port Chicago incident were dropped, and all of the sailors convicted by a General Court Martial Board in the aftermath of the Guam "mutiny" were freed. The NUL noted in a press release that the Navy had indeed initiated a new policy toward Negro personnel, as shown in the reversals of the court martial convictions.[87]

The Navy made no further moves in the direction of full integration between the end of World War II and 1948. But following Truman's decision to support equality of opportunity in the armed services, the Navy Department seemed more willing to integrate enlisted men than the Army did. Granger not only criticized past Navy policies that discriminated against Negroes, but he also asked of naval officials their views of future integration. During one of the hearings conducted by the President's Committee on Equality of Treatment and Opportunity in the Armed Services, Granger alluded to Navy officers' lack of consistency in supporting integration. He also reminded Defense Department officials of the fact that they had not as yet ordered the Navy Reserve Officer Training Corps (NROTC) units on the predominantly white college campuses to admit Negroes.[88] Captain Fred Stickney, one of several witnesses that Granger questioned, admitted that the Navy did not plan to order the admission of Negroes to NROTC units on white campuses, and that no NROTC units were planned for Negro college campuses. He argued that only fifty-two units were mandated under law, and that these had already been established on white college campuses.[89]

Throughout 1948 and into 1949, Granger and other Negro leaders chided the Navy for not operating NROTC units on Negro college campuses. Granger also recommended that the Navy commission Negro dentists and physicians in the regular Navy, and that the Navy order NROTC units on Northern white college campuses to admit Negroes.[90] Granger's call for the commissioning of Negro naval officers did not become a reality until 1949, but the Navy did take steps to eliminate the widespread segregation among enlisted men before the Army did. The reluctance with which NROTC units accepted Negroes and the token integration policy of the Naval Academy after 1948 tarnished the Navy's otherwise successful integration programs.

Negro leaders agreed as early as 1939 that equality of opportunity in the armed forces was impossible to achieve without the elimination of segregation.[91] Their strategies for desegregating the armed forces differed markedly. Randolph believed that civil disobedience was a viable tactic to force armed forces desegregation. The threat of civil disobedience had led to the Fair Employment Practices Executive Order in 1941. Not all the Negro leaders agreed with Randolph, however. Walter White of the NAACP disapproved of Randolph's strategy, saying that "the Association will continue to campaign against segregation and discrimination within the framework of the United States Constitution."[92] In the wake of Truman's announcement that steps were being taken to desegregate the Army, Navy, Marine Corps, and Air Force, White repudiated Randolph's call for civil disobedience. He said that "throughout its 39 year history, the Association had opposed defying authority or flaunting the banners of revolution."[93] Granger did not repudiate Randolph's strategy of ending armed forces segregation. But he gave himself a larger role than he credited to Randolph and other Negroes in the events leading to the desegregation of the armed forces. Granger wrote that:

> When James Forrestal, as Secretary of the Navy, borrowed me from the National Urban League on a part-time, dollar-a-year basis, to help the Navy tackle its racial problems toward the end of the war, we made an agreement at the very start that we wouldn't talk about interracial justice. Why? Because it would have been difficult to find Navy officers who would admit to being concerned about interracial justice. But they were concerned about an efficient Navy, one that would win the war as fast as possible. So that was my theme song as I travelled 60,000 miles and talked to 10,000 Negro servicemen and their officers. And it paid off—this efficiency theme—when first Admiral Chester W. Nimitz, and then Admiral Louis E. Denfeld and finally, Secretary Forrestal approved my recommendations. A year later, the Navy had adopted an effective policy of no segregation and no discrimination in recruitment, enlistment, training, promotion, assignment, housing or recreation of Navy personnel. Once the Navy adopted the policy and put it to work successfully, the rest of the armed services came along. This was an Urban League job, and Urban League success applied to what would have seemed to be a most unlikely field of effort.[94]

That Granger exaggerated his and the Urban League's role in the desegregation program is unquestionable. This does not, however, diminish the enormous role that Granger played in the desegregation process.[95] In the final analysis, it was the combined efforts of Granger, White, Randolph, Truman, the Negro and white press, and large numbers of Negroes and whites that closed the chapter on legally enforced racial segregation in the U.S. armed forces.

7

The Urban League and the Postwar Era, 1945–1953: Civil Rights and Racial Confrontations

During the Truman presidency, 1945–53, the NUL's general program was that of protecting and expanding job opportunities for Negroes and ameliorating racial tensions in urban centers. The specific programs of the NUL were to urge the enforcement of Negroes' constitutional rights, to prod the federal government to take a more active role in Negroes' search for equality, and to continue its efforts of reforming existing governmental structures. These efforts reflected Granger's influence on the direction of the NUL.

Granger's views of the NUL's role in the search for equality were conditioned by at least two factors. With the war over, he feared that the momentum of policies that expanded Negroes' economic and employment rights, largely the result of executive orders, would dissipate and even retrogress. Granger also viewed racial discrimination as one of the most undemocratic features of American society. This chapter discusses NUL successes and failures in reforming existing governmental structures, and it also examines the reasons why Truman backed civil rights. Finally, this chapter discusses how the continuing process of the urbanization of Negroes and Truman's bold moves in the civil rights arena led to new departures among scores of Negro leaders and their followers.

I

Sustained opposition by the white population to equality of opportunity in housing and employment during World War II foreshadowed "a greater opposition in time of peace."[1] Hence by 1945 League officials supported a permanent FEPC, and called upon the federal government to protect the rights of Negro citizens. Calls for additional federal action reflected the NUL's growing impatience with job bias. Despite two executive orders that had banned employment discrimination between 1941 and 1945, Negro workers had encountered numerous employment obstacles during the war. Fully aware of Executive Order 8802 of June 1941, in testimony before a Congressional Committee during 1942, a Glenn Martin Corporation executive nonetheless argued that it was impractical to employ Negroes because white workers would object.[2] Granger and others in the Urban League Movement also had not been able to convince AFL officials that it was in their interests and in Negro workers' interests to show a united front in negotiations with industry. Some CIO unions too had denied Negroes union protection, and their members had objected to working with them.

The 1942 nonferrous mine strike at Butte, Montana, was a case in point. This CIO local went on strike when the U.S. Army furloughed four thousand soldiers, thirty of whom were Negroes, to ease the labor shortage.[3] The miners stated that they would not return to work "as long as a single Negro was below ground."[4] The federal government did not enforce Executive Order 8802, and the National CIO's Executive Committee did not uphold its nondiscriminatory pledge. Despite the strike at the Butte mine, the CIO more readily admitted Negroes into labor's ranks than the AFL did. Granger knew that without an FEPC, union and nonunion whites alike were free to insist upon an all-white force. It should be remembered that the FEPC lacked the authority to increase Negro union membership, but it did prod employers to end job discrimination. In 1945 the FEPC, but not Executive Order 9346, expired at the hands of the U.S. Congress.[5]

That the FEPC was allowed to die was a serious setback for the NUL. Nonetheless, Granger and members of his executive staff called for equal opportunity. They embraced patriotism, using it as an instrument to combat prejudice against Negro workers in general and Negro veterans in particular. The United States Veterans Administration (USVA) was one of the agencies to which NUL officials turned, seeking its assistance in promoting equal opportunity—this strategy won few friends in the USVA. Little help was also forthcoming from the American Legion (AL). A majority of the Negroes in uniform during World War II came from the South, and it was assumed that they would resettle there. Local veteran organizations in the sixteen Southern states were segregated, and Negro veterans in six of these states were prohibited from establishing their own AL posts. Hence the NUL urged David Glasscoff, national adjutant of the AL, to amend the charter to allow for separate Legions.[6] This Glasscoff would not do; subsequently NUL officials urged that the AL's officers appoint Negroes to the national staff, only to be hurriedly rebuffed.

Not to be outdone, NUL officials called upon Brigadier General Frank T. Hines, administrator of Veterans Affairs, to invoke the Four Freedoms in the distribution of funds to veterans for health, hospitalization, rehabilitation, and educational purposes. Hines promised NUL officials that the Veterans Affairs agency, under his direction, would not countenance segregation and discrimination, but he left the enforcement of the pledge to the states. Subsequently, and as a last resort, Granger and his administrative staff sought Truman's assistance in guaranteeing minority-group veterans and other Negroes equality of opportunity in the postwar programs.

A memorandum, "The Racial Aspects of Reconversion," which was submitted to Truman in 1945, painstakingly documented housing and employment discrimination, as well as the educational biases faced by Negroes. The report showed that nearly 750,000 Negroes, excluding armed forces personnel, had migrated across state lines between 1940 and 1945. Also found in the memorandum were specific recommendations that urged Truman to: (1) create a permanent FEPC; (2) guarantee that Negroes could work in the Southern United States Employment Services (USES) offices and could share in policy-making and program-planning; (3) expand Social Security coverage to include Negroes laid off during the conversion to peace, who had had this coverage during the war years; (4) consider extending unemployment insurance for domestics and agricultural workers; (5) remove racially restrictive covenants from all federally assisted housing; (6) urge federal aid to education; and (7) ask congressional enactment of compulsory and adequate medical care programs, financed partially from federal funds.[7] These proposals not only were revolutionary for the era, but they also showed that the NUL had increasingly come to rely upon politics in the struggle against inequality. Under Granger's leadership, and despite his repeated denials, the NUL lobbied for the passage of legislation that would close the economic gap separating Negroes and whites. But Granger and other NUL officials were also intent upon maintaining the NUL's social work orientation, a factor that distinguished it from the legalistic NAACP. Yet reliance upon mediation, conciliation, fact-finding, and face-to-face meetings with the power structure had not appreciably advanced the goal of integration.

Unemployment, as NUL officials well knew, created a sense of frustration among the urban Negro population. By the end of 1945 nearly 600,000 had been dismissed from their wartime jobs, and approximately 800,000 had been affected by cutbacks. Added to these startling figures were voluminous reports documenting job discrimination and incidents of personal indignities experienced by Negro veterans.[8] Taken together, NUL leaders feared that urban racial violence was inevitable. Other racial reform leaders also concluded that violence could become a tool for change if the Negroes' demands were not met.

During April of 1946 the American Council on Race Relations (ACORR) convened a national emergency conference in New York City to discuss unemployment among Negroes. Julius A. Thomas, an NUL representative, told those assembled that the veterans organizations were not concerned with the job needs of Negro veterans, but were referring them to Urban League offices.[9] Furthermore, Thomas characterized the high unemployment rate found among the Negro ex-servicemen as inexcusable. In the aftermath of the conference, NUL officials contacted the Congress, urging it to pass legislation to alleviate the high unemployment rates found among urban Negroes.

As talk of a bill to underwrite housing surfaced, the NUL sought out those who would construct the publicly assisted housing. The anticipated passage of the Taft-Ellender-Wagner housing bill prompted NUL officials to reopen discussions with AFL leaders and members. They sought from the Brotherhood of Electrical Workers Union and from the United Association of Journeymen, Plumbers, and Steamfitters Union a pledge that Negro ex-servicemen would be employed on all their construction sites. As an added measure, Granger also petitioned Emanuel Lerner, Branch Director of the National Housing Agency, "to utilize Negro building trade workers in the emergency housing program."[10] Neither the unions nor Lerner gave a firm pledge. And the Taft-Ellender-Wagner housing bill met with defeat in the Congress, temporarily ending NUL leaders' hopes of placing Negro veterans in the construction unions. Despite these and other setbacks, the NUL continued to remind the federal government of its role in thwarting the drive for equality and equality of opportunity.

The USES's actions were a case in point. The Labor Department announced that the USES would revert to state control during November of 1946. It had been centralized in the nation's capital during World War II; and therefore as long as the FEPC received federal funding it had been able to monitor the activities of the USES. Unquestionably the USES had not strictly adhered to the executive orders. The NUL charged Robert C. Goodwin, director of USES, with approving racial discrimination in the referral of individuals to jobs and employers. Even after these practices had been brought to Labor Secretary Louis B. Schwellenbach's attention, USES policies remained unchanged, much to the dismay of Granger. Commerce Secretary Henry A. Wallace, however, examined the data collected by the NUL on racial discrimination within the USES, and he also urged Schwellenbach to discuss the matter with NUL officials.

In the wake of the Wallace correspondence, Schwellenbach agreed to meet with NUL officials, but he would not air his views on how he planned to safeguard and expand Negroes' employment opportunities. In the ensuing months, NUL officials experienced partial success in reforming the USES. During September 1945 Schwellenbach consented to end discrimination in the District of Columbia's USES offices, but refused to end discrimination in job referrals. Schwellenbach's intransigence on the issue of discriminatory job referrals was one reason why NUL officials concluded that federal agencies would not advance Negroes' rights unless the President ordered them to do so.

Granger and other NUL officials were encouraged by reports being leaked from the White House. These reports were encouraging to NUL officials because they told of Truman's concerns of deteriorating race relations in America. On December 5, 1946, the President issued Executive Order 9808, creating the President's Committee on Civil Rights. The Executive Order confirmed rumors that Truman did have an interest in protecting all Americans' civil rights. Truman explained why he created the Committee on Civil Rights:

> I took this action because of the repeated antiminority incidents immediately after the war in which homes were invaded, property was destroyed, and a number of innocent lives were taken. I wanted to get the facts behind these incidents of disregard for individual and group rights which were reported in the news with alarming regularity, and to see that the law was strengthened, if necessary, so as to offer adequate protection and fair treatment to all of our citizens.[11]

Truman instructed the fifteen-member Committee to recommend to him ways of protecting the rights of Americans who were denied equal justice under the law on account of "their racial origin or religious beliefs."[12] It goes without saying that Granger and other NUL officials approved of the appointment of Sadie T. Alexander and Channing H. Tobias, both Negroes, to the Committee. They also applauded the executive order, calling it the most important committee since Reconstruction days "to advance the civil rights of the people."[13]

Truman was the nation's first President to speak boldly of the federal government's role in safeguarding every American's constitutional rights. His belief was that Negro advancement had "to take place within the framework of a biracial or a nonsegregated social structure."[14] But Truman vehemently denied that he supported social equality of the races, insisting that he supported only the Negroes' constitutional rights.

Truman's support of Negroes' constitutional rights was a disappointment to many white Americans, and especially so to white Southerners. Moreover, a number of his closest advisors believed that Truman stood a good chance of being defeated in the 1948 presidential election if he did not retract or soften some of his earlier statements on civil rights. Truman later confirmed that his closest advisors warned him not to risk defeat by speaking boldly on civil rights. He wrote that:

> Members of the Cabinet and others warned me that I was riding to a defeat if I stuck to my FEPC orders and if I did not let up on the battle for civil-rights legislation. But I wanted to win the fight by standing on my platform, or lose it the same way.[15]

The extent to which Truman was guided by political considerations is unclear. The Northern Negro vote was essential to a Truman victory, at least after it was apparent that Truman had lost the Southern white vote. Truman denied that he supported civil rights for any political gains, but rather because of his belief that party platforms—the Democratic Party's 1944 and 1948 platforms called for civil rights legislation—were contracts with the people; and that they had to be carried out.[16] In the ensuing years Truman was successful in implementing some of the planks of the 1948 platform. His successes were largely in expanding Negroes' employment opportunities in federal jobs.

Ensuring equal opportunity in employment in the federal agencies became one of Truman's civil rights goals. He seemed troubled by the fact that the government in Washington condoned segregation and discrimination. Of the nearly 300,000 Negro government employees in 1945, approximately 70 percent were in unclassified positions.[17] Agencies such as the Public Health Service, the International Bank, the Patent Office, the Federal Security Agency, and others, publicly acknowledged that they did not employ Negroes except as cafeteria workers, porters, and the like. The NUL and other organizations chided the President for allowing federal agencies to engage in such racial discrimination. Then, on July 26, 1948, Truman issued Executive Order 9980, banning employment discrimination in the agencies of the federal government.[18] An accompanying message indicated that the President had issued the executive order because employment discrimination in the federal government clearly violated those principles upon which the United States was founded.[19]

The executive order did not prohibit state governments and private industry from practicing employment discrimination. For this reason, representatives of the NUL reminded Truman that Executive Order 9346, issued by Roosevelt, remained in effect. The Congress had refused to appropriate money to revive the FEPC. Any executive order that Truman might have issued to ban employment discrimination in private industry would suffer a similar fate at the hands of the Congress. Therefore Truman urged the Congress to renew FEPC funding. In 1948 President Truman seemed certain that only government action would equalize job opportunity and "eliminate the influence of prejudice in employment."[20]

The economic recession of 1948–49 resulted in additional barriers to Negro employment, and also contributed to a further widening of the economic gap separating Negroes and whites. An Urban League study, released in 1949, documented the recession's impact on the Negro wage earner. Negroes in New York City constituted 19 percent of the jobless, although they were only 8 percent of the city's total population. About 34,000 of the 67,000 unemployed in St. Louis were Negroes. More than 11,000 of the 49,000 persons without jobs in Pittsburgh were Negroes.[21]

Employment opportunities for urban Negroes did not improve throughout 1949 and into 1950. Alarmed over the situation, in the fall of 1949 NUL officials hammered out an agreement with the USES, which called for a joint attack by both agencies to fight "employers' prejudices against Negroes."[22] This agreement proved to be an empty gesture on the part of USES. Of necessity, local Urban Leagues' industrial relations secretaries and the executive secretaries then arranged conferences with employers, at which they demanded that Negroes and other minority laborers be retained and utilized on the basis of the skills they possessed. Initially their demands fell on deaf ears. It took an international crisis and executive orders to advance the concept of equality of opportunity.

The nation once again had its attention diverted by a war. The Korean conflict injected a new and in some ways a propitious factor into the racial situation. White America expected that Negroes would fight for their country and would not allow their grievances to stand in the way of national unity. The Korean War, just as had World Wars I and II, spurred Negro demands for equality. Negro leaders in the NUL, as well as those in the NAACP, did not abandon their rhetoric of national unity, but they did capitalize on the crisis atmosphere to press for an end to segregation and racial discrimination. Segments within white America resisted the calls for full and complete equality, believing that an international Communist plot threatened American democratic ideals more than segregation and discrimination did.

The view that Communism was a threat to Western democracy was not totally unfounded. Communism theoretically offered Negroes more than American democracy did. Its calls for a classless society, an end to racism, segregation, and discrimination, and its claims of equality for all struck a responsive chord among some Negroes. During the Korean conflict, both the Communist Chinese and North Koreans bombarded Negro soldiers with anti-American propaganda, much of which pointed to democracy's shortcomings. Democracy's shortcomings also attracted the attention of one NUL founder, who said that: "If I were a Negro, I think I would join the Communist party. The Communist party has for its cardinal principles, equality, nonsegregation and equal justice for men of all colors."[23] Officials of the NUL refrained from stating that Communism theoretically offered Negroes more than democracy did. But they were ever mindful of the fact that the United States had to grant Negroes more equality and justice than in the past, if the Communist propaganda was to be countered effectively. Their approach was to warn of the possibility of renewed racial violence in urban centers if Negroes were barred from employment in the war industries.

Neither the Communist propaganda nor the possibility of urban racial violence led to a quick end to employment discrimination. Therefore, in January of 1951, Negro leaders convened in New York City to explore ways in which they could bring additional pressure to bear on the Truman administration. The NUL officials decided that the tactics of scientific social work—fact-finding and analysis—remained viable in the drive to ban racial discrimination in the defense industries. During a meeting with the Secretaries of Defense, Labor, the Interior, Agriculture, Commerce, and the Treasury, NUL officials proposed specific programs to ensure "a fair deal for the race in the present emergency [Korean conflict]."[24] Cabinet officers were told that Negroes expected that all government contracts awarded to private industry would contain nondiscriminatory clauses, and that the federal government would enforce those clauses. In no uncertain terms, NUL officials bluntly informed federal officials that continued discrimination against Negroes was a luxury that the United States could not afford. A follow-up NUL publication, "The Price We Pay," showed that ghetto residents accounted for only 6 percent of the taxes collected in major cities. The report also showed that cities spent nearly 55 and 35 percent of their budgets on police costs and fire protection in the urban ghettoes, and that 55 percent of the urban juvenile delinquents resided in ghettoes.[25]

Truman's actions on civil rights issues during 1951 won the applause of Negro leaders. The President acted despite the fact that the Eighty-First Congress had buried civil rights legislation, and the Eighty-Second "would not even think the issue worthy of consideration."[26] On February 2, 1951, Truman issued Executive Order 10210, which directed the Defense Department to place nondiscriminatory clauses in all of its contracts awarded to private industry.[27] This executive order was followed by five others between March and August of 1951. The five orders were intended to end discrimination in the agencies of the federal government: National Advisory Committee on Aeronautics; the Public Printer's Office; the Tennessee Valley Authority; the Defense Materials Procurement Agency; and the Federal Civil Defense Administration.[28] But the extent of these orders' effectiveness in ending employment discrimination based on race, color, religion, or national origin is debatable because they lacked enforcement powers.

Congressional hostility to civil rights legislation was what made Truman decide to issue executive orders banning employment discrimination. He was justified in issuing the orders inasmuch as Executive Order 9346, which Roosevelt had issued in 1943, remained in effect. The refusal of Congress to appropriate funds to finance the FEPC had relegated the Executive Order to near obscurity. It should be pointed out that nondiscrimination clauses had been inserted in all government contracts awarded between 1943 and 1951, but again they had not been enforced.[29] On December 3, 1951, Truman issued Executive Order 10308, which created the Committee on Government Contract Compliance; in addition, the order placed the responsibility of enforcing nondiscrimination clauses on federal agency heads.[30] It should be noted that under the First War Powers Act of 1941 (Section 201, 55 Statute 839, 50 U.S.C. App. 611), the President was granted emergency power to provide for the national defense. This piece of legislation, as amended in 1947 by 66 Statute 295, did not expire until June 30, 1953.[31]

Following the issuance of Executive Order 10216 on February 23, 1951, Granger reminded Truman that the Atomic Energy Commission (AEC) discriminated against Negro job seekers.[32] An NUL report, issued during 1951, cited the Kennewick-Richmond (Washington), the Paducah (Kentucky), and the Oak Ridge (Tennessee) AEC projects as being among the chief violators of the federally mandated, nondiscrimination clauses.[33] Truman was slow in both answering the charges and directing AEC officials to desist from any further discriminatory hiring practices. A point of interest is that before Executive Order 10216 was issued, Julius A. Thomas and Warren Banner, from the National Office (NUL) and the Seattle Urban League (SUL) executive secretary, had already met with AEC officials to discuss the employment situation in the vicinity of Hanford, Washington.[34] Representatives of the General Electric Corporation, the prime contractor for the AEC project, claimed that whites had enacted an ordinance that banned Negroes from living in Hanford and in the surrounding communities. The League found, following a study, that such an ordinance did exist and concluded that "the real problem lay in the attitude of the townspeople."[35] At the same time, however, the Board members of the NUL discussed alternative approaches, that is, if the AEC and General Electric failed to comply with the antidiscrimination clause. They were to: (1) resort to legal action; (2) conduct a study; (3) arrange another face-to-face conference with the AEC and the General Electric Corporation; and (4) urge the President to act on the matter.

Granger decided, over the objection of the Board, that the study method was most appropriate, but the Board voted that the findings be promptly forwarded to the AEC. On March 15, 1951, William Dean of the NUL Research Department made a detailed presentation to the Board. To the surprise of several Board members, the information collected by the Research Department had not been submitted to the AEC as had been directed; whereupon Board member Judge Irvin Mollison asked why this had not been done.[36] Granger blamed budgetary problems for the delay. Following a lengthy presentation, the Board again directed Granger and his staff to make the proper presentation to the AEC.

In this instance Granger did follow the dictates of the Board. During September of 1951 he reported to the Board that Fletcher C. Waller, director of personnel of the AEC, had agreed to end segregation at the Paducah site, and that some progress had been made toward ending employment discrimination at the other AEC installations.[37] As it turned out, however, AEC officials had falsified the employment figures in order to curb criticism of their discriminatory hiring practices.

The contractors and subcontractors did likewise. During April of 1951, Charles T. Steele, the Louisville Urban League's executive secretary, reported that Mr. Bryon Neilson, works director of the McGraw Construction Company, had greatly exaggerated the number of Negroes employed at the Paducah AEC project. Neilson put the number at four hundred, but Steele identified only 150 Negroes, divided as follows: forty-one carpenters, one bricklayer, one electrician, and the remainder as common laborers.[38] Moreover, according to Steele, there were no Negro clerical workers, despite the fact that AEC officials had publicly announced that there were. Meanwhile the Union Carbide Company, a holder of an AEC contract at Paducah, maintained that it had not hired any Negro workers because it desired experienced workers, and that its policy was to exhaust "the local labor market before seeking employees outside of the immediate area."[39] Finally Steele revealed that the local USES office had refused to refer qualified Negroes to the AEC construction site because the McGraw Company had asked for only white workers.

By 1952 Negroes seeking employment at the AEC Paducah project were faced with additional problems. M.M. McGrath, superintendent of carpenters, did everything imaginable to create dissension among the members of Local 1912, a Negro union.[40] He urged Negroes who were members of the local to disaffiliate from it, and promised that they would have a job at the Paducah project as long as he was the superintendent. After officials of the NUL were apprised of McGrath's tactics, Harry L. Alston, industrial secretary of the Southern Field Division, NUL, maintained a watchful eye on the events at the AEC site, and insisted that housing for Negroes be built in the vicinity of Paducah.[41] Housing, NUL representatives concluded, remained the key to forcing the AEC to employ Negroes.

The NUL's staff did not have to contend with the AEC's stalling tactics alone. The NAACP too assumed an active and vocal role in the struggle with the AEC. On March 28, 1950, the AEC, in Washington, D.C., announced plans for the construction of a hydrogen bomb installation in Aiken and Barnell Counties, South Carolina, on the Savannah River, at a cost estimated at about $600 million.[42] Clarence Mitchell, director of NAACP's Washington Bureau, corresponded with the AEC on December 4, 1951, insisting that the Southern pattern of employment not be followed at the H-bomb site.

The entry of the NAACP into the AEC controversy appeared to have provoked jealousy in at least one NUL official. Julius A. Thomas, in correspondence with a colleague, pointed out that "they [NAACP officials] got the jump on us with this operation."[43] But he was also quick to point out that the NUL should discuss with the NAACP the possibility of closer collaboration because it was necessary under the circumstances. The Urban League affiliates' officers, unlike Thomas, were pleased that the NAACP had contested the AEC's hiring practices. The Louisville (Kentucky) Urban League's executive secretary praised Curlee Brown, president of the NAACP, for being "very active and vocal in attempting to secure employment for qualified Negroes."[44]

For the most part, representatives of the NAACP and the NUL worked closely together as general patterns of discrimination unfolded at the H-bomb site in South Carolina. The AEC and the Du Pont Corporation, the prime contractor, practiced racial discrimination in the hiring of workers. The Du Pont Corporation trained a white woman as an IBM operator rather than hire a Negro who was already a skilled IBM operator. Despite repeated promises to NUL and NAACP officials, Du Pont and the AEC would not advertise for skilled and semiskilled workers in the Negro weeklies.[45] W.W. Holly, business agent, Carpenters Local 283, informed NAACP and NUL officials that "no damn body is going to come up here and tell me how to run the Carpenters' Local. No one looks out for Jews, Italians or white people."[46]

With these and other obstacles to surmount, representatives of thirty-six national organizations met in Washington, D.C., during 1951. The delegates lobbied for civil rights legislation, and they urged the Congress to change its rules for ending debate on civil rights legislation. Inevitably the problems with the AEC were also touched upon during the meeting, and the delegates urged Truman to issue another executive order banning job discrimination in industry.[47] It is worth pointing out that the NUL sent representatives to the meeting, despite the fact that it was a lobbying effort.

How best to win AEC compliance with the nondiscrimination clauses became a perplexing problem for the NUL. Some progress had been achieved at the South Carolina H-bomb project by September of 1951, as discrimination in the use of rest-room facilities had been discontinued.[48] But much to the chagrin of NUL and NAACP officials, qualified Negroes had not been hired as electricians' helpers, mechanics, plumbers, pipefitters, welders, heavy equipment operators, iron workers, and clerical workers. Officers of the local NAACP concluded that neither Du Pont "nor the union locals [had] any intention of being fair to Negro workers and job applicants unless made to do so."[49] For reasons that remain unclear, NAACP officials switched tactics, asserting that segregated rest rooms would lessen white objections to equal employment opportunities at the H-bomb sites. With the approval of the national office, local NAACP officers urged the NUL to support segregated rest room facilities.[50] Harry Alston, an official of the Southern Regional Office, NUL, privately denounced the NAACP's new strategy, and argued that only sustained pressure would win the AEC and Du Pont's cooperation.[51] Two things were abundantly clear by 1952: the AEC did not intend to abide by Executive Orders 10216 and 10308; and its officials had little fear of President Truman. The NUL soon learned that other defense contractors were also intent upon evading Truman's executive orders.

The Lockheed Aircraft Corporation had received Air Force contracts. Yet James V. Carmichael, a vice president of the corporation's Marietta, Georgia, plant, decreed that "Lockheed will live the Southern tradition."[52] Representatives of the NUL notified Carmichael of their objections to segregating Negro and white workers.[53] The aircraft plant at Marietta had a work force of ten thousand; five hundred were Negroes, but they held only unskilled jobs.[54] It was only after repeated calls to Lockheed's main office in Burbank, California, that Carmichael agreed to meet with NUL and NAACP officials and discuss the situation.[55] Nothing of a concrete nature came out of this and subsequent conferences with Lockheed officials. Throughout 1950 and 1951, Granger and other NUL representatives reminded the Defense Department of Lockheed's defiance of Executive Order 10308, but to no avail. In the meantime they investigated employment discrimination in other industries.

The brewery industry was not war-related; nonetheless its hiring practices came under NUL scrutiny during 1951. A study directed by J. Harvey Kerns, associate director of the NUL's Research and Community Projects Unit, found that only five hundred of the thirty-eight thousand brewery workers were Negro.[56] The situation was no better in the nonproduction jobs; only twenty-five of the eighteen hundred clerical workers were Negro Americans. Nearly all of the brewery industry's Negro employees were laborers, sweepers, yard and maintenance workers, or messengers. Kerns concluded that most of the brewery production workers, who for the most part were of German extraction, believed that their industry was the exclusive domain of whites.[57] The leadership of the CIO union, however, held an entirely different view than that of the rank-and-file union membership.

The Brewery Workers International Union (BWIU), whose constitution forbade racial discrimination, pledged to assist the NUL in achieving a greater representation of Negroes in the production jobs.[58] Kerns released a second study on the brewery industry toward the end of 1951, praising the union for its cooperation. Granger insisted that the League's interest in expanding jobs for Negro workers in the production of beer had resulted in "definite policy changes by certain leading breweries, with a promise of further important changes in the future."[59] Two years later, however, Granger was hard pressed to defend what was an optimistic appraisal of the brewery industry's support for equal employment opportunities in 1951. Not all CIO unions, despite their claims of supporting equality of opportunity, readily opened skilled jobs to Negroes. The fact that Negroes were found in greater numbers in the CIO than in AFL unions was because there was a variety of unskilled jobs in the plants in which a CIO union was the bargaining agent. By the 1950s, most CIO unions had purged union officials who, because of their socialist proclivities, preached worker solidarity across racial lines. A lack of Negro-white worker solidarity had led to race strikes in the defense industries during World War II, several of which involved CIO unions. The racist attitudes that had sparked the race strikes during the Second World War were not completely absent from the minds of the white CIO and AFL members in 1953.

II

The NUL had endeavored to win craft unions' (AFL) cooperation since its founding in 1910. In some instances the AFL did not hesitate in entering into informal agreements with the NUL and its local affiliates, but it rarely did anything more than verbally support the programs of the NUL. In Denver the only union to support equality of opportunity was the Tramway Union, which voted "to admit Negro trolley-bus operators when they were first hired."[60] The New Orleans Urban League's executive director reported that the AFL Council would not embrace integrated unions, but sought the cooperation of the local Urban League in "giving assistance to the rapidly growing organized labor movement in the new State of Israel."[61] Leaders of the Los Angeles Urban League chronicled that they had a "splendid relationship in the way of 'lip service' with the American Federation of Labor."[62] Marion M. Taylor, executive secretary of the Omaha (Nebraska) Urban League, reported that "the AFL will make no pretense at cooperation. They simply do not desire and intend for Negroes to get apprenticeship training in this state, except occasionally in the field of cement mixing."[63] Correspondence from the Pittsburgh Urban League recounted the tactics "used by craft unions designed to deny apprenticeship and membership opportunities to qualified Negro applicants."[64]

Nelson C. Jackson, Southern Field Director, NUL, had solicited these
views from the affiliates' executive directors and local industrial relations
secretaries in advance of a speech delivered to the AFL unions on April
28, 1953. The local affiliates' officers were quick to point out that AFL
unions resisted opening their ranks to Negroes; but they, like NUL officials, held out hope that at some point in time craft unions would fully
support the concept of equality of opportunity. The fact that the Urban
League had consistently maintained an optimistic posture toward the AFL
without any concrete results to show for its optimism was cause for alarm
among several Negro leaders.

As early as World War II, some Negroes and some whites concluded
that the techniques and strategies of the NUL and the NAACP would not
win equality for Negroes. In 1942 a small group of Negro and white
intellectuals decided to rely upon nonviolent, direct-action techniques to
challenge the white power structure.[65] As one author stated, the nonviolent movement for desegregation "was born during World War II."[66] In
1942 Bayard Rustin, a member of the pacifist Fellowship of Reconciliation, staged a one-man sit-in, protesting segregation and racial discrimination in the Northern and border states. During the same year, James
Farmer, a Negro and the race relations secretary of the Fellowship of
Reconciliation, "proposed to the Fellowship that it attempt to create an
organization, composed of both pacifists and non-pacifists, committed to
non-violent actions against racial discrimination."[67]

Farmer's idea gave birth to the Congress of Racial Equality (CORE). In
the ensuing years its members confronted segregated housing owned by
the University of Chicago, and attempted to desegregate swimming pools
and theaters in Chicago, Columbus, and Cleveland, among other Northern
cities.[68] It would be several years before CORE attacked segregation in
the Southern states.

In 1947 Rustin and a small group of CORE members defied North
Carolina's segregation laws. A North Carolina judge not only admonished
them for disobeying a state law, but he also imposed a thirty-day jail
sentence on them. In the wake of the sentencing, CORE officials served
notice on the South that other attempts would be made to overturn Jim
Crow.

Both the NAACP and the NUL took notice of CORE's impact on urban
Negro America. Its nonviolent, direct-action approach soon won wide
acceptance among the young Negroes in general and the expanding urban
Negro middle class in particular. It appears that the NAACP's leaders
adopted a more aggressive posture as CORE's program received national
attention. Under Walter White's leaderhip, the NAACP joined with partisan political groups and pressed for equality, ignoring the fact that the
NAACP's constitution prohibited its officers from supporting partisan po-

litical candidates and causes. White's activities as the NAACP's chief executive officer did not escape the attention of the Board members. In 1946, a Board member wrote to White:

> But I have a complaint—and a hot one! What I have in mind is the sudden and rather startling political activity in which you are at the present time involving the NAACP. I have no objection to what you may do personally as a citizen, for freedom of action is your inalienable right. But I would raise the question as to whether the NAACP as an organization should be involved. Again and again I read in the newspapers that the NAACP is one of the organizations joining this activity or that, and I am not aware that we have officially authorized such actions at all.[69]

This stern reprimand did not stop other NAACP officials from going their separate way, often without the approval of the NAACP Board.

In 1949 Roy Wilkins, the NAACP's acting secretary, raised the ire of an NAACP Board member, Judge Hubert T. Delany, by accusing him of being a persistent antagonist of the national office of the NAACP. Wilkins believed that Delany was primarily responsible for the New York NAACP's decision to warn the NAACP not to meddle in its internal affairs. Moreover, Wilkins charged that the New York NAACP refused to cooperate in working out national NAACP programs and in raising money for national projects. Wilkins then implied that the New York NAACP's drop in membership was because of the local NAACP's reluctance to cooperate with the national association.[70]

Delany disagreed that the New York NAACP chapter was to blame for its drop in membership, pointing out that the NAACP's membership had also declined, from about 500,000 members in 1945 to about 150,000 by 1949. Delany reminded Wilkins that the sudden drop in the (national) membership was not attributable to the recession alone, as Wilkins said that it was.[71] As the relations between Wilkins and Delany deteriorated, Delany told Wilkins that as acting secretary he had no right "to attempt to upbraid a member of the Board."[72] Delany also informed Wilkins that his "high and mighty Hague attitude of 'I am the law' will no longer work with either the branches, the union or the staff."[73]

Whether or not Delany and Wilkins resolved their differences is unclear. But it is clear that there were those in the NAACP who felt that the NAACP's sudden involvement in partisan politics was an unwise strategy, and that Wilkins did not have the final say on NAACP policies and strategies. Moreover, the NAACP's approach to civil rights was being questioned, because not everyone was convinced that legalistic strategies would rid the society of attitudes that had fostered racial segregation and discrimination.[74]

Not everyone had faith in the NUL's social service approach either.

Therefore the NUL's and the NAACP's strategies for change were called into question by their Boards and by an increasing number of urban Negroes. The evidence suggests that the NUL Board members, or at least several of them, were more critical of the NUL than the Board members of the NAACP were critical of the Association. In 1951, for example, NUL Board member Sidney Hollander questioned the "non-attendance of the NUL at the Civil Rights Mobilization, organized by the NAACP and co-sponsored by sixty other organizations."[75] Granger explained that the NUL's constitution prohibited its officers from engaging in activities designed to influence the passage of legislation. For the moment his answer appeared to be satisfactory. But in 1953, Hollander wanted to know why the NUL did not send representatives to a Washington, D.C., meeting at which fifty-two national organizations met with the U.S. Attorney General, seeking the Eisenhower administration's help in certain areas of civil rights.[76] Granger simply stated that he and other NUL officials had not received an invitation to attend the meeting. Hollander then questioned Granger's decision to pass on to key political figures, who were not members of the NUL, resolutions passed at the 1953 annual NUL meeting before the Board put its stamp of approval on these resolutions. Granger apologized for the mistake, but it was clear that he objected to Hollander's remarks and was piqued that his decisions had come under Board scrutiny. The very fact that Hollander, other NUL Board members, and several of the affiliates' executive directors and boards saw fit to question Granger's actions meant that he had lost their confidence in his ability to guide the Urban League Movement.

Bitter infighting between Charles E. Eason, executive secretary of the Urban League of Flint, Michigan (ULOFM), and members of the local board led to Eason's firing on February 1, 1952. In the wake of the dismissal, the NUL learned that ULOFM's board of directors had charged Eason with "lobbying outside of the Board, instead of discussions within it."[77] Earlier the local board had asked Eason to resign without informing the NUL, an action that violated a prior agreement hammered out between the NUL and Urban League affiliates. Rescinding the firing, Eason received correspondence from the Board, demanding that he tender his letter of resignation, effective July 1, 1952.[78] Granger was informed of the ULOFM board's latest actions, and he was displeased. On February 1, 1952, Granger made a personal appearance before the ULOFM's board, insisting that it reconsider its decision regarding Eason. The local Board stood firm, informing Granger that he could not interfere in the decisions of the affiliate Urban Leagues. Not to be outdone, Granger offered Eason the executive secretary's job in the Philadelphia Urban League.[79] Granger's action indicated that he would, if necessary, interfere in the decision of a local Urban League, and that he believed he had the power to decide who the local executive secretaries would be. The ULOFM's board actions showed clearly that an affiliate could defy the NUL executive secretary without fear of reprisal.

The actions of the ULOFM's board were not a challenge to Granger's authority. It should be remembered that the NUL did not establish local Urban Leagues, but upon founding the locals affiliated with the Urban League Movement. Accordingly, as one former local Urban League executive secretary pointed out, the local Urban Leagues did not take kindly to individuals from the national staff coming in, telling them what they ought to do, giving them advice, and offering their assistance in resolving internal problems.[80]

The affiliates' officials guarded their loose relations with the NUL; several charted their own course; and several executive secretaries ignored any advice that Granger gave them and agreed wholeheartedly with the nonviolent, direct-action strategy associated with CORE.[81] A number of the affiliates' leaders were of the opinion that for the Urban League Movement to survive, it had to keep its "feet in the ghetto and its hands in the power structure."[82] Granger did not share this view. Rather he believed that the NUL and the Urban League Movement could not engage in direct action and nonviolent protest without alienating the power structure. Granger did not question the capacity of scientific social work to raise the status of Negroes, and he believed that the Urban League Movement had successfully addressed civil rights issues without deviating too far from its social service orientation. And while Granger saw a need for the NAACP's legalistic approach and the nonviolent, direct action of CORE, he did not believe that the NUL also had to engage in these tactics to win full equality for Negroes.

Granger, like Wilkins of the NAACP, often acted as though he was the sole determiner of the NUL's strategies, techniques, and targets. Moreover, he confessed that he was perfectly satisfied to be called an "Uncle Tom" or a "Commie," "as long as he got the job done."[83] On more than one occasion Granger reminded his detractors that he was a member of the NAACP, and that this was sufficient proof of his support of civil rights causes.[84] Yet he was unwilling to alter radically the NUL's approach to civil rights, believing that the NUL's contribution to equality was to continue in its social service tradition. Granger argued strongly that the NUL did not need to bat people over the head to foster racial advancement. One of the NUL's ex-presidents related that Granger believed that the NUL was not founded "to fight the Southern system of segregation overtly; it was a job for the NAACP."[85] Moreover, Granger attempted to silence his critics by suggesting that NUL programs were indeed resolving what had been strained racial relationships in the South, and that these improvements were achieved without direct action strategies.

By 1947 Granger believed that the South was making rapid strides in improving relations between the races where employment was an issue. In the aftermath of a tour of several Southern cities, Granger reported that the barriers to Negroes gaining meaningful employment in the sixteen Southern states were on the decline.[86] On another level, however, he feared that the tactics associated with CORE, if embraced by the NUL and its affiliates, would jeopardize the affiliates' financial support from the Community Chest and similar agencies. Local Urban Leagues depended heavily upon the Community Chest for their funding. Granger also feared that the NUL would lose its tax-exempt status if it openly engaged in activities that might be considered political. He believed that the tactics of CORE contributed to a further polarization of the races in the South. Denying that these considerations guided his actions, Granger insisted that the NUL's first emphasis was that of getting men to work so that they would perform the man's role in the family.[87] In retrospect, he was justified in pursuing equality of opportunity in a cautious manner. After he had spoken out on civil rights issues in 1954, the NUL and its affiliates in the South were denied Community Chest funds for several years. That the Community Chests temporarily ended their support of the Urban League was disheartening, but the Negro middle classes' disenchantment with the NUL was the serious issue.

III

The Negro middle classes had been the NAACP's and the NUL's staunchest backers since their foundings in 1909 and 1910. Many of the gains credited to both organizations had primarily benefited middle- and upper-class Negroes. Most Negroes, however, remained in either the unskilled or low-paying jobs. Nonetheless, statistics compiled by the Labor Department illuminated the rise in Negro families' income between 1943 and 1945. By 1950, however, "the median annual income of Negro families was $1,869 or about 54 percent of the $3,445 average for white families."[88] An examination of Negro employment in the high-status jobs, as illustrated in Table 14, shows the economic disparities that separated Negroes and whites.

For the years 1940–47, the Negro workers' economic gains were unimpressive when compared to those of white workers. The same can be said of their employment opportunities, as seen in Table 15. Despite all that has been written on the rise of a Negro middle class during World War II, white-collar jobs generally remained the domain of whites. Hence in 1948 the NUL created a Pilot Placement Project to assist Negro college graduates in finding employment in technical and white-collar jobs,[89] but discrimination against Negroes limited this program's potential. A report released by the NUL's Research Department showed that Harvard, Yale,

A Search for Equality

Table 14. Race and Class of Employed Persons, by Occupation and Sex, United States, 1950[a]

Sex and Occupation	White	Negro	Negro as Percentage of White
Male, employed	36,830,187	3,499,697	8.6
Professional, technical, kindred workers	2,886,870	75,436	2.5
Architects	23,594	135	0.6
Accountants and auditors	319,503	900	0.3
Chemists	66,082	667	1.0
Designers and draftsmen	140,709	633	0.4
Lawyers and judges	172,710	1,367	0.8
Pharmacists	79,500	1,147	1.4
Teachers	266,340	18,763	6.6
College presidents, professors, instructors	92,861	2,522	2.6
Craftsmen, foremen, kindred workers	7,256,143	269,373	3.6
Carpenters	871,588	34,582	3.8
Electricians	303,429	3,236	1.0
Toolmakers and diemakers, etc.	151,003	522	0.3
Plumbers and pipefitters	267,374	8,290	3.0
Service Workers	1,882,822	464,075	19.6
Police, sheriffs, and marshals	208,455	4,050	1.9
Firemen, fire protection	107,938	1,441	1.3

[a]Data extracted from *1950 Census of Population, Characteristics of Population, United States Summary, 2, Part 1* (Washington: Government Printing Office, 1953), Table 128, pp. 1–276–277. The employment data on black and white females can be mined from Table 128, pp. 1–278. All occupations engaged in by males are not shown in this table. The professions were randomly chosen.

Columbia, Michigan, the University of Pittsburgh, and the Massachusetts Institute of Technology encountered considerable difficulty in placing their Negro technical and professional graduates in industry.[90]

Unskilled and semiskilled Negro workers were faced with even greater obstacles in industries in which craft unions were organized. If the Negro middle class had begun to find fault with the programs, strategies, and techniques of the NUL and the NAACP, the urban masses had even greater reasons to complain. Continued employment discrimination, poor

Table 15. Race of Employed Females and Males, Selected Occupations, 1950ᵃ

Sex and Occupation	White	Negro	Negro as Percentage of White
Female, employed	13,794,932	1,869,956	11.9
Professional, technical, and clerical workers			
Actresses, dancers, entertainers	19,978	733	3.5
Authors, editors, reporters	29,054	394	1.3
Chemists and natural scientists	34,395	222	0.6
Lawyers and judges	6,165	83	1.3
Nurses, professional	357,427	12,550	3.2
Nurses, student professional	71,931	3,231	3.1
Physicians and surgeons	11,323	257	2.2
Bookkeepers	552,373	2,993	0.5
Salespersons, retail	1,170,649	19,750	1.7
Males, employed	36,830,187	3,499,697	8.6
Professional, technical			
Dentists	71,062	1,525	2.1
Physicians and surgeons	175,783	3,769	2.1
Designers and draftsmen	140,709	633	0.4
Natural scientists	33,593	488	1.4
Engineers, electrical	104,742	337	0.3
Engineers, mechanical	109,068	326	0.3

ᵃData extracted from *1950 Census of Population, Characteristics of Population, United States Summary, 2, Part 1* (Washington: Government Printing Office, 1953), Table 128, pp. 1–276–278. This table accounts for only a partial listing of Negro males and females engaged in professional, technical, and clerical pursuits.

housing and schooling, and inadequate recreational facilities heightened racial tensions and increased frustrations among the poor. The Truman era had its share of racial confrontations. Not all of the racial confrontations during the Truman presidency resulted from job-related grievances; some were sparked by whites' objections to Negroes using public facilities. Between June and mid-July of 1949, the nation's cities had to contend with racial conflicts. In St. Louis, Negroes, led by the St. Louis Urban League, pressured city officials to open all public swimming pools to all of the city's residents, and without regard to race or color. In 1949 the director of public welfare of the city of St. Louis ruled that the pools henceforth were open to blacks and whites alike. Whites denounced the decision, and white lifeguards threatened to strike if the ruling was enforced.[91] The guards did not follow through on their threat, but they encouraged white youths to attack Negroes who attempted to use the pools on an integrated basis. The result was a series of racial clashes, but the city of St. Louis did not rescind the desegregation order. Other cities also were plagued by racial clashes as Negroes increased their protests against segregated, publicly owned recreational facilities.

In 1949 the Washington, D.C., recreation department desegregated the pools and other recreational facilities that it had jurisdiction over; but not before the Washington Urban League, the Washington NAACP, and other groups pressured it to do so.[92] This pressure followed in the wake of a Red Cross report, issued in 1948, which showed that between 1945 and 1948 thirty-seven Negro children had drowned while swimming in the unsupervised waters of the Anacostia River and in Kingman Lake.[93] Washington's Negro citizens had every reason to complain: only four pools were open to them, yet they constituted 33 percent of the population. The change in policy, as expected, resulted in racial clashes.

A drive to desegregate the swimming pools in Youngstown, Ohio, during the summer of 1949, also led to racial confrontations. There were no laws in Youngstown that required segregated pools, but over the years whites in Youngstown had come to regard a pool located in an integrated neighborhood as the "Negro pool" for the entire city. In addition, an unwritten city law prevented the lifeguards at the "Negro pool" from being rotated to the other public pools. Youngstown's city officials did not deny that the segregated pool was unlawful. But when officials of the Youngstown Urban League called for an end to segregation in the use of the city's pools, the local newspaper accused them of rushing the situation.[94] The local newspaper's statements did not have a calming effect on the situation, as racial clashes marred Youngstown during the summer of 1949.

Sizing up the situation in Youngstown and other cities, the NUL urged Truman to speak out as forcefully against segregation in the use of public facilities as he had on the denial of equal employment opportunities. A memorandum from NUL officials to the President, titled, "An Urgent Call to Action to Enforce the Rights of All Citizens—Without Discrimination," underscored their determination to rid the society of racism.[95] Truman's reply to the NUL memorandum contained assurances that he supported equal rights for all Americans. His reply indicated that he fully understood why millions of Negroes were impatient about continued segregation and racial discrimination. But the precise extent of Truman's cooperation with the NUL in its attempts to reform existing governmental structures remained to be seen.

The mood of Negroes changed markedly between the end of World War II and the year 1953. Several factors account for the changes in the mood of Negro America. First, urbanization had altered the perceptions of Negroes. They were more apt to view their rights on the basis of being American citizens rather than Negroes. Second, Truman's civil rights stance had encouraged Negroes to press for even more changes in the society than those wrought by the executive orders. Third, urban Negroes had come to regard economic equality as a right granted them by the Constitution, and spoke in bolder terms and took more direct steps toward the goal of full equality than ever before. Fourth, the younger urban Negro leaders and an increasing number of urban Negroes had, since about 1945, begun to question the desirability of pursuing equality by traditional methods—voting, pleading, and the like. Their doubts stemmed from the fact that more and more urban Negroes questioned the capacity of government to resolve their longstanding grievances against a society that was permeated with racism. Finally, while not rejecting the social work strategies of the Urban League Movement, urban Negroes had doubts about the old civil rights organizations' capacity to reform the existing governmental and nongovernmental structures. Increasingly, scores of urban Negroes believed that the time had come for new departures in the civil rights movement, and they did not exempt the NUL from their criticisms of the strategies used in the search for equality.

The Pains of Maturation: Internal Dissension within the Urban League

The NUL and Urban League Movement's officials have argued persuasively that inequality, segregation, and racial discrimination are inconsistent with democratic ideals. This argument emerged in 1910, the founding year of the NUL, and has been repeated ever since. However, opinion was divided within both the NUL and the ULM about which strategies would win complete equality for Negroes.[1] During the 1950s, for example, several of the NUL's Negro Board members argued for a complete reexamination of the strategies and techniques that the NUL had employed in its efforts to promote racial advancement. And there was disagreement on whether or not the NUL had been successful in its efforts to reform existing governmental structures and to end racial discrimination and legally enforced segregation. These dissenting Negro Urban Leaguers hoped that Granger would at least weigh the value of direct action, since racial discrimination and segregation obviously remained persistent problems in American society. Indeed some Negro Board members had come to question the assumption that reliance primarily upon fact-finding, analysis, and investigation would appreciably change the status of Negroes.

Their call for new departures did not set well with Granger. He held firm to the belief that the NUL should, with few exceptions, continue the search for equality in much the same vein as had its founders. Under Granger's direction the NUL had remained basically a social work organization, although it did of course address civil rights issues, and attempt, whenever the need arose, to reform existing governmental and some nongovernmental structures. During the 1940s, in fact, the NUL and several of the Urban League affiliates did become major civil rights organizations.

Chapter 8 discusses the reasons for the dissension within the Urban League during the 1950s. The fact that the NUL and several of the affiliates actively pursued civil rights necessarily made the Urban League a vital force in the civil rights revolution, whose origins can be traced to the stirrings among urban Negroes during the 1940s. This chapter also will show why Granger would not cooperate with the NAACP, and why several NUL Negro Board members were critical of Granger because he would not seek a rapprochement with the NAACP and its officials. It then examines the activist-oriented Urban Leagues in order to show how their policies and those of the NAACP and the newly created civil rights organizations were compatible with each other. Finally, the chapter analyzes the impact of the internal dissension on Granger's role within the Urban League Movement, and the extent to which the internal dissension altered the course of the NUL and the Urban League Movement.

I

If there had been internal acrimony within the NUL Board between 1910 and 1950, it was kept from the public. During the 1950s, however, differences of opinion on which strategies the NUL should rely upon to rid society of segregation and racial discrimination led to a public disclosure of dissension within the NUL. The decision of several NUL Board members to exercise a greater degree of authority in the establishing of NUL priorities angered Granger. Further, at least three Negro Board members attempted to alter the racial composition of the NUL Board. When NUL Board members concluded that they, rather than Granger, should be the policy-makers of the NUL, the internal dissension was brought into public view. The NUL constitution clearly designated the Board as the NUL's chief policy-maker.[2] But for several decades the executive director and his staff had largely determined NUL policies.

Granger resisted efforts by the NUL Board to exercise its duties as spelled out in the NUL constitution. Because he became heir to the NUL leadership in the midst of an international crisis, the Board did not seem to care that it was Granger who determined the direction of the NUL. But with the advent of organizations that advocated direct action and confrontation, several NUL Board members began to question Granger's decision not to cooperate with the NAACP, and not to incorporate direct action into the NUL's strategies for change. Whereas the NUL of the era 1911–1941 had endeavored to improve the image of Negroes so that whites would not fear them, several Negro NUL Board members now wondered why they should keep on trying to convince whites that there was no need to fear Negroes.[3] And while nearly every NUL Board member solidly approved of Granger's efforts to reform existing governmental structures, there was little support for his belief that above all else the NUL's major tasks were to engage in the traditional and preventive social work programs.[4] In short, by the 1950s several Negro Board members, with considerable support from urban Negroes, expected the Negro-oriented organizations, NUL included, to challenge aggressively the white power structure.[5] Granger of course believed that under his leadership the NUL *had* aggressively challenged the power structure—by using the traditional social work tactics of fact-finding, analysis, and observation.

Granger, a professional social worker, rejected the direct action approach. Perhaps this accounts for his reluctance to alter in any significant way the strategies of the NUL. Moreover, Granger's aloofness was a source of irritation to the newer and younger local executive secretaries, whose relationships with officials of the NAACP, CORE, and other civil rights organizations were more solid than Granger's. The fact that Granger refrained from forming a united front with the NAACP at a time when rising expectations among Negroes peaked was the single factor that contributed most to the internal acrimony found in the Urban League Movement.

An examination of the Granger years, and of Granger's personality, reveals several of the sources of the dissension that plagued the NUL and the ULM from about 1944 to about 1960. While Granger was not known in NUL circles as an able administrator, the NUL Board did praise him for his ability to communicate with the nation's white elites. R. Maurice Moss, the associate executive director of the NUL, ran the day-to-day operations. But Moss could not change the course of the NUL, as several on the Board wished, because Granger did not believe that it was crucial for the NUL to attain greater visibility among the urban Negro masses. But Granger did believe that it was necessary for him to meet with and to court the support of white elites. He also rejected the view that an enlarged Negro membership was vital to the NUL's survival.

Granger's refusal to listen to several Negro Board members, and his reluctance to defer to the NUL Board on policy decisions, alienated his backers. Sophia Y. Jacobs, for example, recalled that "Granger was insensitive to the Board and its role as policy maker."[6] Her view was shared by most of the people on the Board. Even the affiliates' executive secretaries found fault with Granger, because of their belief that he was apt to reject their views on which racial advancement strategies were most appropriate, even without first giving careful thought to them. Instead, any local executive secretary who did not accept Granger's views was labeled a "rebel."

The internal controversy of 1943–44 revolving around the Memphis Urban League's (MUL) executive secretary, Benjamin Y. Bell, Jr., and the local Board indicates the low level of tolerance that Granger held toward the "rebel" affiliates' officers. Bell was one of several local executive secretaries who were attempting to transform a local Urban League into an organization that would be a vital force in the community.[7] Upon learning that employers had forced Memphis's laundry workers to contribute 5 percent of their annual earnings to the Community Chest, Bell spearheaded a drive to organize them into a union. That most of the laundry workers were Negroes also influenced Bell's decision to attempt to unionize them. The fact that the local Urban League received most of its operating budget from the Community Chest was immaterial to Bell, as he believed that the employers had no right to dictate to their workers how much of their annual pay should be donated to the Community Chest.

Memphis's business community saw the situation in an entirely different light. This was a civic project that they cared about, and they therefore believed that the workers were contributing to a worthy cause. And the fact that Bell was attempting to unionize the laundry workers threw fear in the minds of the business community. Southern white businessmen's opposition to unions needs little discussion. They disguised their dislike of unions by charging that Bell's union-organizing activities were improper for a social service agency to engage in.[8]

Key members of the business community first approached Bell, urging him to abandon his plans for unionizing the laundry workers. When Bell rejected their advice, they then began applying pressure on the MUL's Board to censure him. The Board would not censure Bell, but it did advise him that he was engaging in an unwise activity. When all else had failed, the Memphis white business community informed Granger of Bell's activities. Granger sent word to Bell that the "Board is the last court of directive authority."[9] Bell ignored Granger's advice. Subsequently an NUL representative arrived in Memphis, met with Bell, and explained that his union-organizing activities were in violation of NUL policies. Although the NUL representative praised Bell for encouraging Negroes to join the labor movement, he informed Bell that the local executive secretaries of Urban Leagues were not labor organizers.[10]

Bell resented both the reprimand and the fact that the white business community in Memphis had drawn the NUL into a local dispute. In the heat of anger, he served notice on the white business community and on the Memphis City Hall (the two were indistinguishable) that neither group could interfere with the local Urban League's program.[11] Moreover, Bell informed the Community Chest that the MUL could do without its yearly contributions, an act that angered Granger and other NUL officials. NUL officials then warned Bell against attempting to build a one-man Urban League in Memphis. Bell rejected the advice, pointing out that the powers that be in Memphis wanted the local affiliate to remain weak and impotent.

Granger and his staff turned against Bell when it became clear that he would neither follow their dictates nor allow the local Board to determine the policies of the local affiliate. They concluded that he had moved too hurriedly in Memphis, and that his youth and vigor were limitations on his effectiveness as an Urban League executive director.[12] Bell's punishment included removal from the executive director's post and an assignment in an industrial relations department of another Urban League, where he could be trained to be a "good" Urban Leaguer.

Granger did not view the Memphis incident as an aberration within the Urban League Movement. Rather he believed that unless the Urban League acted to head off future incidents of this kind, other Urban League executive secretaries would plan similar confrontations with city halls. Granger contacted Mayor La Guardia of New York City, urging his support in convincing other mayors of the need to discuss interracial situations and programs at their next conference. La Guardia rebuffed Granger, leading him to conclude that La Guardia was afraid of his reactionary brothers from the South.[13] Granger pointed out that La Guardia "smelled as any other fake liberal would."[14]

NUL officials and many other Negroes were disappointed that both white liberals and conservatives rejected NUL proposals that, during the 1940s and 1950s, could have conceivably ameliorated racial tensions in urban centers. Granger's continuing to court the support of white liberals invited unnecessary criticism of NUL programs; at least this was how some of the NUL's critics perceived the situation. However, a blanket condemnation of white liberals was a mistake. An examination of the activities of white liberals associated with the Urban League Movement indicates that many of them proposed programs or supported Urban League policies that did indeed ameliorate racial tensions in urban centers. Several of the local Urban Leagues addressed issues and involved themselves in controversies that, in an earlier era, would have been handled by a local NAACP chapter.

The Portland (Oregon) Urban League (PUL), for example, willingly investigated a racial situation that involved white teachers, officials, and Negro students. Harold York, the principal of the integrated Roosevelt High School in Portland, used the term "nigger heaven" during an assembly, apparently referring to the fact that a number of the Negro students chose to sit in the balcony of the auditorium, segregating themselves from the white students. The Negro students were understandably hurt, shocked, and humiliated at York's racist remark, and were enraged that their principal had subjected them to such an indignity. Following the assembly, a score of Negro students confronted York, who apologized for having used the term "nigger heaven." But York's apology did not satisfy the students, and they then marched to the Portland Urban League offices to inform Edwin C. Berry, the executive director, of the incident. Meanwhile, a group of students discussed York's remark with a Miss Craig, the dean of girls of Roosevelt High School. While she abhorred York's use of the term "nigger heaven," she reminded the students that "this is not the first time such things had happened here, and it will not be the last."[15] Her explanation, like the York apology, further irritated the Negro students and Berry.

Berry met with York, who readily confessed to having referred to the balcony of the high school auditorium, where scores of the Negro students sat, as a "nigger heaven." But York insisted that the remark was not intended as an offense to the Negro students, explaining that he had lived among Negroes and held no prejudice toward them. During the meeting Berry also learned of additional interracial difficulties at the school and within the Portland school system.

One of the incidents at Roosevelt High involved a Mr. DeLotto, a physical education teacher, and Willie Johnson, a sixteen-year-old Negro student. DeLotto had called Willie "a black bastard" after the student told DeLotto that he resented being referred to as "boy." When informed of the name-calling incident, York explained to Willie that "DeLotto was from the South and naturally did not like Negroes."[16] It was also revealed that one of Roosevelt High's teachers had publicly declared that Negroes have a peculiarly offensive body odor. A male teacher at the George School had slapped five Negro girls, and in another incident a teacher at the Lincoln High School had made racial references so offensive that the Negro students in her classes wanted to transfer to another high school.[17]

The PUL's Board applauded Berry's involvement in the racial problems; so much so that Mrs. Hilman Grondahl, the Board secretary, informed Paul A. Rehmus, Superintendent of the Portland School System, that the ill will generated in the community as a result of the situation at Roosevelt High School and other schools in Portland could not be resolved without Berry's cooperation.[18] Berry, one of the acknowledged "rebels" during the Granger years, was convinced that the Urban League affiliates should perform such community functions in addition to establishing employment bureaus, maintaining day care centers for children, and attempting to win the cooperation of the white labor movement.

The Urban League affiliates that won the financial backing of local Community Chests addressed issues that promoted racial advancement, racial pride, group consciousness, and self-determination in a narrowly defined manner. Throughout the 1950s, the financially secure Urban Leagues also saw their role in urban America to be that of promoting programs in order to gain power, develop leaders, and obtain benefits.[19] Although Granger insisted that the NUL's programs sought identical goals, his methods and tactics differed markedly from those of the activist local Urban Leagues. The one thing that Granger seemed to forget was that the NUL was operating in an era unlike the one when Wood and Jones were at the helm.

II

From 1917 to 1941, Jones and Wood ran the NUL, but after 1941 Granger let it be known that he, rather than the NUL president, was the major force in the NUL. Theodore W. Kheel was the only NUL president who between 1941 and 1961 challenged Granger. Perhaps Kheel would not have been the activist NUL president that he was had there not been internal dissension within the Urban League. Except for Kheel, the NUL presidents between 1941 and 1956 served as fund raisers and presided over the Board meetings.[20] These were largely the extent of their powers.

The fact that the white Board members and NUL presidents were Granger's choices enabled him to ignore those Negro Board members who were critical of the manner in which the NUL pursued full equality. Moreover, the NUL's Negro staff members and those Negroes on the Board who met with Granger's approval were all establishment moderates.[21] This clear majority led Granger to conclude that he could ignore the dissident voices that called for a change of course for the NUL. Yet Granger was unwise; while most of the Negro Urban Leaguers supported him, they nonetheless believed that he had to be more forceful in his relations with the larger society than he had been during the 1940s.[22] They even thought that Granger was not as adamant on the race question as he should have been.[23]

Granger saw himself in an entirely different light. He once remarked that "if you get the attention of people you are interested in, you generally will get their support."[24] He held certain notions about whom to seek out for help and assistance. Although the NUL was not troubled by a cult of personality as were several of the other civil rights organizations, it did reflect the personality of its executive director. Thus Granger attempted to attract individuals to the NUL who shared his views about the value of scientific social work as opposed to direct action.

Granger's personality and his impact on NUL programs not only attracted certain individuals to the organization but also became a source of annoyance to a few Board members. Much of the annoyance was because Granger did not see any value in cooperating with the NAACP. He attempted, without success, to silence his critics by pointing out that the NUL's programs of racial advancement were based on NAACP objectives.[25] Granger's political beliefs also came under close scrutiny, particularly in the area of national politics.

Granger's critics disliked his repeated boasts of his affiliation with the Republican Party, and that he did not try to hide his contempt of Democrats. Granger was an Eisenhower supporter in the 1952 presidential election, while NUL president Lloyd K. Garrison openly backed Adlai E. Stevenson, the Democratic candidate. Most of the Negro Board members were also Stevenson backers, much to Granger's dismay. Whether or not

Granger took remarks made by several Negro Board members as personal during the height of the 1952 presidential campaign is unclear. But one Urban League observer noted that during 1952 Granger "exhibited neurotic tendencies at times."[26] Because Granger perceived himself as a liberal, he resented the fact that several Board members called him a conservative. A former Urban Leaguer stated that as Granger grew older he felt that his adversaries should "fight the enemy rather than turn on him."[27] He was particularly resentful of any criticism of his work that came from the Left. One person known for his Leftist leanings remarked that Granger was "exceedingly paranoid toward the end of his career in the NUL."[28]

Granger and several of his backers on the NUL Board were well aware that the changes in American society expected by urban Negroes would come slowly, if at all, if they were pursued by the Urban League's traditional methods. Yet Granger seemed unwilling to abandon completely the social work orientation and to employ direct action strategies and techniques in the search for equality. He even resisted efforts by several of the Negro Board members to alter the course of the NUL, after it was abundantly clear that scores of urban Negroes had rejected gradualism and scientific social work as tools of racial advancement. Granger insisted that the NUL was not intended as a mass movement organization, and therefore the fact that several civil rights organizations were quite attractive to urban Negroes was not a sound reason for the NUL to change course. When it was obvious that Granger would not cooperate with the NAACP and would not consider direct action as a viable strategy, the Board then began questioning his authority to set policies for the League.

Unfortunately the dissension over NUL tactics and strategies, and the question of whether the final say on NUL policies rested with Granger or the Board, surfaced partially as a racial issue rather than one directed toward a critical examination of old concepts versus new directions. Although Negro-white cooperation had made the NUL a noteworthy social work and civil rights organization, this alliance had always been an uneasy one. As early as the 1920s, for example, Marcus Garvey and other separatist-oriented Negro spokesmen raised the ire of a number of Urban Leaguers by suggesting that the NUL did not represent Negroes because it was controlled by white liberals. This argument resurfaced during the late 1940s and the early 1950s, and this time it found fertile ground among a growing number of upwardly mobile Negroes. This was particularly true of those articulate urban and educated young Negroes who backed direct action in the search for equality. Many Negroes no longer viewed white liberals in the same vein as did Negro founders of the NUL in 1910.

Increasingly, after 1950, the NUL and several of its affiliates were denounced by the Negro separatist groups because of their ties with liberal whites and moderate Negroes. And for a good reason: the NUL's philosophy was not forged during the 1950s but during the Progressive Era—a period of moderate, middle- and upper-class reform. Following a tradition established during the Progressive Era, NUL leadership and its Board members were still drawn largely from the white upper classes, as well as from the Negro middle classes and from Negro professional groups.

That Granger rarely, if ever, invited representatives of the urban Negro masses to serve on the NUL staff and the Board was a mistake. Separatist leaders capitalized on this oversight and painted the NUL as an elitist organization. Several on the NUL Board, and particularly the community-oriented Negro Board members, urged Granger to at least consider that separatist ideology was on the rise in urban Negro America. Moreover, this group of Negroes believed that the NUL was out of step with the times because whites remained the majority on its Board. A rumor circulated that the NUL was beset with dissension because of the white majority on the Board. Some NUL Negro Board members became even more dissatisfied when Robert Dowling, a white, was named the NUL president.

Dowling succeeded Garrison as the NUL president on May 15, 1952. Born in New York City on September 9, 1895, to Robert E. Dowling and Minetta Linck, Dowling passed up college, entered the Army during World War I, and pursued a business career following his discharge. His father was founder of the City Investment Company, a real estate holding company in New York City. In addition to his business activities Dowling was active in the National Conference of Christians and Jews, and was a former director of the Boy Scouts of America.[29]

Dowling's credentials were impeccable, except for his financial interests in apartment complexes that barred Negro occupants. One of these apartment complexes was built in 1943 by the Metropolitan Life Insurance Company, with which Dowling had financial connections. Much to the dismay of dozens of NUL and NAACP members, Metropolitan Life decided that: (1) Negroes would not be permitted to occupy apartments in the development; (2) all streets and parks in the development would be marked "private" and therefore would be closed to nonresidents; (3) a public school would not be constructed in the project because Negro children from surrounding areas might try to enroll in the school; and (4) a community auditorium would be deleted from the original plans, because Negroes might try to use it.[30] Although Metropolitan Life did not attempt to hide the fact that the development was closed to Negro occupancy, the New York City Board of Estimates approved not only the construction plans, but also acceded to Metropolitan Life's request for a 25 million dollar tax exemption, spread over twenty-five years. The Board of Estimates took this action despite the objections raised by the NAACP and the NUL, along with other sympathetic groups. Many Negroes and whites disapproved of the rules governing this Stuyvesant Town development, which was built at a cost of some $50,000,000 and housed some 24,000 persons.

The Stuyvesant Town housing development, coupled with other housing developments with which Dowling had financial connections and which denied Negroes occupancy, caused some individuals in the League to question Dowling's commitment to integrated housing. He was nevertheless named the NUL president over the strenuous objections of several NUL Board members. They argued, but to no avail, that the NUL had indeed compromised its credibility in the area of integrated housing. Their objections to Dowling as NUL president were valid. The fact that he was associated with housing developments that barred Negroes could be interpreted as supporting segregated housing. Hence, naming Dowling as NUL president was, to some Urban Leaguers, a source of embarrassment. Granger's continuing support of Dowling, after the facts were made known, angered several NUL Negro Board members. Even before the Dowling controversy, several Negro Board members had claimed that Granger's housing policy was unworkable. While Granger may well have understood why these Board members resented Dowling's becoming the NUL president, he believed that his (Granger's) stand on integrated housing was above reproach. Granger came to believe that the insults and charges hurled at Dowling were mere smoke screens, and that he was the real target of the indictments and insults. Whatever the truth of the situation, in the ensuing months, rumors were circulated in the major Negro newspapers that the NUL Board was divided into pro- and anti-Granger supporters. Granger of course denied the rumors. On May 22, 1954, several Negro newspapers carried an unsigned syndicated column that elaborated in detail on the internal dissension within the National Board. The *Pittsburgh Courier* predicted that a purge of dissenting Board members was forthcoming.[31] The dissension, the column reported, stemmed largely from the NUL's softness on segregated housing. In addition, the paper stated that Granger had not backed a forceful housing policy because of Dowling's financial interests in real estate.

As usual Granger denied that the NUL Board was beset with internal problems, insisting that there was complete harmony among the Board members. It is uncertain whether the editorial staff of the *Pittsburgh Courier* was aware of a memorandum that Granger was circulating among his friends on the Board. It charged several Board members with attacking the NUL leadership, with voicing suspicions about industrial, business, and real estate whites who were associated with the NUL, and with denouncing those Negro Board members who refused to "join in the attacks."[32]

A follow-up story, appearing in the *Chicago Defender,* further added to the rumors that had won wide currency in Negro America. It alleged that

Dowling and Granger were cooperating to dissuade NAACP Secretary Roy Wilkins from pushing his application for an apartment in United States Steel's Delaware Valley (Pennsylvania) housing development.[33] In addition, the newspaper reported that Granger had ousted several Board members who had criticized him.[34] Granger denied that he had purged any Negroes from the NUL Board. On June 8, 1954, Theodore E. Brown gave an exclusive interview to James Booker of the New York *Amsterdam News,* confirming reports of a Granger-led purge of dissident Board members.[35] The League's internal problems were now in full public view. Brown maintained that Granger wanted him removed from the Board because of his "vociferous views on the question of racial rights."[36]

In the aftermath of the *Amsterdam News* article, other equally damaging issues emerged. During one of the Board sessions devoted to the Brown controversy, Granger in a fit of anger informed the Board that it had no control over how he spent NUL funds. During the same session Frank Evans, a Cleveland Urban League Board member, sought recognition to speak. Granger denied his request, pointing out that membership in a local Urban League did not necessarily make one a member of the NUL. Needless to say, Granger's remarks annoyed several Board members. Their anger, and their suspicions of Granger's competence in leading the NUL, were intensified when the *Amsterdam News* reported that, as of 1954, there were "approximately 2500 members of the NUL."[37] It would seem that several of the Board members attributed the low membership directly to Granger's abuse of power.

These revelations, coupled with Brown's earlier interview, sparked additional anger within the NUL Board, and also made Granger the target of newspaper reporters. When questioned, all Granger would say was that he expected cooperation only from those who agreed with the NUL rationale, and from those who were intelligent enough to understand what it was he was doing. Granger did, however, lash out at Brown, telling an *Amsterdam News* reporter that the Brown interview was an effort on the part of dissidents to discredit the name of the NUL "by smearing the reputation of its chosen leaders."[38] As expected, this and other remarks Granger willingly gave newspaper reporters heightened tensions and produced additional discord within the NUL Board of Directors.

Privately Kenneth B. Clark, a Negro Board member, attempted to persuade the Board to censure Brown for having given the interview, but not to purge him from the Board; but to no avail. Publicly Clark depicted Brown's interview as "a regrettable incident which had exposed Urban League internal affairs to public scrutiny."[39] When pressed to explain why there were thirty-eight whites and only twenty-two Negroes on the NUL's Board of Directors, Clark remained silent.

As the events surrounding Brown's ouster from the NUL Board unfolded, it became clear that it was Granger and Dowling who had ordered the purge. The nominating committee, composed of Board members, began accepting names for the slate of nominations for "new" Board members, beginning about the middle of January 1954. A dozen names had been received by March, and Brown's was among them.[40] By April several names, including Brown's, had been deleted from the list for undisclosed reasons. Upon learning that his name no longer was on the slate of candidates, Brown asked why. The nominating committee would only say that an additional meeting was needed to clear the air. Later meetings did not lead to a resolution of the controversy, and the issue was placed on the agenda for the full Board to resolve at its June 10, 1954, meeting.

More than one Board member inquired as to why Brown was no longer a candidate for reelection. Benjamin Wood, a Granger supporter, insisted that the committee had "agreed to keep its decisions confidential."[41] Granger was less timid, explaining that the nominating committee had voted to authorize a "rest period" for Board members upon completion of two terms. He also pointed out that the nominating committee had voted to reduce the cumbersome Board membership from fifty-nine to forty members. Regarding Brown's name, Granger explained that it was removed from the original list after the nominating committee had "reconsidered individually each nomination it had passed on previously."[42]

The committee, as Granger later pointed out, recommended that Brown be dropped from the Board for these three reasons: his interview with the *Amsterdam News*; his call to Beulah Whitby informing her that the nominating committee had decided to remove her name from the slate of prospective Board members; and his remarks to Whitby that the committee's decision not to renominate her was for reasons that "reflected on her character and connections."[43] It is clear why he endeavored to remove Whitby from the NUL Board. Whitby was one of those who had stated publicly that the NUL was not in tune with the mood of Negro America. While she was careful not to attack Granger and his views of how to pursue full equality, Granger, as he often did, took Whitby's remarks personally. He used the situation to punish Whitby, remaining hopeful that her problems with the Detroit mayor would disguise his true intentions—the removal of Whitby from the Board.

Mayor Albert E. Cobo of Detroit had rejected Whitby's application for the post of director of the city's Commission on Human Relations. He told the newspapers that Mrs. Whitby was "too close to organizations not in line with the thinking of his administration."[44] Detroit's newspapers interpreted the mayor's statement to mean that Whitby was associated with Communist organizations. Mayor Cobo ultimately corrected the newspaper statements. He informed the public that Mrs. Whitby, as chairman of the Community Services of the Detroit Urban League, had "endorsed violence if necessary in order to break down the city's segregation pattern in public housing projects."[45]

There is little doubt but that Granger was distressed over the publicity generated by the Whitby controversy. As in the past, he was ready to protect the NUL's good name at all costs. Granger seemed convinced of Whitby's guilt before hearing the facts, stating that the events in Detroit involved "not only members of the National Board of Trustees but also the public relations of the Urban League of Detroit."[46] In the aftermath of the statement, Granger scurried to Detroit, but he promised that no decision on Whitby would be forthcoming until the Board had its say. Rather than following through on his word, Granger instructed the nominating committee to delete Whitby's name from the list of Board candidates.

Removing Whitby's name was a mistake. She had many friends on the Board who saw her as an able and dedicated worker. When it was a certainty that Granger intended to purge Whitby from the Board, her friends reacted swiftly, annulling the nominating committee's decision. Whitby was not only returned to the Board but was also elected as one of the NUL's vice presidents. Having handed Granger and his conspirators a resounding defeat, at least four of the Board members were then intent upon voiding the nomination committee's decision to remove Brown. The move failed. One reason was that Brown was unpopular within the Board. As Granger had reported, Brown had expressed suspicions of white Board members in private meetings, and in doing so had engaged in character assassination.[47] While it is a certainty that Brown's Negro supporters on the Board did not approve of his tactics, they disliked Granger as much as if not more than Brown did.

By the end of June of 1954, newspaper headlines reported the resignation of two Negroes from the NUL Board. Irvin C. Mollison, Judge of the U.S. Customs Court of New York City, and George D. Cannon, a Harlem physician, both denied that the Brown controversy had influenced their decision. Judge Mollison maintained that he tendered his letter of resignation because:

> The National Urban League has no program of any real benefit to Negroes. The League, its officers, and its staff are completely out of touch with Negroes and their desire to participate as full-fledged American citizens in our American democracy.[48]

Dr. Cannon's letter of resignation read as follows:

> I did and do now recognize that some objectives can be obtained by other than militant means. However, the over-cautious policy of not giving support by statements or participation in conferences, other than as an occasional "observer," where programs for Negro advancement are being formalized, processed, or activated, is a criticism that has more than once been discussed in

board meeting. Nothing has been done to correct this reluctance to put the organization in the vanguard for the advancement of Negroes.[49]

While Mollison and Cannon insisted that Granger's purge of Brown did not influence their decision to resign from the Board, the fact that they announced that they were leaving the Board soon after the Brown case broke linked the two events.

The dispute between Granger and several Board and ex-Board members intensified in the ensuing months. Granger busied himself and his staff with preparing and issuing statements that put the blame for the internal dissension on the activities of Brown, Mollison, and Cannon. A memorandum, presumably written by Granger in 1954, pinpointed the origins of the internal problems to the year 1949, at which time the NUL and the Urban League of New York,* rarely on friendly terms, undertook a joint fund-raising set-up in order to avoid duplication. According to Granger's recollection, the dissension arose out of this joint venture. One of the League's former presidents, however, disputed Granger's conclusion, stating that throughout the time of the joint fund-raising effort there was close cooperation between the NUL and the local affiliate.[50] James Felt of the NYUL and representatives from the NUL met weekly to discuss issues of mutual concern. And Elmo Roper and Winthrop Rockefeller of the NYUL assisted in coordinating the activities of the national office and the affiliate, so as not to duplicate efforts.[51] Granger also claimed that by 1949 Judge Mollison objected to the white majority on the Board of Trustees. Consequently, as Granger explained it, Mollison was named to chair the nominating committee.

By 1952, a total of nine Negroes had been added to the NUL Board; Theodore Brown and George Cannon were among the group. During 1952, according to Granger's recollection, Mollison complained that the NUL had not aggressively lobbied for a permanent FEPC. Meanwhile Cannon began sparring with Dowling because he was unable to secure an apartment in a development financed by the Equitable Life Insurance Company, a business in which Dowling had connections.[52] Because Cannon did not gain admission into the housing development, Granger contended, he and others began spreading rumors that the NUL would not fight for integrated housing with Dowling as its president.

Public statements from Granger and publicity releases from his staff were of little avail in curbing criticisms against the NUL's overall program. One of Granger's closest friends correctly advised him to rethink his approach toward civil rights in light of the Supreme Court's *Brown* v. *Board of Education* decision.[53]

---

*Each of the New York City boroughs had a local League until the 1950s, at which time they merged to form the Urban League of Greater New York (ULOGNY).

The *Brown* decision unquestionably had placed the NAACP in the driver's seat as far as the desegregation of public education was concerned. Southern Negro educators in particular hailed the Supreme Court decision. John H. Lewis, president of the Morris Brown College in Atlanta, said of the ruling: "America no longer places herself in the equivocal position of preaching democracy while practicing its reverse."[54] William R. Strassner, president of Shaw University, Raleigh, North Carolina, said that the ruling "was a vindication of Democracy in the eyes of the world."[55] These statements accurately reflected the Southern Negro intellectuals' views on segregation, and also showed a meeting of the mind of Northern and Southern Negro intellectuals with regard to ridding the society of an educational caste system and of legally enforced segregation itself.

Granger's initial reactions to the decision are not known; he seemed preoccupied with defending himself rather than with anticipating the *Brown* decision's impact on race relations in America. He did not mince words in lashing out at his detractors, stating that Mollison had spread a "fat black lie" in charging that the League had failed to cooperate with the NAACP and other organizations.[56] He attributed the conduct of Mollison, Brown, and Cannon to personality aberrations, insisting that they ought to see a psychiatrist. Granger rejected Brown's allegation that the NUL had not kept pace with the local branches in other cities.[57] He also disclosed that both Mollison and Brown had been "forced out of their respective local NAACP branches, a fact we did not discover until too late."[58] Further, the beleaguered Granger declared that the three were emotionally unsuited to serve on the Board. To this charge Earl Brown, a columnist for the *Amsterdam News,* replied: "What is needed on the NUL Board is a large helping of emotionalism and less social service gobbledygook. That is, if the League plans to gain a niche in the battle for human equality and justice in the United States."[59] While Brown's column might have been an overstatement, it nonetheless underscored the urban Negroes' growing aversion to NUL tactics and strategies.

Privately Granger confessed that the Board controversy had caused the NUL to receive unfavorable publicity. Publicly he insisted that his policies were the correct ones for the League. But in the 1954 annual report, Granger stated that the NUL should revise its policies and programs to accommodate the great changes that were anticipated as a result of the 1954 Supreme Court decision.[60] Granger also linked the plight of the Negro American to the struggle for freedom then under way in Africa. He wrote that: "Nkrumah and his fellow leaders of a new Africa had placed the rest of the free world deeply in their debt, for if we remain free, it will be because Africa attains freedom, and they are on the road to attainment."[61] Granger endeavored to separate the NUL and himself from the techniques and strategies of earlier Negro leaders, exclaiming that:

Booker T. Washington, W.E.B. Du Bois, James Weldon Johnson, Eugene K. Jones—all of these made their contribution to the revolution of American thinking, and they all passed off the stage while History changed the setting and got ready for the next phase. That phase is now upon us. Now the fight is for integration, and has been for a couple of decades, without the aware knowledge of some of us.[62]

Granger should be applauded for attempting to bring the NUL more in line with the views of other civil rights organizations, that an end to colonialism in Africa would enhance the status of the American Negro. Granger was correct in believing that the Negroes' search for equality was inextricably bound up in the struggle to free Africa of European colonialism.[63] Yet neither Granger nor Dowling could resist directing additional blows at their detractors. Granger, for example, remarked that "any organization like the NUL is always open to attack by psychotic headline-hunters and similar critics."[64] Dowling insisted that no change was forthcoming in NUL programs, techniques, and targets, pointing out that: "Our program of education and persuasion has been good for 43 years, and we think we have made a lot of progress. We have made more friends through our methods and will continue our approach."[65] But these and other remarks made by Granger, by Dowling, and by the dissidents added fuel to the fire.

Tempers flared and feelings were further ruffled between June and September of 1954. Frank Evans, whom Granger had denied permission to speak at the June 10, 1954, meeting held in the National Office, indicted the NUL by alleging that it was antiunion.[66] Granger refuted the allegation, calling Evans "an emotionally disturbed individual, who had a reputation around Cleveland of being off in a number of ways."[67] As a parting shot, an angry Granger insisted that Evans was acting as a stooge for Mollison who, according to the executive director, was "intensely suspicious and hating—almost to the point of psychosis."[68]

At no time did the Board members join Granger and Dowling in their public denunciations of Cannon, Brown, and Mollison. Perhaps it was because even Granger's friends saw him as a prima donna who often made decisions without consulting the Board of Trustees.[69] While a majority of the NUL trustees deplored the methods of Brown, Mollison, and Cannon, there was general agreement that NUL tactics and techniques were in need of review. The charges hurled at Granger and the NUL pointed to admitted weaknesses in the League's role in the search for equality.

In one sense the accusations of Mollison, Brown, and Cannon had not been in vain. A former Board member admitted that "Mollison and Cannon shook things up and made the League a more visible organization than in the past."[70] While agreeing with their ultimate motives, a second Urban Leaguer characterized Mollison as a cranky old Midwesterner whom Truman had made a Customs Judge, and Cannon as a New York radical.[71] In another sense the internal feud was little more than a name-calling contest. Granger and his supporters on the Board avoided discussing any contemplated changes in the League's strategies and techniques for racial advancement.

In the aftermath of the feud revolving around Granger, Mollison, Cannon, and Brown, the Board reluctantly instituted structural changes. It was decided that: (1) each local affiliate was entitled to one voting delegate at the annual conference; (2) the NUL Board would be reduced from fifty-nine to a maximum of forty-two members; (3) Board members would be automatically retired after two consecutive three-year terms; and (4) Negro representation on the NUL Board would be increased.[72] All of these reforms were in effect by 1956.

The shouting and turmoil within the Board were noticeably absent by 1956. Yet the progressive Negroes in the organization remained dissatisfied because the NUL continued to rest its hopes for changes in the Negroes' economic and social condition largely on educational protest, persuasion, investigation, and cooperation from white labor. But more important was the fact that Granger's power to rule had been broken. It was Dowling, however, who fell victim to the internal dissension. It was announced in 1956 that Theodore W. Kheel would become the NUL's president, replacing Dowling who had held the post for four years.

Born on May 9, 1914, in New York City, Kheel received the A.B. and the LL.B. degrees from Cornell University.[73] His involvement in civil rights and social service activities had won him the respect of Negroes and whites alike. Kheel had served on the President's Committee on Equal Opportunity, chaired the Mayor's (New York City) Committee on Job Advancement, and was a member of the President's Committee for Human Relations. As the NUL's new president, Kheel was expected to call for wider employment opportunities for Negroes and to end the bickering between NUL and NAACP officials, because he was a member of the NAACP as well as the NUL president.

Kheel's leadership as president of the ULOGNY had been impressive. He had personally led the battle to force the airlines operating out of New York to hire Negro pilots and stewardesses. His wife, Mrs. Ann Kheel, the ULOGNY's present Board secretary, informed me that Kheel had also pressured law firms in New York City to employ qualified Negro lawyers.[74] Kheel recalled that when he assumed the NUL presidency, no help in the area of equal employment opportunities was forthcoming from the federal government. He agreed with the "objectives which Granger had set for the NUL, but questioned the pace with which the executive secretary hoped to realize certain objectives."[75] Kheel attributed the League's limited success in the field of equal opportunity to the fact that both the NUL and its affiliates were small operations until the 1960s. Most of the affiliates had no more than three salaried workers as late as 1956,[76] a revelation that dispels the myth that big business has been generous in its support of the Urban League Movement.

The internal dissension within the NUL Board and within the Urban League Movement stemmed from several sources. Until the 1950s there does not appear to have been much concern over the fact that the NUL Board was overwhelmingly white. Beginning in 1949 or thereabouts the aspirations of the American Negro included, among other things, a growing belief in self-determination. This meant that Negro-oriented organizations should be under the control of Negroes. Second, the younger and more vocal Negro Board members believed that the time had come for the NUL to reexamine its strategies and techniques in light of the new demands that some Negro leaders were making on the political process. Third, several Negro Board members were of the opinion that the white majority on the Board was too great a moderating influence on NUL policies and strategies, and that their majority status was in direct conflict with the growing belief among Negroes in self-determination as a viable strategy in the search for equality. Not that Negro professionals and the middle classes were rejecting integration, but rather that they believed strongly in Negro control of organizations that promoted racial advancement in Negro America.

Granger, like most of the white NUL Board members, seemed unaware of the fact that there was growing cooperation among Negro separatists, integrationists, and self-determinationists. Nor did Granger and the white NUL Board members seem aware that these crosscurrents were increasingly present in the actions and thoughts of the Negro Board members; at least this can be said of ex-NUL Board members Brown, Mollison, and Cannon. At the same time, Brown, Mollison, and Cannon can be criticized for not perceiving the valuable differences between the work and programs of the NUL and the NAACP. They and their supporters on the NUL Board and in the Negro community at large failed to credit the NUL with at least limited successes in opening various employment opportunities heretofore closed to Negroes. The NUL under Granger's direction put to good use scientific social work, civil rights techniques, and pressure group tactics. Granger's zeal for reforming existing governmental structures, coupled with his interest in civil rights and his use of pressure group tactics, gave the NUL no reason to be ashamed of their role in the Negroes' search for equality.

9

The Watershed Years of the Urban League, 1953–1961: Polite Protest or Direct Action?

Lester B. Granger was undoubtedly pleased that a Republican, Dwight D. Eisenhower, was elected to the presidency of the United States. And he made little attempt to hide his disdain of an earlier Democratic President, Franklin D. Roosevelt, whom Granger characterized as being actively anti-Negro. Granger's remarks about Truman were less pointed, although he did state that "you can have a desegregation that is so far from integration as to be a waste of time."[1] With the election of a Republican, Granger was indeed hopeful that Negroes would be integrated into the mainstream of American society, and that segregation and racial discrimination would be overturned with a minimum of resistance from the die-hard white supremacists.

Granger expected that Eisenhower would give the NUL the fullest cooperation in integrating Negroes into every facet of American society, as well as supporting programs to reform governmental structures that heretofore supported racial discrimination and segregation. Chapter 9 examines the extent of the Eisenhower administration's assistance to the NUL in the search for equality and in reforming existing governmental structures.

I

The Eisenhower administration inherited a myriad of employment and housing problems from the Truman presidency. Employment discrimination remained a serious problem. And Negroes still "[received] less housing value per dollar than [did] whites."[2] Realtors, lending institutions, and builders were guilty of excluding nonwhites from the better existing housing and especially from newly developed neighborhoods. Mortgage money from private sources generally was unavailable for improving the housing conditions of urban and rural Negroes; and most private lenders had refused to invest in nonsegregated housing. Between 1935 and 1950, approximately nine million housing units were erected by private developers; of these about one hundred thousand, or only slightly over one percent, were open for nonwhite occupancy.

The NUL's late entry into and expanding interest in the dispute over segregated housing has already been documented. By 1944 Granger and his staff, together with the NUL Board, began investigating the racial problem in housing. Not until 1952, however, did the NUL create an Office of Housing Activities, with Reginald A. Johnson as its director. Under his leadership the Office of Housing Activities dealt with the "problem of private home building and ownership by Negroes under racially nonsegregated conditions."[3]

Contesting segregation in privately financed housing set the NUL on a collision course with the United States Steel Corporation, among others. The housing controversy had its origins in the Truman administration. In 1951 the corporation made known plans to construct a modern steel plant at Morrisville, Pennsylvania, at the cost of $4 million. In addition, U.S. Steel spent about $15 million for a new community, Fairless Hills, to house workers. Discussions between the NUL and U.S. Steel began as early as 1951 in regard to open housing and equal employment opportunities. Little progress was made during 1951, and the officials of the NUL and U.S. Steel agreed to meet again in 1952. On November 18, 1952, Robert W. Dowling and Winthrop Rockefeller of the NUL met privately with Clifford Hood, president of U.S. Steel, and E. Earl Moore, the corporation's vice-president. Both Hood and Moore declared that Negroes would be employed on the same basis as other workers, but they remained silent on the issue of open housing at Fairless Hills.[4] During subsequent meetings, U.S. Steel officials informed the NUL that Negro workers could not reside in Fairless Hills. In response, Moore and Hood urged that the NUL press the Levittown Corporation to alter its housing policies.

A Levittown housing development was under construction in the vicinity of Morrisville, Pennsylvania, but located in New Jersey. Reginald A. Johnson of the NUL met during 1952 with the Levittown builders—William Levitt and John Galbreath—and were informed that the development was closed to Negro occupancy. Despite the fact that a New Jersey law forbade racial discrimination in housing, Levitt and Galbreath held firm, realizing that the federal government did not support integrated housing even when federal mortgages were used to purchase homes. This fact made it all the more difficult for Granger, since he was already under fire for not having formulated a workable housing program.

The housing crisis with U.S. Steel surfaced at about the same time that the NUL Board was in the throes of an internal dispute, much of which centered around charges that Granger and NUL president Dowling were "soft" on segregated housing. The allegation was not entirely incorrect. Granger thwarted the Board's efforts to pressure the U.S. Steel Corporation to open Fairless Hills to Negroes who were employed by the corporation at its Morrisville plant. Yet the NUL, despite the claims of its critics, was not to blame for Negroes having been barred from buying and renting housing in the Fairless Hills and Levittown developments. The federal government was the principal culprit, inasmuch as it had guaranteed loans even after learning the decision of U.S. Steel and Levitt to bar Negro residents from the developments. As a result of federal inactivity in the area of open housing, neither Levitt nor the U.S. Steel Corporation held any real fear of the NUL. Even after Granger seemed convinced that the federal government would not side with the NUL on this issue, he nonetheless believed that his affiliation with the Republican Party would turn the tide in favor of the NUL. Therefore he kept a tight rein on the housing issue.

Indeed Granger did not give the NUL's housing committee, a task force comprised of Board members, a free hand in challenging U.S. Steel's housing policy. The committee included Sophia Y. Jacobs, Sadie T.M. Alexander, William H. Baldwin, III, Theodore Brown, John L. Snyder, Jr., Edward Stanley, and Mrs. Arthur Hays Sulzberger. With the exception of Brown, they were loyal Granger backers. Granger had few objections to the committee protesting housing discrimination at Fairless Hills, but he disapproved of direct action and confrontation as strategies for resolving the dispute with U.S. Steel.

A majority on the Board held an entirely different view, and therefore instructed the Bucks County Committee to seek an end to housing discrimination. Aware of this new mood of the Board, Granger instructed the committee to press for the placement of Negroes in skilled and technical jobs at U.S. Steel. In that way a confrontation with the industry might possibly be avoided, inasmuch as previous executive orders prohibited U.S. Steel and other companies from engaging in discriminatory employment practices. The placing of skilled and professional Negroes in U.S. Steel would not be a strategy of confrontation. But the placing of Negroes in housing built by U.S. Steel was another matter.

The NUL's president, Robert W. Dowling, appointed the Bucks County Committee, and he, like Granger, was hopeful of avoiding a confrontation with U.S. Steel. While the two men's actions saved the corporation from public embarrassment, their tactics did serve to spread dissension within the NUL Board. The members of the Bucks County Committee would not disobey Granger, and they momentarily affirmed the assertion that it was the executive director who ran the NUL.

At the September 17, 1953, Board meeting Mrs. Jacobs informed the full Board that the ultimate goal of the committee remained unchanged; but for the purposes of strategy, it argued that employment opportunities for Negroes at the Morrisville plant took first priority. Board member Kenneth B. Clark inquired as to why U.S. Steel had delayed in employing technical and skilled Negroes in the new plant. Julius A. Thomas, industrial relations secretary of the NUL and a partial supporter of Granger, explained that it was the custom of several corporations to place new technical and professional personnel in plants "where they can get adequate training before [they are assigned] to a particular operation."[5] Clark did not hide his anger over the fact that the Bucks County Committee had ignored a Board directive, inquiring as to why the committee no longer deemed integrated housing an important issue.[6] Granger came to the defense of the committee by asserting it was essential that the task force (committee) first find qualified Negroes, then see to it that they gained employment at the U.S. Steel plant, to be followed by a program to ensure that those employed at the plant were admitted to the Fairless Hills housing development.

Notwithstanding the logic behind Granger's plan of action for dealing with the impasse revolving around the housing and employment policies of U.S. Steel, the Bucks County Committee's handling of the issues was what provoked several NUL Board members. Mrs. Arthur H. Sulzberger, one of Granger's stronger supporters, disagreed with the Granger plan and urged that legal pressure be resorted to as a way of forcing U.S. Steel to alter its housing policies. Theodore Brown, one of Granger's critics, recommended that the committee's findings be turned over to the President's Committee on Government Contract Compliance (PCOGCC), and that the NUL direct its energies toward a resolution of the housing issue. Granger argued that to follow Brown's advice would hamper rather than enhance the NUL's chances of arriving at a favorable understanding with U.S. Steel. In the final analysis, Granger rejected the advice of even his loyal supporters on the NUL Board, although he only publicly repudiated Brown.

Granger's decision to ignore the Board led to additional tensions within the policy-making arm of the NUL. And the fact that Granger opposed the NAACP's entry into the dispute with U.S. Steel confirmed the views of several Board members, who charged Granger with not seeking the cooperation of the NAACP in matters of mutual concern. In fact, Granger did not want the NAACP's cooperation in resolving the dispute with U.S. Steel, because he was certain that his old nemesis, Roy Wilkins, was responsible for the NAACP's belated entry into the housing and employment dispute. In short, Granger was fearful that in the end it would be the NAACP, rather than the NUL, that would receive the media's attention, that is, if the housing and employment issues were successfully resolved. Granger's views were communicated to those individuals on the NUL staff and Board whom he trusted.

Granger's handpicked NUL representatives, and those sent by the NAACP Bucks County Human Relations Committee (BCHRC), and the American Friends Services Committee (AFSC), met with U.S. Steel officials in Philadelphia on September 24, 1953. E. Earl Moore presided over the meeting. For about twelve minutes he mouthed pious platitudes, after which he pointed out that it was a headache for U.S. Steel to attempt to arrive at any decision with organizations that all had different points of view.[7]

Moore's statement rang with a degree of truth. Prior to the meeting, the four agencies caucused and decided that each was free to act on its own. Unresolved jealousies that had marked the Granger-Wilkins years undoubtedly prevented the realization of a united front. Robert C. Weaver of the NAACP had prepared a statement on the Fairless Hills issue to be sent to President Eisenhower at the close of the meeting with U.S. Steel officers. Representatives of the NUL claimed that they had not been given ample time to study the document, and they refused to sign it. The truth of the matter was that they feared that the publicity from the statement would further enhance the NAACP's image in Negro America.

Despite the bickering between Granger and Wilkins, the meeting with the representatives of U.S. Steel was not a total disaster. Before the meeting, the NUL forwarded to Moore the names of forty-one Negroes who were either skilled workers or held degrees in engineering, metallurgy, and chemistry. During the meeting Moore confessed that the names and the accompanying data had not been reviewed by anyone other than himself. This admission was damaging to the extent that Harvey B. Jordan, a U.S. Steel vice president, later admitted that there seemed to be discrimination in the selection of workers at the Morrisville plant.[8] Yet subsequent meetings between NUL and U.S. Steel officials did not resolve the employment and housing dilemma. Therefore Board member Irvin Mollison recommended that the matter be turned over to the PCOGCC, citing Executive Order 10308 as the precedent.

Between 1953 and 1955 the Eisenhower administration insisted that its equal employment policies were guided by Executive Order 10308, and by the recommendations of the PCOGCC. The PCOGCC, in its report of January 16, 1953, recommended several ways in which the Eisenhower administration could pursue equality of opportunity in employment. They said that persuasion, conciliation, and fact-finding would convince holders of government contracts not to discriminate against Negro workers; that if persuasion did not end employment discrimination, legal actions were to be initiated, but only as a last resort; that education was a valuable weapon to convince employers to abide by nondiscrimination legislation; and that it was the responsibility of the administration to see to it that contractors explain to all subcontractors that employment discrimination clearly violated the executive order.[9]

The Eisenhower administration neither endorsed these proposals nor did it fill vacancies in the PCOGCC that were created during the Truman years. U.S. Steel was a holder of government contracts, and the PCOGCC should therefore have investigated U.S. Steel's hiring policies, but it did not. While several NUL Board members expressed displeasure over the fact that the PCOGCC followed a hands-off policy with regard to the hiring policies of U.S. Steel, they reserved their harshest criticisms for Granger, who believed that the PCOGCC should not enter into the dispute until it received more hard data than the NUL had collected.[10]

A majority on the Board sustained Granger's view of how to resolve the dispute with U.S. Steel. But they also wanted more facts, and sought a meeting with David McDonald, president of the United Steel Workers of America (USW). Moore and Hood had insisted all along that the Negro workers were not eligible for residence in Fairless Hills because it was reserved for employees in the grade classifications of 16 and above. They also had insisted that there were no Negroes in any of the U.S. Steel's plants who were in grade 16. McDonald refuted these assertions by pointing out that hundreds of Negroes in the USW union were above grade 16.[11] As the NUL's investigation proceeded, it was learned that most of the whites residing in Fairless Hills were in fact not classified as grade 16 and above.

For a second time, the NUL's Industrial Relations Department compiled a list of skilled Negro workers and forwarded it to Morrisville plant officials. Again Moore took no action on the list. Largely through Granger's stalling tactics, and those of U.S. Steel officials, the Fairless Hills Village controversy evolved into an explosive issue. Over Granger's objections the full Board voted on January 21, 1954, to present the information collected by the Bucks County Committee to Vice President Richard Nixon, and follow up with a press conference.[12] It appears that Granger instructed the committee to ignore the Board's decision. On March 17, 1954, Mrs. Jacobs informed the Board that a series of events after the January 21 meeting had made it "necessary for the Bucks County Committee to reconsider its previously planned strategy."[13] She explained that U.S. Steel had hired more Negroes at the Morrisville plant, and the NUL should pursue additional employment opportunities for Negroes, rather than open housing. Mrs. Jacobs did not, however, inform the Board that no technical and skilled jobs had been offered to Negroes, that only seventy Negroes had been employed, and that none of these seventy workers resided in Fairless Hills.

Granger's friends and foes alike on the Board were angry that the Bucks County Committee had ignored the Board's mandate of January 21, 1954. What especially angered Granger's critics was the fact that the committee had decided against handing over the findings to Nixon and holding a press conference after it had consulted with Granger and NUL president Dowling. What better proof was required to show that Dowling and Granger were intent upon circumventing the Board's decision.

There was some truth to the allegations that the NUL lacked a workable housing program. But the charge that Dowling and Granger had refrained from pressing U.S. Steel because of its financial contributions to the NUL was unfounded. In fact the NUL did not accept contributions from U.S. Steel while the housing dispute remained unresolved. However, Granger's handling of the controversy made him an easy target for his critics on the Board. Secretary of the Navy Robert B. Anderson sought Granger's services in the capacity of advisor and consultant on the U.S. Navy's desegregation program. The full Board, however, had to make the final determination, and Brown urged the full Board to reject the Navy Secretary's request. Brown pointed out that Negro advisors "were rarely, if ever, called upon to give advice on real, basic problems."[14] His argument was persuasive to the extent that the Board did not approve the Navy Secretary's request. Granger was of course irked by the Board's action; but he did not remain silent after Brown and Cannon asked to review all of the correspondence Granger had written to and received from the Navy Secretary. Granger lashed out at the two Negro Board members, charging them with engaging in character assassination. While it is clear that Granger did not like their request, Brown and Cannon did have the right to review what had transpired between Granger and the Navy Secretary.

That Granger was upset in the wake of the Board vote pertaining to his being loaned to the Navy Department as a consultant is a fact, but the charge that he had formulated an "unworkable" housing program caused him the most anguish. It is true that Granger had experienced limited success with U.S. Steel in altering its employment but not its housing program. The corporation announced on April 24, 1954, that Negro workers had been hired as technical and professional workers at the Morrisville plant. Leon Fennoy, a chemist from Brooklyn, New York, had reported to work at the Morrisville, Pennsylvania, plant on April 12, 1954, and by the end of that year Negroes were at the plant as mechanical engineers, drafters, stenographers, and chemists.

The Eisenhower administration of course capitalized on the partial resolution of the employment problem at the Morrisville plant. As an ex-

ample, Labor Secretary James P. Mitchell praised the Eisenhower administration's equal employment policy in an address to Urban Leaguers during
the 1954 Annual Conference. Mitchell stated that the Eisenhower administration's equal employment program "was not directed toward industry
but was aimed at obtaining industry's cooperation in achieving what is a
just, reasonable and desirable goal from every point of view."[15] His remarks drew polite but unenthusiastic applause from those in attendance.

It was not surprising that Mitchell did not strike a responsive chord
among the delegates to the 1954 Annual Conference, because the Eisenhower adminstration's rhetoric thus far on equal employment and open
housing did not in the least match its record. As in the past, the federal
housing agency heads continued to support segregated housing. Former
Congressman Albert M. Cole, Eisenhower's choice to head the Housing
and Home Finance Agency (HHFA), was no exception.

The President came under severe criticism over the appointment of
Cole to head the HHFA. CIO president Walter Reuther objected to the
fact that Eisenhower had named Cole to head the HHFA, writing to the
President that the former Congressman's "votes in the House on housing
measures were fully in keeping with the unwarranted and exaggerated
attacks which [he] has leveled against public housing and against those of
us who for years have been seeking to improve the living conditions of the
American people."[16]

While Granger, like Reuther, disapproved of Eisenhower's choice to
head the HHFA, it is conceivable that his Republican loyalties and his
deep respect for Eisenhower prevented him from venting his true feelings
to the President. But Granger did not attempt to hide his true feelings
about liberal Democrats such as Reuther. Granger, as stated previously,
did not believe that Reuther and most other liberals, including liberal
Democrats, had any real commitment to equal employment opportunities.
He said of Reuther:

> The United Auto Workers' Walter Reuther, a great liberal! Have you read the
> records of the U.S. Commission on Civil Rights[?] Look at their records on
> employment and see where Reuther's union is down close to being in collabora-
> tion with the Automotive Manufacturers Association of Detroit to bar Negroes
> from training for higher jobs. And this, not one Negro in ten thousand knows.
> The Negro press never played it up. They quoted Reuther as a liberal.[17]

In short, by the 1950s Granger distrusted the motives of white liberals
such as Reuther as much as if not more than he did those of white
conservatives such as Cole.

Despite Reuther's alleged collaboration with forces that denied Negroes
equal employment opportunities, his record on civil rights was decidedly
superior to Cole's. Cole's views on public housing, for example, were

reactionary in comparison to those expressed by Reuther. Cole was reported to have remarked that "the real and dangerous tool now in the hands of the 'little brothers' is the scheme of privileged housing—political housing—public housing."[18] At another point in his undistinguished career as a Congressman, Cole was quoted as having said that "this humanitarian instinct—the elimination of horrible city slums—is warped by some power-hungry planner for the people by selling public housing as slum clearance."[19] Judging from these remarks, Negro leaders were correct in believing that Cole would not challenge segregated public housing, and that he would not urge the federal government to consider the housing needs of urban Negroes. And these views were made known to President Eisenhower at the time that he nominated Cole as head of the HHFA. Reuther, for one, informed Eisenhower that Cole was not the person to head the housing agency. Eisenhower's reply to Reuther was that "Cole is well able to carry out this assignment."[20]

Granger did not, as did Reuther, correspond directly with Eisenhower on the Cole appointment, although word was leaked to the President that Cole was not the NUL's choice to head the HHFA. Rather Granger wrote to Eisenhower that "certain racial problems which had been inherent in the national housing situation for several decades have steadily become so much more serious that they urgently require the sustained official attention of this Administration."[21] Indirectly Granger said two things to the President: that Cole's insensitivity to slum clearance disqualified him to head the HHFA; and that the NUL in the person of Granger expected Eisenhower to take the necessary steps to end segregation and discrimination in both federally assisted public and private housing.

Without Cole's cooperation, the NUL stood little chance of winning the federal government's backing on nonsegregated housing. Things seemed a bit hopeful when on December 10–11, 1954, Cole met with representatives from labor, business, the NUL, and other groups in order to hammer out an agreement on the federal government's role in eliminating discrimination in federally financed housing. Cole sought Granger's reaction to the appointment of an advisory committee on minority housing problems in advance of the meeting.[22] If for no other reason than the fact that Granger was angry because the NUL Board had rejected a request from the Secretary of the Navy for Granger's use as a consultant, Granger informed Cole that "present opinion regards advisory committees on minority problems as out-of-date and now ineffective."[23] Despite Granger's rejection of Cole's idea that such a committee be established, he did support the convening of the December housing conference. Yet Granger and Cole did not see eye to eye on open housing.

Relations between Granger and Cole continued to sour during the early months of 1955, and even more so in August of 1955 when Cole announced that he had relieved Dr. Frank Horne of his job because of budgetary considerations—Horne was considered by Granger and other Negro leaders to be Negro America's foremost housing expert. Granger wired a strong note of protest to Eisenhower, indicting Cole for applying politics "to a situation in which there should be no political considerations."[24]

Eisenhower defended Cole's actions, and directed Special Assistant Maxwell Rabb to inform Granger that Horne was dismissed after Cole had reviewed "his agency's personnel needs for the new fiscal year."[25] Yet Horne and Cole were not on the best terms, as Horne repeatedly criticized Cole's decisions, and particularly Cole's opinions on slum clearance and nonsegregated housing. But in what was a ploy to show that the Eisenhower administration was firmly committed to slum clearance and nonsegregated housing, Rabb assured NUL officials that the reorganization of the HHFA—Horne's dismissal—"did not reflect a change in the Eisenhower Administration's attitude toward providing decent housing for Negroes or of Administrator Cole's on matters affecting racial minorities."[26] NUL officials viewed the reorganization of the HHFA in an entirely different light, arguing that Horne's dismissal was a clear signal that the Eisenhower administration had no intention of supporting integrated housing. A follow-up investigation conducted by NUL officials showed that the HHFA's budget had increased by some two million dollars for the new fiscal year, and that Horne's dismissal was not attributable to fiscal problems.

Cole eventually became a liability to the Eisenhower administration, and Norman Mason was named as Cole's replacement in January of 1959. However, Mason's housing record, like Cole's, gave little cause for rejoicement among NUL officials. Mason had reluctantly agreed to challenge housing discrimination, but only in states where the courts had ruled against segregated housing. The activities of William Levitt of the Levittown Corporation are a case in point. Having won federal approval to construct segregated housing in Long Island, New York, Levitt began a second development in New Jersey that also barred Negroes. The New Jersey State constitution forbade discrimination, and the Newark Urban League's executive secretary reminded Governor Robert Meyner and the State Attorney General of this fact. Between the years of 1953 and 1955, the governor and the attorney general, along with the New Jersey Division Against Discrimination (DAD), refused to use their powers to force Levitt to comply with the state constitution. Therefore in 1958 the NUL brought the matter to Mason's attention, asking him what specific actions he had in mind to desegregate Levittown, New Jersey.

Mason was commissioner of the Federal Housing Administration (FHA) when the NUL brought the Levittown issue to his attention. His job as commissioner of the FHA was to coordinate federal policy with favorable state legislation. In this capacity he maintained that it was not the FHA's responsibility to enforce New Jersey's antidiscrimination housing law.[27] As the HHFA head, however, Mason believed that federal funds should not be used to foster segregation.[28] While applauding his seemingly new-found liberalism, the NUL and the NAACP were unsure that Mason would enforce the law. This skepticism was prompted by the fact that Mason let it be known that he would not seek the advice of Joseph Ray, a Negro, who, as Special Assistant to the Administrator on Racial Relations in the HHFA, had aggressively pressed for federal support of integrated public housing. The new specialist of minority housing was Dr. George Snowden, who was the Intergroup Relations Chief of the FHA while Mason was its head. Val J. Washington, Director of Minorities, the Republican National Committee, believed that it was the New Deal hold-overs rather than Republicans who "were doing a job on Joe Ray in housing."[29] What troubled Negro leadership the most was the fact that the Eisenhower team was content to assist, stimulate, lead, and only moderately prod, but not "to dictate or coerce, the proper exercise of private and local responsibility in ending discrimination in housing."[30]

This fear prompted the NAACP to enter the housing picture. The NAACP's full involvement in the Levittown, New Jersey, housing dispute, however, was kept hidden from NUL leaders. Thurgood Marshall of the NAACP and William Levitt began meeting secretly in 1954. By 1955 they had agreed that a limited number of Negroes would be chosen to purchase homes in the development, after which several get-togethers, teas, and cocktail parties sponsored by neighbors would be arranged for the purpose of introducing the Negroes to the whites in the town. Marshall and Levitt agreed to hold the agreement in strictest confidence, the exception being that Eisenhower's chief assistants would be kept fully informed.[31] However, it was the FHA head, rather than Eisenhower's chief advisors, who was responsible for coordinating federal housing policies with those of the states.

Without a commissioner, the FHA's program of coordinating federal and state antidiscrimination housing laws floundered. Following the announcement that Julian H. Zimmerman had been named to head the FHA, the housing picture brightened somewhat. The new commissioner assured NUL representatives that his agency would enforce FHA regulations, pending Levitt's appeal to the New Jersey High Court. A lower court had ruled that Levitt could not bar Negroes from the development. Zimmerman also promised that the FHA would no longer work with builders "who failed to comply with state laws."[32] Finally, during August of 1959, he ordered the removal of racial restrictive clauses from 221 housing units in the states having antidiscrimination laws, and lifted similar restrictions on college housing units in the Northern states.[33]

The changes in the Eisenhower administration's housing policies, which were announced by Zimmerman, fulfilled at least one of the expectations that Granger felt certain would be realized during the Eisenhower presidency: the reform of existing governmental structures. Whether or not Zimmerman made these changes in anticipation of the 1960 presidential election is unclear. What is clear, however, is that as late as the early months of 1959, President Eisenhower resisted the efforts of Congressmen and Senators who argued that the time had come for the administration to tie the question of housing discrimination to all the federal aid programs.[34] While Eisenhower did not agree that segregated housing and all federal aid programs should be linked, he did believe that the federal government had a responsibility to cooperate with all localities that enacted antibias housing laws.[35] Moreover, Eisenhower's Negro advisors counseled the President to begin overturning federally enforced housing discrimination. In the same vein, the Negro advisors also pointed out to the President that unless his administration vigorously supported both civil rights and antidiscriminatory housing legislation, it would be very difficult for any Republican candidate to appear before Negro audiences to appeal for political support for 1958 and 1960.[36] But the evidence also suggests that what caused the administration to alter its housing policies was the fact that the Democratic Party's chiefs planned to include in their national platform a pledge to seek an end to discrimination in all federally assisted housing.[37] In short, there were several reasons why the Zimmerman-ordered changes could have been politically inspired.

As the 1960 presidential election gained in momentum, Eisenhower and his closest political advisors were aware of the fact that the Republicans had little to show in the way of moving the nation toward the goal of full equality for all of its citizens. Although the 1954 *Brown* decision dismantled de jure segregation in the Southern public schools, little else in the way of civil rights had been achieved. Poll data clearly indicated that the Negro vote remained solidly behind the Democrats, and the fact that Richard M. Nixon would be the Republican Party's presidential candidate meant that little support would be forthcoming from urban and Northern Negro voters. Indeed the fact that Nixon did not support civil rights legislation, and even less public school desegregation, placed the Republican Party in a dilemma as far as the Negro vote was concerned.

II

The fact that the NAACP was successful in overturning the 1896 *Plessy* v. *Ferguson* Supreme Court decision, and that Granger and several of his key advisors were Republicans, had little impact on the Negro vote, as the 1960 presidential election neared a climax. That the NUL was slow in making known its official position on legally enforced (de jure) public school segregation also meant that it could not take any credit for this momentous decision.

Although public perceptions of the NUL were that it did not challenge legally enforced racial segregation in the South, it should be pointed out that both Jones and Granger had opposed de facto segregation in the Northern school systems. They did not, however, actively support nor did they become a party to the NAACP efforts to challenge segregation in the courts. The NUL did not, for example, assist the NAACP in the case against the Charleston (South Carolina) school system, even though the issue was not a dual school system, but rather the fact that Negro teachers were barred from teaching in the Negro schools. The NAACP of course won the case, and Negro teachers found employment in the Negro schools.[38]

That the NUL did not make war on the Southern states for operating dual school systems does not mean that Jones, Granger, and other NUL officials embraced the concept of "separate but equal" schools. It should be remembered that the NUL founders believed that their main task was that of assisting the Negro migrants to cities in acculturating to Northern and urban lifestyles. Because most of the Urban League affiliates were in the Northern cities (during the 1940s there were forty-four Northern Urban Leagues and only eleven Southern Urban Leagues), this meant the NUL's major educational thrust was that of fighting de facto segregation. Hence it prodded the Northern school districts to hire Negro teachers, and convinced Negro parents of the need to involve themselves in the affairs of the schools in their neighborhoods. In short, from 1910 to about 1950, the NUL and most of the Urban League affiliates refrained from becoming parties to the NAACP's challenges to legally mandated public school segregation.

The reverse was true of at least one Urban League affiliate. As a show of its autonomy, the Kansas City (Missouri) Urban League, at the urging of its executive director, Thomas A. Webster, assisted the NAACP in the case *Missouri ex rel. Gaines* v. *Canada.* The U.S. Supreme Court ruled that the State of Missouri and the University of Missouri could not bar qualified Negroes from the state-supported law school.[39] The NUL was unaware of the fact that the Kansas City Urban League was involved in the litigation. In any event, in the wake of the decision, Webster contacted qualified Negroes, and urged them to apply to the law school. In addition, Webster and the local Urban League were a party to a successful challenge of a Kansas City statute that barred Negroes from the municipal golf facilities.[40] It is problematical whether or not NUL officials were informed of the local affiliate's part in this suit that challenged racial segregation in the use of public recreational facilities, although the local social work Survey Board did recommend that Webster be removed as the executive director of the local Urban League. This Board charged that Webster was "too aggressive in advocating social equality between the races."[41] It could not be ascertained whether or not the Kansas City Urban League's Board followed the dictates of the Social Service Board, or that Jones ever repudiated Webster's actions that were taken without the approval of the NUL. Yet within a few years the NUL Board did denounce certain segregationist practices undertaken by interracial agencies.

In 1948 the NUL Board went on record as opposing a plan of the Booker T. Washington Memorial Association (BTWMA) to found industrial schools throughout the nation to train Negro youth. Board members Sidney Hollander, a Negro, and Mrs. Alfred Schoellkopf, a white, both condemned the BTWMA in public for perpetuating segregated education.[42] In 1942 the NUL Board began to field inquiries into the problems that faced Negro students who were unable to participate in extracurricular school activities because of discrimination.[43] The NUL delegates adopted, at the 1953 annual meeting, resolutions that condemned segregation in all private schools, and asked for the repeal of laws that extended tax-exempt status to segregated and private schools.[44] As can be seen, the NUL's policy was that of opposing segregated education. Yet, largely as a result of Granger's belief that the NUL should not be a party to legal actions against segregated education, the NUL did not publicly support NAACP efforts to overturn de jure school segregation.

The U.S. Supreme Court's May 17, 1954, *Brown* v. *the Board of Education* decision forced Granger's hand, and it does not appear that he was prepared for the changes arising out of the decision, particularly the attacks that whites in the South made upon the NUL after it had endorsed the *Brown* decision. Yet the NUL Board was wise to the extent that it took under advisement which strategies to pursue, as a new era of race relations was suddenly thrust upon the American people in the wake of the momentous decision.[45] Judge Waties Waring and other Board members were confident that the Warren Court would reverse the *Plessy* v. *Ferguson* decision.[46]

The NUL membership spent considerable time discussing the impact of the *Brown* decision on race relations at the annual conference, which convened in Pittsburgh during September 1954. And the delegates gave the decision their complete endorsement. Granger withheld his complete endorsement initially, but he did remind those chosen to represent their respective local Urban Leagues that one of the NUL's prime responsibilities was to protect the jobs of Negro teachers in the North and South. Granger also urged the delegates to work for greater cooperation between school boards and the Urban League Movement in order to compensate for the housing patterns in Southern and Northern cities that fostered segregated education.[47]

Granger's advice to the delegates came in the wake of actions on the part of several local Urban Leagues that were designed to end the dual school system in the South and de facto segregation in the North. Indeed, as Brown, Mollison, and Cannon charged, several Urban League affiliates had outdistanced the NUL on civil rights matters in general and school desegregation issues in particular. The Washington (D.C.) Urban League, for example, conducted a survey for the Council of Social Agencies in 1948, which sought opinions from citizens on how to abolish segregated schools in the District of Columbia. Not surprisingly, this local affiliate became the target of die-hard white supremacists, who demanded that the local Community Chest not fund it because of its political activity. Moreover, scores of whites argued that the Washington Urban League was a propaganda tool rather than a social work agency.[48] On April 7, 1949, the Baltimore Urban League, under the leadership of executive secretary Alexander J. Allen, requested the Baltimore Board of School Commissioners to end segregation at the Mergenthaler Vocational High School of Printing, the Baltimore Polytechnic Institute, and the Baltimore Junior College.[49] During December of the same year, Allen urged the Governor's Commission on Negro Higher Education of the State of Maryland to admit "Negro students without restrictions to the existing curricula of the University of Maryland."[50] In both instances Allen upstaged Granger in the continuing battle against de jure segregation.

The aggressiveness on the part of a few local executive secretaries did not stir Granger to action. But the publicity surrounding the NAACP's successful and evolutionary attacks on segregated public education in the South did cause Granger much anguish. It is also uncertain whether he accurately judged the outcome of his ultimate decision to praise the *Brown* decision.

Racist rabble-rousers such as Gerald L.K. Smith and John V. Hamilton lashed out at Granger and the NUL and its affiliates. As spokesmen of the National Citizens Protective Association (NCPA), Smith, Hamilton, and others assailed local Community Chests for supporting a "subversive" organization—the NUL and its affiliates.[51] The appearance of White Citizens Councils, havens for white segregationists, intensified the controversy. On September 21, 1954, the NCPA distributed a leaflet detailing a twenty-one-count indictment against the St. Louis Urban League. The leaflet charged that the affiliate was not entitled to Community Chest support because it had become a partisan political organization.[52] By the spring of 1955, local affiliates in Atlanta, Little Rock, Louisville, Memphis, Miami, Tampa, Richmond, and St. Louis were also uncertain of their standing with their local Community Chests. The NUL's complete endorsement of the *Brown* decision was perceived by Southern whites as a policy that permeated the Urban League Movement.

As the affiliates continued sparring with the segregationist groups, a

1956 court decree ordered the admission of twelve Negro students into the previously all-white high school at Clinton, Tennessee. The State National Guard had to be called out after angry whites had attempted to bar their entry into the school. An explosion demolished the high school, prompting Granger to conclude that some white leaders in certain areas of the South had deliberately "chosen to turn responsibility over to the mob."[53] He also denounced Virginia Governor Thomas B. Stanley following his instructions to the state's legislature to enact laws barring state aid to any local school system that integrated its schools.

Granger's remarks of course sparked further wrath from the White Citizens Council groups. One typical reaction occurred in Jacksonville, Florida. The local Community Chest announced on September 5, 1956, that it no longer supported the Urban League affiliate. While denying that Granger's remarks had led to the decision, Fred Hoffman, the Chest's executive director, did admit that financial support would resume if the local affiliate ended its relations with the NUL.

The actions of the Jacksonville Community Chest were duplicated in other Southern cities. By late 1956 the Norfolk, Virginia, Community Chest severed its connections with the local Urban League. The NCPA had circulated leaflets to the effect that the local Chest supported racial mixing through its funding of the Norfolk Urban League. Granger urged this Community Chest not "to surrender to blackmail by a group who are no better than professional thugs," but to no avail.[54] In the wake of the rupture between the Community Chest and the NUL, officials of the latter visited those cities in which the local affiliates were under attack. In the wake of the visits, Nelson C. Jackson, director of the NUL's Department of Community Relations and Development, declared that the anti-Urban League crusade was "unprecedented in the League's history."[55]

During the fall of 1957, a crisis situation in Little Rock led to a further deterioration of Community Chest–Urban League relations. In the aftermath of a federal court's decision to the effect that eleven Negro students be admitted to the previously all-white high school, a mob gathered on the grounds to block the entry of the Negroes. Rather than employ the National Guard to curb white defiance of the courts, Arkansas Governor Orval E. Faubus used it to prevent the integration of the high school. Granger publicly urged President Eisenhower to use his constitutional powers "to end defiance of the federal government by Governor Orval E. Faubus."[56] The President bided his time, seemingly hopeful that the crisis would somehow disappear. But in the end Eisenhower nationalized the local militia unit, leading Granger to conclude that the federal law and the Constitution had prevailed in the Little Rock school controversy.[57]

Granger's outspokenness on the desegregation of Little Rock High School did not escape the attention of white segregationists. The NCPA went on the attack, threatening personal injury to those who supported the Community Chest if the local Urban League remained a member of the agency. By October of 1957, following an on-site inspection, NUL President Theodore W. Kheel announced the withdrawal of the local affiliate from the Little Rock Community Chest.[58] Kheel summed up the plight of the Urban League Movement when he wrote that "if a 'moderate' program, such as the Urban League, is a target for bitter subversionists no constructive interracial program is safe."[59]

It appears that it was Granger's decision to withdraw the Little Rock Urban League from the Community Chest. Kheel, unlike Granger, believed that the Community Chest-Urban League controversy could in the end prove helpful in altering the NUL's image in the public mind.[60] He also confided that it was his intention to make it appear that the "siege" was more than it actually was, by capitalizing on the publicity surrounding the issue. Sophia Y. Jacobs shared Kheel's view, pointing out that the Board was not particularly bothered by the White Citizens Councils' activities.[61]

This was not so of a number of the Urban League affiliates' executives and Board members. Perhaps this explains why the Baltimore Urban League was the only Southern affiliate to call for a strict enforcement of the *Brown* decision. In contrast, the New Orleans Urban League Board decided to state that most Louisiana newspapers had urged compliance with the decision, but not to commend them publicly for taking this rational position.[62] Privately, the local Board did discuss "what the Urban League program will probably mean in the next five, ten, or fifteen years."[63] Harry L. Alston, director of the Southern Division, NUL, advised the Winston-Salem (North Carolina) Urban League (WSUL) not to involve itself in desegregation controversy. Winston-Salem was targeted as one of six cities in the South to which the NUL and other organizations would send representatives to expedite the *Brown* decision.[64] Alston reminded Samuel D. Harvey, the WSUL executive secretary, that the volunteer leadership within the Winston-Salem Urban League "would be in much better position to initiate any program or plan toward integration of schools, at least more so than some outside representative."[65] In reply, Harvey told Alston that he and the WSUL Board were in full agreement that Granger and the NUL Board's policies were not always in concert with those of the local Leagues.[66] The Memphis Urban League's executive secretary, J.A. Daniels, was quick in pointing out that there was no pressing need for anyone from the NUL to attend local conferences and meetings with Chest officials and other leading citizens.[67] It was the Portland (Oregon) Urban League that affirmed the local Leagues' autonomy, informing the NUL that it (the Portland Urban League) "is autonomous, operating under the direction of an interracial board of twenty-one outstanding Portland citizens."[68]

It is not at all clear how Granger viewed the independence that more than one local affiliate exercised during the Community Chest crisis. But Granger steadfastly argued that the 1954 Court decision underscored the effectiveness of "moderation" in promoting racial advancement, and that the decision also produced a healthy condition in the United States, "despite bitter controversy, corrupt political leadership and shameless violence."[69] It is unlikely that Granger viewed Eisenhower's handling of the events revolving around the *Brown* decision as an example of corrupt political leadership. Yet Granger was disappointed because Eisenhower only endorsed the *Brown* decision in the most casual way. However, Granger's belief that Negroes would witness significant changes in their status during the Eisenhower years remained unchanged.

III

Granger was not the only Negro leader who believed that Negroes would make remarkable strides during the Eisenhower presidency. In 1948 Walter White of the NAACP not only praised Eisenhower as a promoter of armed forces integration, but also stated that he believed in equal justice for all Americans.[70] Therefore the NAACP leadership, like Granger, expected Eisenhower to promote full equality during his presidency. As the Eisenhower administration neared completion of its first four years in office, Negroes did not hesitate to express their disappointment in the progress of racial advancement under this administration.

The Eisenhower administration, like the Granger-led NUL, was out of touch with urban and urbane Negroes' hopes and dreams. Eisenhower and his advisors either championed moderation or only hesitantly addressed the issue of civil rights. Eisenhower and his advisors, except for his Negro advisors, seemed unaware of Northern and urban Negroes' firm determination to achieve economic parity with the larger society. Nor was there any discernible evidence that the men around the President were keeping abreast of the rising unrest among rural and urban Southern Negroes because of their second-class status. Yet criticism of Eisenhower from the Negro leaders had been surprisingly mild, and this was because the President had not entirely ignored discriminatory employment practices.

During his first term in office, Eisenhower issued two executive orders that prohibited holders of government contracts and agencies of the federal government from denying Negroes employment. Executive Order 10557, issued on September 3, 1954, declared that:

> The contracting agencies of the United States Government are required by existing Executive Orders to include in all contracts executed by them a provision of obligating the contractor not to discriminate against any employees because of race, creed, color, or national origin.[71]

Between 1954 and 1956, defense contractors who violated Executive Order 10557 went unpunished. The President's Committee on Government Contract Compliance (PCOGCC), established to monitor defense contractors' compliance with the executive order, did little in the way of forcing contractors' compliance with the order.

Eliminating discrimination in the federal agencies had also proved to be a failure. President Eisenhower issued Executive Order 10590 on January 18, 1955, informing federal agency heads that:

> It is the policy of the United States Government that equal opportunity shall be afforded all qualified persons, consistent with law, for employment in the Federal Government; and . . . this policy excludes and prohibits discrimination against any employee or applicant for employment in the Federal Government because of race, color, religion, or national origin.[72]

The President's Committee on Government Employment Policy did not aggressively investigate employment discrimination, and therefore it was charged with not carrying out its mandate.[73] In particular, the PCOGEP drew sharp criticism from Negroes: Clarence Mitchell of the Washington Bureau of the NAACP, stated that the PCOGCC and the PCOGEP were made up "of retired or elderly individuals who are considerably out of step with the times."[74] There was considerable truth to the statement made by Mitchell. More often than not, the PCOGEP and the PCOGCC ruled Negro applicants unqualified for jobs, but refused to initiate thorough investigations of the charges that racial discrimination seriously limited the employment opportunities of qualified and unqualified Negroes alike.[75]

The PCOGCC was all-white at the outset. Little change was forthcoming in the decisions that the committee rendered even after Negroes were added to it, and after Vice President Richard M. Nixon was named its chairman. Under Nixon's leadership, the PCOGCC engaged in stalling tactics to prevent Negroes from making greater inroads in jobs and occupations that had been closed to them. Hence Nixon found few admirers within the NUL and the Urban League Movement. Board Member Sophia Y. Jacobs insisted that "Mr. Nixon was not interested in civil rights."[76] Theodore W. Kheel characterized the Vice President as one "who did not wish to rock the boat."[77] Board member Judge Waties Waring revealed that Senator Wayne Morse, who disliked Nixon, once stated that in the area of civil rights he would rather deal "with a smart demagogue like Nixon than a stupid demagogue like Eisenhower."[78]

Senator Morse's observations of Eisenhower and Nixon should not be dismissed as intellectual arrogance on his part. They rang with a degree of truth. Eisenhower displayed little common sense in his dealings with Negroes. For example, while addressing the National Negro Publishers Association in the spring of 1958, Eisenhower urged that Negroes exercise patience and forbearance in gaining equality.[79] It appears that he completely forgot all the years in which Negro Americans exercised patience and forbearance, only to have so little to show for their patience. Conceivably, had it been Nixon who was addressing the same gathering, he would have commended Negroes on their restraint in waiting to enjoy full equality, and would also have reminded them that confrontation and direct-action tactics could not ensure instant and full justice. It is also unlikely that Nixon would have failed to remind Negroes of their constitutional rights as American citizens, as Eisenhower failed to do during the address.

Jackie Robinson, in an emotionally charged letter to Eisenhower, wrote:

17 million Negroes cannot do as you suggest and wait for the hearts of men to change. We want to enjoy now the rights that we feel we are entitled to as Americans. This we cannot do unless we pursue aggressively goals which all other Americans achieved over 150 years ago.[80]

It does not appear that the President ever comprehended the reasons why Negroes rejected his advice. Eisenhower replied to Robinson: "While I understand the points you make about the use of patience and forbearance, I never urged them as substitutes for constructive action or progress."[81] If anything, his reply to Robinson was even more insulting than the advice he had offered the Negro press corps during his address. Eisenhower approved of the tactics associated with the NAACP and the NUL—legalism, persuasion, fact finding, moderation, and the like. Unquestionably he judged the direct action and confrontation strategies of the Southern Christian Leadership Conference (SCLC), CORE, and other groups as not being constructive. Even Granger, an Eisenhower supporter, denounced the President for offering ill-conceived advice. Granger concluded that it "had come from a good man who is either without a plan or is unwilling to share it if he has one."[82]

The men around the President saved him from further embarrassment. While not necessarily agreeing with the Negroes' new belligerence, they nonetheless recognized its presence. On May 29, 1958, the Reverend Dr. Martin Luther King, Jr., wired the President seeking a White House Conference.[83] Eisenhower's key advisors seized upon this request to make amends with the Negro leaders. King had politely informed the President that neither he nor his staff could avoid school desegregation and other equally important civil rights issues.

A preparatory meeting was convened on June 9, 1958. In attendance were White House Assistant Rocco Siciliano, E. Frederick Morrow, a Negro advisor, Deputy Attorney General L.E. Walsh, and the Reverend King. Those representing the White House came close to sabotaging the impending meeting with the President. Morrow wanted to limit the meeting with the President to King and A. Philip Randolph.[84] This King would not consent to, pointing out that the NAACP, which had spearheaded the fight for school desegregation, could not be left out. Therefore King insisted that an invitation be extended to Roy Wilkins, explaining that with the NAACP executive secretary present the leadership would be "diversified enough to be representative of the Negro Community."[85]

It was not accidental that King made no mention of Granger as a participant in the White House Conference. The NUL executive director had not endeared himself to urban Negroes, despite his belated outspokenness on the *Brown* decision. By 1958 Granger was not viewed in Negro America as a member of the black vanguard. But as a loyal Republican, the NUL executive director could not be totally ignored by Eisenhower, and Siciliano urged the President to invite Granger. Yet there is reason to believe that the hurriedly arranged meeting between the President and Negro leaders did not mark a change in direction of the Eisenhower presidency. Siciliano reminded the President that "the elections are some months away."[86]

During the planning session, King reminded the White House aides of Eisenhower's avoidance of Negro leaders. The President had tentatively agreed to meet with Randolph in 1953, and with Congressman Adam Clayton Powell, Jr., and others in 1957, only to renege on his promise. Indeed King had requested the White House meeting in the first place because of a growing belief among Negro leaders that Eisenhower did not wish to meet and talk with them.

The White House summit meeting took place on June 23, 1958. Eisenhower received from the four Negroes a nine-point proposal, five of which dealt with their immediate concerns. These urged the President to: (1) convene a White House Conference of Negroes and whites, at which ways and means of implementing the *Brown* decision could be discussed; (2) issue a presidential statement affirming his support of school desegregation; (3) authorize the Justice Department to investigate vigorously the bombing of churches, synagogues, and homes in the South; (4) expand the Negroes' voting rights; and (5) bar federal funds to schools that practiced segregation.[87]

Eisenhower's immediate response and his commitment to these proposals are not known. White House protocol forbade the "direct quotation of the President or any commitment of the President to an agreement or specific opinion."[88] Hence all that the four Negro leaders said to the press corps following the meeting was that the President had "indicated a sympathetic interest in the program presented to him."[89]

Granger was less cautious in communicating his feelings on the White House meeting to the NUL Board, and to the affiliates' Boards, presidents, and executive secretaries. He wrote that Eisenhower "was not well informed on the day-to-day developments that were our concern as either of his two predecessors in office would have been."[90] Two inferences can be drawn from Granger's observations: Granger either credited the isolation of the presidency with shielding Eisenhower from the realities of the American racial crisis, or by 1958 he had serious doubts that Eisenhower's intellectual capacity matched that of Roosevelt's and Truman's. In any event, Granger expressed his dissatisfaction over Eisenhower's general responses. The Negro leaders left the meeting with the impression that Eisenhower did not seem troubled over the white South's continuing to defy the federal government.

The white South continued its defiance of the 1954 Supreme Court's decision throughout 1959. Equally tragic were NUL statements claiming that substantial gains were being made toward improving the position of Negroes in American society. In a forty-four-page report entitled, "Building for Equal Opportunity," the NUL endeavored to show that most Americans were willing to work toward racial equality.[91] Meanwhile the urban masses believed that Negro and white Americans had drifted farther apart, the federal government was not committed to equal opportunity and equal justice under the law, and that Negroes' economic position had steadily deteriorated. Although more Negroes than ever before had crossed and were bridging the threshold from poverty to a middle- and professional-class status, Negroes remained pathetically underrepresented in most professional, skilled, clerical, and union jobs, as Table 16 documents. Federal inactivity in the areas of civil rights and equality of opportunity had helped to spark the Negro Revolution.

The white South did not take kindly to the new activism that the Negro and some white college students had exhibited in their drive to overturn Jim Crow laws and racial segregation. Whites looked to their local police forces to restore calm. Despite the brutality used by police to end the demonstrations, Negroes were intent upon serving notice on society that they would no longer abide by segregation laws. This sentiment was particularly in evidence among Southern Negro college students by 1960, the year in which the sit-ins were launched.

In 1960 a small group of black students from the North Carolina Agricultural and Technical College in Greensboro staged a sit-in at a Woolworth lunch counter. Similar demonstrations were repeated in other Southern cities. It was not that the NAACP and the NUL had stood idly by as segregation and Jim Crow laws prevailed, but rather that neither organization had seemed willing to provoke a confrontation with the white South and the nation. Reminding Negro and white Americans alike that it neither condoned nor participated in public demonstrations, the NUL nonetheless took note of the importance of the sit-ins. Granger maintained that they were natural outgrowths of hostilities against a system that had failed to provide equality for all.[92]

Table 16. Race of Employed Males, by Occupation, 1960[a]

Male, Employed	Northeast		North Central		South		West		Negro as a Percentage of White
	White	Negro	White	Negro	White	Negro	White	Negro	
Accountants	123,893	892	110,168	668	88,125	443	66,688	317	.697
Architects	7,973	60	7,342	40	7,264	106	6,234	27	.81
Lawyers and judges	66,593	475	51,604	731	55,454	593	28,756	205	.99
Pharmacists	25,374	308	23,278	520	21,834	495	12,317	139	1.76
Chemists	25,700	606	20,182	378	17,569	356	10,117	199	2.09
Physicians and surgeons	64,643	1,083	55,183	1,225	50,677	1,527	34,441	381	2.06
Bookkeepers	38,385	680	39,049	307	47,897	410	20,979	211	1.03
Mail carriers	49,480	4,103	53,820	6,154	42,123	7,202	26,158	2,591	11.69
Electricians	85,783	1,516	94,586	1,007	90,347	1,741	56,808	714	1.51
Carpenters	172,028	3,935	205,913	2,541	261,544	27,004	133,864	2,350	4.63
Plumbers and pipe fitters	86,737	1,475	83,367	1,335	77,238	6,614	44,414	696	3.47

[a]Data extracted from *U.S. Census, 1960, Characteristics of the Population, U.S. Summary, 1, Part 1* (Washington: Government Printing Office, 1963), Table 275, pp. 1–717. Even if the Negro female professional and skilled workers are added to the totals presented here, Negroes are still vastly underrepresented in most of these job categories. All geographical areas of the U.S. are not included here.

President Eisenhower called for the creation of community biracial conferences as the sit-ins spread. He believed that the lines of communication between Negroes and whites were no longer open.[93] Granger applauded the President's suggestion, but at the same time reminded him of the role that the President should play in ushering in true equality.[94] Eisenhower came under severe criticism for his attempts to create the machinery for reopening the dialogue between well-meaning Southern Negroes and whites. O.U. Roberts, president of the Oil and Gas Properties of Houston, Texas, wrote to Eisenhower:

> It is inconceivable to me, yea even shocking, that the President of the United States would openly advocate and commend the actions of negroes in their so-called sit-down demonstrations which have led to mob violence and the breach of peace. I have heard it said that you have said you would do more for the negroes than Abraham Lincoln did for them. What have negroes done for you, what have they done for America, what have they done "period" to justify your attempts to force them down the throats of the people of the South?[95]

As it turned out, the President's moderate position became a source of irritation to white Southerners and Negroes alike.

The sit-ins continued. In a brief span of time, Southern Negro college students, supported by white collegians, had preempted the NAACP's role as the nation's premier civil rights advocate. Their actions also shifted the civil rights movement from a traditional Northern to a Southern beachhead, not to mention the fact that their direct action and confrontation tactics had contributed further to the NUL's loss in popularity among urban Negroes.

Granger did not despair, and he set about revitalizing the social service agency's image by concentrating on issues that had been responsible for the NUL's birth. Granger remained wedded to the belief that white labor would eventually support equal opportunity. In 1956, at the urging of the Washington, D.C., NAACP and the Washington Urban League, the PCOGCC undertook an investigation of the employment practices of Local Union No. 26, an affiliate of the AFL-CIO International Brotherhood of Electrical Workers. The government had begun a massive building program in the nation's capital, and Local 26 was awarded a number of federal contracts despite the fact that it had openly violated the executive orders banning discrimination on account of race. After four years of negotiations, Local 26 remained all-white.[96]

In 1960 the NUL entered the picture and discovered that Labor Secretary James P. Mitchell was uncommitted to equality of opportunity in employment. A member of the PCOGCC, Mitchell, like Nixon, did not wish to antagonize labor leaders.[97] Moreover, the Labor Secretary, like Nixon, was a foe of compulsory Fair Employment Practices legislation. Both men also held a negative view toward the presidential orders that had as their objective the full realization of equal employment opportunities.[98]

Granger and the NUL began prodding the PCOGCC, but to no avail. Subsequently the General Services Administration (GSA) was made aware of the fact that Local 26 was in violation of the executive orders.[99] Following its investigation of the charges, GSA administrator Franklin Floete informed the NUL that Negroes had not been hired by Local 26 because they lacked the necessary skills to work on the job.[100] Conducting its own investigation, the NUL staff uncovered the fact that Floete had relied solely upon the information supplied him by the union, and had not given skills tests to any of the Negroes. Upon receipt of this information, an angry Granger charged Floete with avoiding his responsibilities as a member of PCOGCC.

Although Floete had not acted responsibly, the NUL Board could not speak in a unanimous voice on how to win the cooperation of the PCOGCC. At least four NUL Board members urged that a press conference be held in Washington, D.C., at which the PCOGCC, the GSA, Eisenhower, and labor leaders would be held up for scorn before the public. Harry Van Arsdale advised against attacking labor leaders in public, because he felt that the charges could not be justified by the facts which had been gathered by the NUL.[101] A press conference was not held, due to the Board's reluctance to take any action that might have alienated organized labor.

While the employment discrimination controversy was hanging fire in Washington, Americans' attention was directed to the upcoming presidential election. At the conclusion of what was a generally lackluster primary, Richard M. Nixon and John F. Kennedy emerged as the candidates of the Republican and Democratic Parties. At the outset Negroes were unenthusiastic over the prospect of either Nixon or Kennedy occupying the White House. But as the campaign moved into the final weeks, the concern shown by the Kennedy family about the safety of the Reverend Dr. Martin Luther King, Jr., raised Kennedy's stock in Negro America. By the narrowest of margins, which was aided by strong Negro support, Kennedy became President.

Granger was hostile toward Kennedy. He remarked that "Kennedy had not one single credential to warrant his getting one single Negro vote. He was a [Joe] McCarthy supporter, as you know."[102] Granger respected and acknowledged the enormous power wielded by the occupant of the White House. During January of 1961 the NUL submitted a memorandum, "The Time is Now," to Kennedy, containing the following recommendations: (1) the PCOGCC either should be abolished or reorganized because of its past failures in expanding equality of opportunity for Negroes; (2) federal funds should be withheld from urban renewal programs unless discrimination and segregation were abolished; (3) all contracts of the federal government should contain nondiscrimination clauses; and (4) the President should maintain a vigilance on discrimination in federal agencies.[103]

The tone of the memorandum indicated that Granger's target of winning white labor's cooperation, even if gained through governmental actions, remained basically unchanged. Indeed winning the cooperation of the white labor movement was consistent with the NUL founders' views of what was required to advance Negroes' social and industrial needs. But the problem facing the NUL in 1961, in contrast to 1910, was not so much winning white labor's cooperation as it was striking a formula for combining direct action and confrontation with moderation.

Kheel, as the NUL president, did combine these elements, and with considerable success. When Kheel declined to seek reelection to the NUL presidency in 1960, it surprised several of his backers. On September 7, 1960, the *New York Times* carried an announcement to the effect that Henry Steeger, a publisher from New York City, was the new president-elect.[104] With Granger remaining at the helm, few changes were anticipated in the thrust of the NUL's programs.

Kheel's greatest disappointment as NUL president was the fact that he was unable to convince Granger of the need to rethink and revamp NUL strategies and techniques in light of the changing times. He stated that he would have preferred to serve under Whitney M. Young, Jr., than under Granger. Kheel regards the role that he played in maintaining "the organization in a period of change and [delivering] it to Whitney Young as the NUL's major accomplishment under [his] presidency."[105]

That the NUL and the Urban League affiliates had remained small operations until the 1960s, as Kheel noted, had indeed limited their chances and effectiveness in promoting substantive changes. Yet Granger boasted of the Urban League Movement's growth between 1941 and 1961. There were thirty-seven League affiliates when he became the executive secretary and sixty-six upon his retirement in 1961, with two in the making. In 1941 there were 216 salaried employees in the Movement; there were 504 in 1961. The budget of the NUL and the Urban League locals had grown from about $650,000 in 1941 to a record $3,550,000 in 1961.[106]

Granger had impressive statistics to show for his years as the NUL's chief executive officer. But apparently he had not yet realized that the 1950s were far different from the years in which urban Negro and white reformers had conceived of the idea of the NUL. Negroes had not shared in the gains made possible by the unprecedented growth of the industrial system. If anything, the Urban League affiliates had done little more than to assist urban Negroes in integrating themselves into the lowest levels of the industrial world. It appears that the younger and more aggressive affiliate executive secretaries had realized this as early as the 1940s, and it was then that they rebelled against Granger. Having reached the mandatory retirement age, Granger was eased out of the NUL leadership without the bloodletting that would have accompanied this change in leadership in 1956. Steeger informed the news media that effective October 1, 1961, Whitney M. Young, Jr., would become the NUL's executive director.

Young was born on July 31, 1921, at Lincoln Institute, Kentucky, on the campus of a Negro boarding school of which his father was president. He graduated from high school at the age of fourteen, enrolled at Kentucky State College, and received a degree four years later. Young enlisted in the U.S. Army, serving with the 92nd Infantry during World War II. At the close of the war, Young entered the University of Minnesota and received the M.A. degree in social work. In 1947 he was named the director of industrial relations and vocational guidance of the St. Paul, Minnesota, Urban League. Young was chosen as the dean of the Atlanta University School of Social Work, serving in that post from 1951 to 1961.

Undoubtedly Kheel had a large voice in the selection of the NUL's new executive director. Kheel argued strongly that Young "was militant without being irresponsible."[107] Guichard Parris, at one time the NUL's director of publicity, maintained that Young's greatest appeal to the Board was his insistence upon unity within diversity.[108] The Chicago Urban League's executive director, Edwin C. Berry, pointed out that the affiliates' executive directors were drawn to Young because he encouraged them to adopt a more aggressive style of confronting society than Granger had. As a result of Young's leadership, the Urban League Movement became an active partner with other civil rights, direct action, and human relations organizations.[109]

The change in executive directors and the expectations of new departures that it nourished ushered in a new phase of Urban League history. A chapter on the Young years was not included in this study for several reasons: first, the Young papers remain closed to scholarly research; second, the Young years merit a book-length treatment; and third, the end of the Granger years was an appropriate time to end this study.

Young's immediate importance to the Urban League Movement, however, should be acknowledged. He defused the internal dissension with the NUL Board and the Urban League Movement, and smoothed relations between the NUL and the NAACP. His long-term contribution to racial advancement was the fact that he built a bridge of understanding between those who favored and those who rejected social work as a tool for racial advancement. Young informed white and Negro America alike that social work techniques had served the cause of racial advancement well; therefore the NUL, under his direction, would not abandon its social work tradition. But Young knew that the process begun by Lester B. Granger—the League's concentration on both civil rights and social services—had transformed the NUL into a major national civil rights organization. Young seemed proud of the fact that white America viewed the NUL as a civil rights organization, but would nonetheless continue to support its activities through the Community Chest, as well as through individual and corporate contributions. In the final analysis, Young, more than any other single Urban League director, cemented the relationships of the NUL and big business, and made the Urban League a respectable organization in Negro and white America alike. The NUL as it is known today is indeed the work of Whitney M. Young, Jr.; Vernon E. Jordan, Jr., who was named the NUL executive director in 1971, readily acknowledges this fact.

All told, Eisenhower was a bitter disappointment to Lester B. Granger and to most other Negro leaders as well. His stance on school desegregation, open housing (publicly and privately financed), and equal employment opportunities was quixotic. On the one hand, the Eisenhower administration endeavored to make it appear that it backed Negro advancement. Time and time again, Eisenhower assured the American public that he would protect the constitutional rights of the American people. On the other hand, the President avoided meeting with Negro leaders who had the documented evidence to show that Negroes' constitutional rights were being violated. Eisenhower's vacillating position seems to indicate that he did not want the Republican Party saddled with a pro-civil rights program, partly out of fear that such a program would weaken the Republican Party in the South. It would be unfair, however, to conclude that Eisenhower sought to avoid addressing civil rights issues. While Eisenhower endeavored to minimize the extent of his administration's involvement in civil rights, he was at the same time fully aware of the growing political importance of civil rights, both in the United States and in the international political arena. In the final analysis, Granger's belief that with a Republican in the White House the Negroes' search for equality would receive a sympathetic hearing was unfounded, to say the least.

10

Conclusions:
The Changing of the Guard

Several major themes of this study will be summarized in this chapter. The first is the question of the Urban League's ideological foundation. Because both the Urban League and the NAACP were authentic products of the Progressive Era, their ideological basis cannot be attributed solely to Booker T. Washington and William E. B. Du Bois. The fact is that several individuals made enormous contributions to the ideals of both the Urban League and the NAACP. Both organizations drew from ideologies that embraced and rejected the status quo, although their founders subscribed to the dominant value system and the institutional structures of American society. Second, this chapter examines the factors that led to strained relations between the Urban League's Negro and white founders. Third, it offers a brief yet comprehensive commentary on the racial ideology of William H. Baldwin, Jr., his links to Booker T. Washington, and his impact on the ideals that were incorporated into the movements that merged to form the Urban League. Fourth, the chapter shows how the founding of the Urban League and the NAACP resulted in large part from the progress that Negroes made from about 1830 to about 1905 in developing a sense of racial pride and racial unity. This progress enabled their leaders to speak out in bolder terms and to take more direct steps toward the goals of complete equality. The fifth theme is the impact of socialism on the thinking of several of the NUL's founders. The final theme of Chapter 10 is the effect of Jones and Granger on the course of action taken by the NUL from 1910 to 1961 in its search for equality.

No single racial ideology undergirded the Urban League and the NAACP at the time of their founding. It can be argued, however, that the Negro intellectuals who contributed to the creation of both the Urban League and the NAACP were the ideological descendants of Frederick Douglass.[1] They, like Douglass, believed that both industrial and classical education could help advance the Negro. The Negro founders of the Urban League and the NAACP urged federal protection of the Negroes' constitutional rights, called for justice and equal opportunity for the poor and the unskilled urban dweller, and denounced both a racial caste system and racial discrimination. Douglass, like the Negro founders of the Urban League and the NAACP, preferred a pragmatic approach to resolving racial problems, and subscribed to social control. Implicit in the term social control is a belief that not all members of society are capable of self-direction or self-restraint. Social control as conceived during the Progressive Era was that in the society a group of educated and materially well-off individuals believed it was their responsibility to direct or restrain the undisciplined masses. While Douglass and the Negro founders of the Urban League and the NAACP generally rejected violence as a solution to the racial problem in American society, they did subscribe to revolutionary change in the society: revolutionary change when the Constitution is enforced, and when the rights of a minority are protected by the Constitution.

Neither Douglass nor the Negro founders of the Urban League and the NAACP believed that the goal of complete equality would be realized without a protracted struggle with the larger society. But Douglass and the Urban League and NAACP Negro founders did not lose hope that white Americans would ultimately support the rights of Negroes and other minorities, and they believed that the Negroes' search for equality had been, was, and would continue to be both evolutionary and revolutionary.

Douglass commented on the past and future of the Negroes' search for equality during a speech in 1883 at the Fourth Congregational Church in Washington, D.C. He perceived two groups of Negro leaders—those of his generation and those of the postbellum era. Douglass remarked: "I represent the past, they the present. I represent the downfall of slavery, they the glorious triumph of liberty. Their mission begins where mine ends."[2] He concluded that Negro leaders were ever mindful of what was possible to achieve and what was not, and he reminded his audience that as Negroes made progress, their leaders would speak in bolder terms and take more direct steps toward the goal of complete equality.

The Negro founders of the Urban League and the NAACP represented the present with regard to Negroes' hopes, dreams, and expectations. Their mission began where Washington's and Douglass's ended. Their emergence as spokesmen for Negro America signaled a new direction for racial advancement organizations. The founding of the Urban League and NAACP indicated a growing awareness on the part of Negro and white racial reformers alike of the pervasive nature of institutional racism in American society.

The conclusion that institutional racism is the Negroes' single most powerful enemy can be traced to Douglass, as well as to the postbellum urban institutional church and the nonsectarian agencies that labored among Negroes. The idea that institutional racism is a deterrent to Negro advancement can also be traced to socialist thought and to some segments of Progressivism. While socialism and Progressivism were not totally devoid of racism, both schools of thought advanced the belief that social progress and social control would unite disparate groups in America. Although the Progressives and socialists were not in agreement on the best way to curb the power of the capitalist classes, the NUL founders, like the Progressives and socialists, believed that scientific social work was an instrument of social control.

In 1910, while few Negro intellectuals in the NUL questioned scientific social work's value in resolving racial and urban problems, there was sharp disagreement as to the extent to which the Socialist Party in America and its ideology held out hope for Negroes. The disagreement revolved around the question of whether or not the Socialist Party and socialism itself had the capacity to eliminate segregation and racial discrimination from American life. The Socialist Party refused to acknowledge the special needs of Negroes, viewing them only in terms of the larger problem of workers versus capitalists.[3] Yet international socialism's repeated calls for worker solidarity and an end to racism were the only instances when interracial cooperation received political backing during the Urban League's infant years. Despite the calls for worker solidarity across racial lines and an end to racism, the supporters of socialism did not hold as large a perspective on the plight of the Negro in America as did the many Negroes and whites who undertook scientific social work activities among the urban Negroes.

Countless numbers of social workers, racial reformers, and social activists gained extensive knowledge of the problems of urban Negroes by undertaking field work. This knowledge, more than any other single factor, prompted several Negro and white intellectuals and racial reformers to found the Urban League. They believed that sociology and scientific social work would assist Negroes in the transition from rural to urban life, and would also be mechanisms for maintaining domestic tranquility.

Efforts to promote and achieve domestic tranquility among the diverse groups in urban America did not become the Urban League's exclusive domain, as the NAACP was also interested in the same goal. The leaders of the NAACP, however, turned to public propaganda methods in hope of resolving America's explosive racial and urban crisis. The Urban League's modus operandi was both scientific social work and publicity. During its infancy it used these strategies to acquaint the larger society with the needs and desires of the urban Negro population. In short, there was unity of purpose within the Urban League and the NAACP, but there was also a range of beliefs concerning which strategies and tactics could best advance the Negro cause. Ultimately the white and Negro founders of both the NUL and the NAACP believed that interracial cooperation was the desirable way of pursuing full equality for Negroes.

This cooperation became the cornerstone of both the Urban League Movement and the NAACP. Yet, in time, interracial cooperation led to discord. Negroes and whites in both organizations held different views about what equality was and how it could be achieved. The white founders of the Urban League and the NAACP were primarily interested in the creation of an orderly society, after which the constitutional, economic, and social rights of Negroes would be realized gradually. But both organizations' Negro founders objected to any further postponement of those rights guaranteed by the Constitution, though they realized that complete equality was not achievable in 1909 and 1910. The Negro founders of the NUL and the NAACP also objected to denial of equality of opportunity for Negroes, because whites insisted that the social separation of the races was the desired state of affairs.

In spite of the different ways in which Negroes and whites in the NUL and the NAACP perceived and worked toward equality, they launched a sustained attack on institutional racism. This attack came in the wake of changing attitudes that were wrought by a modern, urban-industrial society. Scores of urban Negroes and whites no longer subscribed to many of the racial beliefs that continued to govern Negro-white relations in rural and Southern America. Pierre Van der Berghe, for example, pointed out that paternalistic forms of race relations, though complex, are generally found in "pre-industrial society, in which agriculture and handicraft production constitute the basis of the economy."[4] In contrast, he concluded that competitive relations are generally associated with industrial and urbanized society.[5] William J. Wilson argued in a similar vein, pointing out that industrialism not only leads to whites viewing Negroes in a more favorable light, "but [it] also tends to lead to changes in minorities resources—educational advances, occupational opportunities heretofore restricted—and a greater political awareness and participation."[6] He concluded that industrialism provides minorities with a greater chance for developing their own institutions than preindustrial societies.[7] In short, the formation of the NUL and the NAACP was in large part a response to changing conditions and aspirations that came in the wake of industrialism and urbanization.

While industrialism and urbanization created more enlightened perceptions among Negroes and whites alike, the problems inherent in urban society clouded these perceptions. The urban intellectual classes believed that social control would strike a happy balance between the more enlightened perceptions and the realities of urban life that sparked racial, class, ethnic, and political tensions. Accordingly, the urban intellectual classes sought to instill in the minds of the new immigrants and the Negro migrants the Protestant work ethic, as well as to change the class status of urban political leadership. In short, the changes in society that the urban intellectual classes were hopeful of realizing could not be achieved, in their opinion, without attention to the problems of urban Negroes and to the "decadent" urban governments. They wanted urban governments under the control of Anglo-Saxons who were of middle-class and upper-class origins.

William H. Baldwin, Jr., like the whites who assisted in the founding of the NUL, was a leader of the drive to change the class status of urban political leaders, and to address the problems of urban Negroes. Although Baldwin did not live to witness the creation of the NUL, he did make outstanding contributions to urban reform programs that were associated with the Progressive Era, and to those ideals that led to the creation of organizations for racial advancement. Baldwin wrote that the municipal governments had failed largely because of

> an indifference on the part of the educated classes to civil responsibilities, toward a state of affairs wherein the very governmental agencies which were designed to restrain the individual within proper bounds foster and encourage the evil use of his liberties for the sake of gain.[8]

Baldwin believed that it was the responsibility of the educated classes to lead the way in the institutionalization of social control procedures in modern industrial society, and that it was the responsibility of these classes to lead the way in the elimination of needless barriers to Negro advancement.

Baldwin advocated social control, and the NUL was a mechanism for this aim from the outset. But Baldwin's views of the city differed markedly from those held by some urban-oriented Negroes and whites. Baldwin viewed the city's social environment as the least favorable "to the normal moral development of the individual,"[9] while scores of urban Negroes and whites believed that the city made one a more complete individual. Despite Baldwin's Jeffersonian view of urban America, he and other Negroes and whites who were concerned about city living concluded that leaving the migrants to their own efforts would be an act fraught with danger. Therefore Baldwin and other Negroes and whites of middle- and upper-class backgrounds took it upon themselves to address the social, political, and industrial problems of the migrants and the immigrants. While they did not promote social equality between the races, they did urge an end to the needless inequalities in urban and Northern life that denied Negroes equal political and industrial opportunity.

Baldwin's racial views can be summarized as follows: he called for the protection of the rights of Negroes as American citizens; and he believed that Negroes should have the same chance to realize their aspirations as whites. Baldwin did not support industrial-type programs for rural and Southern Negroes because he saw them as being peculiarly suited for Negroes, but rather because he viewed industrial education as a form of social control. It was Baldwin's hope that Southern Negroes and whites could be educated so that they "could live together in mutual helpfulness."[10] Baldwin, like the NUL founders, viewed publicity as the reformers' primary weapon for changing racial attitudes and for promoting the interests of Negroes. Baldwin and the NUL founders repeatedly insisted that "reforms can be made only through the pressure of enlightened public opinion."[11] The historical problem, then, is to decide whether Baldwin and other whites and Negroes who relied upon scientific social work or publicity as tools of racial advancement were racial conservatives or pragmatists. In short, did they know what was possible to achieve and what was not?

A speech delivered by Baldwin at the 1899 American Social Science meeting has been widely quoted in order to portray him as a racial conservative.[12] When this speech is examined in its entirety, and when his remarks are examined in the context of the prevailing racial views held by most whites during the 1890s, a different picture of his racial ideology emerges. Baldwin argued that social equality for Negroes was "demanded by sentimental theorists, who would be the last to grant such recognition if they were to live with the problem."[13] A number of whites who advocated social equality between the races were socialists who were committed to this cause. But for the most part, those whites who promoted social equality were theorists rather than practitioners of their belief in social equality. Baldwin eschewed social equality, but he was not a racial conservative. He was a Social Darwinist and therefore argued that the intelligent, educated Negro was no more likely to treat the ordinary, uneducated Negro as a social equal than the "educated white [was likely to socialize with] the uneducated, shiftless white man."[14] Baldwin did not advocate integration in the fullest sense, nor did he advocate the complete separation of the races. He remarked that if Negroes were educated it would be difficult "to keep them so separate and apart that not a single Negro of whatever distinction would have any possible direction or superintendence over any white man."[15]

Baldwin's Social Darwinism did not tarnish his humanitarian views. A

New York Times editorial concluded that he was a brother to those who suffered from the terrible heritage of oppression, prejudice, and contempt.[16] Somewhat contradictorily, perhaps, Baldwin believed that Anglo-Saxons represented the best of mankind, and expressed complete confidence in the ability of Anglo-Saxon institutions and principles to "mold human individuals, from whatever shores, as in the past, to accept and apply our standards."[17] In short, Baldwin's view toward the new European immigrants and the Negro migrants was not totally devoid of paternalism, as the editorial reveals.

The urban and Northern Negro intellectuals were hard pressed to harmonize their own racial views with those of the urban white racial reformers and Progressives. The educated Negroes objected to the white reformers eschewing social equality between the races, because it was their view that their constitutional rights were denied them in order to institutionalize the social separation of the races. Responding to the 1899 Baldwin address, T. Thomas Fortune, editor of the *New York Age,* remarked:

> You cannot eliminate the social question, and you cannot eliminate the Negro from politics. I cannot eliminate myself from politics. It is impossible for me to do it, and still preserve my self-respect and my identity as a citizen.[18]

Fortune's remarks were significant because they echoed the urban and Northern Negroes' determination to be treated the same as all other Americans.

Urban Negro racial reformers believed that their call for complete equality was not a call to violate the private rights of American whites. Therefore they stated clearly that American citizens had the right to exclude other private persons from their private domain. But they concluded that racial segregation in public and industrial estates was indefensible, politically and economically. The Negro founders of both the NUL and the NAACP did not object to self-imposed segregation, such as separate churches, social clubs, and fraternal organizations, and on occasion embraced separate institutions with considerable enthusiasm. Du Bois, for example, readily admitted that "of course, some segregation must come, but we do not advertise it, and we do not think it in itself is a good thing."[19] Not all Negro leaders agreed with Du Bois.

While there was divided opinion among Negro intellectuals and others on the desirability of social segregation, they were of one mind on the evils of economic and political segregation. What distinguished the Negro intellectuals from the urban white racial reformers and the urban Negro masses was their rejection of the view that the color line was regrettable but unassailable. Because of this different perception, the Negro intellectuals resisted the efforts of friendly whites who were content to adjust "their endeavors for amelioration of the Negro, even though the color line persisted in its vaunted stubbornness."[20] The Negro founders of the NUL moved beyond Washington's racial advancement agenda, and advocated full economic and civil equality for Negroes in general and for themselves in particular.

The historiography on the NUL read as follows until the early 1970s: (1) that Booker T. Washington's racial ideology undergirded the formation and the program orientation of the NUL;[21] (2) that the views of William H. Baldwin, Jr., and Washington about the Negroes' place in American society were essentially the same; (3) that Ruth S. Baldwin brought her husband's conservative racial views into the NUL; and (4) that the NUL founders were all conservatives and were allies of Washington. Historians and social scientists in increasing numbers now reject these interpretations, because new evidence suggests otherwise.

The NUL was founded by Negroes and whites who were interested in containing and resolving racial conflict, reducing the incidents of industrial strife, and improving the social, economic, political, and health conditions of a rapidly expanding urban Negro population. These were the ideals that Ruth S. Baldwin brought into the NUL, and these were also the views that her husband subscribed to. Baldwin, like his wife, played a large role in the creation of the movements that ultimately combined to form the NUL, and a number of his reform views were incorporated into NUL ideology and program orientation. Baldwin argued persuasively that social reform work should not be made partisan or political, and that its object should be that of improving conditions for the poor and less fortunate in the society.[22] Hence the NUL, in accordance with Baldwin's social philosophy, has operated on the premise that public opinion must be informed through investigation and reports compiled by reasonable persons "who have the confidence of the community."[23]

Ruth S. Baldwin and the other NUL founders were the reasonable men and women who compiled reports and undertook investigations, and they were also the men and women who had the confidence of the larger community. They, like the socialists, urged the solidarity of the working classes across racial lines. But the NUL founders, unlike the orthodox and internationally minded socialists, did not endeavor to indoctrinate the working classes in order to make them lose sight of their basic loyalty to America and its institutions.[24] Each of these ideals were reflected in the NUL's program orientation. Foremost in the thinking of the NUL founders was the notion that the problems of the "Negro are social and economic and that any approach to their solution which is not predicated on an analysis of these factors must ultimately fail."[25] These were the beliefs of liberals, rather than conservatives, at the time of the founding of the NUL.

One indication of the liberal views found among the NUL founders was the argument that social problems know no racial lines, but that racial prejudices accentuate them, and mar the development of harmonious relations between Negroes and whites in America in general and in the cities in particular.[26] This belief, more than any other factor, was what cemented the union of urban Negro and white racial reformers and Progressives who founded the NUL and the ULM.

As it turned out, the Negro founders of the NUL and the ULM did not exercise control over programs and policies, because whites controlled the purse strings directly or indirectly. Thus the NUL's and the ULM's program orientation was "the ameliorative method which hopes that in the long run smooth working relations will be effected on the basis [of] mutual forbearance and good will."[27] While it can be argued that Washington's program of racial advancement had an identical objective, this fact does not necessarily link the NUL and Washington. The Progressives also held these views, and many of them were not supporters of either Washington or the NUL and the ULM. The NUL founders, unlike Washington, were not concerned with arriving at an accommodation with the white South, did not advise urban Negroes to eschew politics, and did not counsel Negroes to make their home in the South. More important, the NUL founders sought to end the color line in craft unions and in the industrial world.

Expanded educational opportunities and solid vocational guidance were among the programs initiated by the NUL and the ULM to promote equality. Added to these were the institutionalization of programs and ideals in order to harmonize the interests of the working classes and the privileged classes. Unfortunately these programs were of little value, and these ideals were unattainable within the system of government then found in most American cities, both the Negro and white NUL founders concluded. Accordingly, they advocated a system of government that set for itself a rigid standard of conduct for individuals and groups, as well as for the business community.

The fact that NUL founders embraced ideals that called for the best in individuals meant that education had to be considered as a tool of social control. No single type of education captured the attention of the NUL founders. But in the area of social work, they did turn to the liberal arts colleges and sought their support in training Negroes to work among the urban poor. They also looked to the liberal arts colleges to train leaders of thought and action. A 1923 *Opportunity* editorial strongly endorsed higher education for Negroes, declaring that "college training is, of course, a requisite for entering all the professions in which Negroes are so seriously needed, and is fast becoming a requisite for business."[28] The NUL founders, like Du Bois, argued that Negroes should pursue both classical and industrial education.

The extent to which Du Bois's racial ideology influenced the economic and social justice movements arising out of the Progressive Era is of course difficult to gauge. But his belief that the social sciences and social work would serve the cause of racial advancement carried equal weight with his views of the value of politics in the struggle for racial equality. Referring to the applicability of scientific social work in studying the Negro urban condition, Du Bois wrote: "We know of no instrument that has been more effective in interpreting the problems of the Negro, in securing recognition of the need for action, than the well-conceived social study has been in recent years."[29] Du Bois, however, expected concrete action in the wake of the scientific studies of the Negro problem. The same was true of the NUL's founders and supporters.

Both the NUL and the NAACP have relied upon publicity and investigation to acquaint the larger society with the needs of the Negro. They have shared a common assessment of priorities, although from 1911 to 1941 the NAACP primarily addressed political questions, while the NUL preempted industrial and social issues. Sometimes their concerns overlapped. The allegation that the NUL and the NAACP have been divided by profound ideological differences is not sustained by the evidence. Roger N. Baldwin noted that the two organizations were not always on friendly terms, and his statement is often cited to show that their periodic unfriendliness was grounded in ideological differences. But Baldwin's remark referred to a personality conflict revolving around Granger and Roy Wilkins.[30] It was not unusual for Granger and Wilkins to lash out at each other, but it did not follow that they were at odds ideologically. The minutes of the Boards' meetings do not reveal major ideological differences that could have led to acrimony between the NUL and the NAACP.

The programs of the NUL and the NAACP have been both complementary and supplementary. Both organizations have relied upon the interracial methods of protest, propaganda, and persuasion to promote integration. The NAACP has been referred to as the War Department branch of the struggle for racial equality, and the NUL the State Department. At the same time, Negro supporters of the Urban League acknowledged that the tactics of agitation and coercion have their place and value in the search for equality.[31] But these tactics were not viewed as useful in the work that the NUL undertook on behalf of the Negro masses in the urban centers. Granger once remarked:

> If only one organization could survive, and I had to choose one, I'd choose the NAACP, because the NAACP was not out necessarily to get change, but to shout aloud a grievance, and in the long run some of this would get to the conscience of the people.[32]

In short, he recognized the importance of agitation in winning equality. And Granger was quick to note that every program associated with the NUL has been based upon NAACP objectives—full equality and integration.

The NAACP's officers shared Granger's views that the NAACP and the NUL pursued identical goals. In 1925 James Weldon Johnson, the NAACP executive secretary, stated:

> Perhaps there are those who feel that the two great national organizations, the NUL and the NAACP, are working along different lines. The two great organizations should supplement and complement each other. The problem with which we are all concerned is divided into two parts: Colored people of the United States must make themselves fit for all the common rights of American citizenship. They must be economically fit, educationally fit and morally fit, and no race can ever become great which is not strong physically. On the other hand, American Negroes must find a way to compel a recognition of their fitness when they are fit. One program is valueless without the other. For what use is fitness if one is not allowed to enjoy it? Within the scope of this the Urban League functions and this dovetails into the second proposition. There are those who teach that all that is necessary is to become fit and automatically the matter of rights will take care of itself. Such miracles do not happen. If this were the case the problem would have been solved a generation ago. And again there are those who speak of abstract rights like gas in the air—intangible. Material things cannot be maintained except with abstract rights.[33]

Johnson rejected the view that the NAACP and the NUL were ideologically at odds with each other, and that Washington's ideology undergirded the NUL. He, like Du Bois, urged Negroes to pursue industrial and classical education, and warned them against believing that they could survive in a modern civilization without assimilating its cultural norms and developing leaders of universal perspective.[34] Johnson argued for a continuation of the work begun by Washington among the rural and Southern Negroes. Yet he also cautioned Negroes and whites alike against believing the industrial education or any other type of education was a panacea for America's race problem. In short, the creation of the NAACP and the NUL was a rejection of the belief that industrial education or classical education alone would solve America's racial crisis.

During World War II, fourteen Negroes, leaders or academicians, confirmed the view that education was not a panacea for America's racial crisis, and showed clearly that Negroes as a people wanted equality of opportunity and equal justice. This had been Negro America's aim for centuries. An essay written by Roy Wilkins, the editor of the *Crisis,* has generated the most controversy, and is also the one cited most in historical works that comment on the historical progression of Negro advancement. Wilkins wrote:

> They asked then, and they ask now, simply complete equality in the body politic. They could not in self-respect ask less. If it has seemed in the past that certain segments of the Negro population and certain leaders have demanded less, closer study will show that the goal has always been complete equality. There is considerable evidence that the master politician on the race question, Booker T. Washington, carelessly nominated as the "half-loaf" leader, envisioned complete equality as the goal for his people. A shrewd man, thoroughly in tune with his time and its people, Washington appeared to be an appeaser and did his great work under that protective cloak.
>
> It was inevitable that there should emerge, as the Negro made progress, a group which felt the time had come for bolder words and more direct steps to the goal.[35]

Basil Matthews casually referred to the Wilkins essay in his biography of Washington, stating that Wilkins argued that the "*Crisis* magazine and the NAACP 'really arose from Washington's great work.' "[36] As can be seen, Wilkins wrote something totally different, but Matthews did capture the spirit of Wilkins' essay. In 1960 Elliott M. Rudwick claimed Wilkins said that "Booker T. Washington's contributions were important in the creation of the Association."[37] And in an extended essay, Rudwick endeavored to disassociate Washington from any of the ideals that the NAACP has pursued.

Despite what Rudwick and others have written in an attempt to separate Washington from the NAACP, Washington's interest in the Association was more than met the eye. Replying to the charge that the NAACP had become reactionary by 1914, Mary White Ovington reminded Du Bois: "As to our being reactionary—I don't think we are nearly as reactionary as when we started. Why, think, we had to fight to keep *BTW* off the committee in those days."[38] Washington remained on friendly terms with most of the NAACP's founders, including Du Bois, although he was not above publicly denouncing their tactics and strategies.

The Wilkins essay appeared in print the same year Gunnar Myrdal concluded that Washington was not an all-out accommodating leader.[39] The importance of the Wilkins essay was not so much that it, like the Myrdal study, called for a reexamination of Washington's contributions to Negroes' search for equality, but that it also urged historians to acknowledge the revolutionary and evolutionary aspects of racial advancement. In the same essay Wilkins chastised those historians who not only dimmed Washington's image but also misrepresented his contributions to the evolution of racial protest that led to the creation of the NUL and the NAACP. The essay also advised scholars to consider the extent to which progress on the part of Negroes raised aspirations, and how these aspirations are reflected in the words of Negro leaders and in the various programs of racial advancement. Finally, the essay pointed out that the tactics and strategies of all Negro leaders are to win full equality for Negroes, and that terms such as conservative, accommodationist, militant, and radical do not adequately reflect the ways in which Negroes have pursued equality.

An examination of the NUL's programs and policies is an ideal place to test the major theses of Wilkins' essay. Although the Urban League Movement in 1910 was primarily concerned with the economic and social problems that urban Negroes faced, the fact that its founders turned to scientific social work to address these problems indicated that Negroes had decided that there was no single panacea to the race problem. Moreover, the founding of the Urban League Movement and its ultimate reliance on vocational guidance cast doubt on the utility of Washington's racial ideology to equip Negroes to survive in an urban and industrial society.

The NUL founders believed that Negroes would not improve their lot in American society as long as a racial caste system prevailed. While the Southern-based Urban League affiliates did not openly advocate integrated work forces, as did the Northern-based Urban League affiliates and the NUL, their executive secretaries did reject legally sanctioned segregation and racial discrimination. The leaders of both the Northern and Southern Urban League affiliates expected the larger society to endorse wider employment opportunities for Negroes. With this goal as a high priority, the NUL leaders embraced solidarity of the working classes—in the hope of reshaping attitudes that limited Negroes' employment opportunities. The fact that the NUL promoted the solidarity of the working classes across racial lines meant that institutional racism was under attack. But it cannot be said that every NUL founder who subscribed to the belief of worker solidarity across racial lines was a socialist.

Socialist ideology did not play as great a role in the shaping of the NUL's programs and tactics as did modern scientific social work, even though the early settlement-house work and social work programs were first undertaken by the Fabian Socialists in England. A goodly number of Americans involved in settlement-house work and social work programs from about 1880 to 1910 were also socialists. Their impact on programs and reform efforts of the Progressive Era has not been discussed fully.

The extent to which socialist thought influenced the thinking of several of the NUL founders has also not been fully acknowledged. Since its founding the NUL has "tenaciously held to the theory and practice of scientific social work as the basis for the ultimate adjustment of racial difficulties in America."[40] NUL leaders have consistently argued that any improvement in the Negroes' occupational status "must be predicated on a change of attitude on the part of employers and on the part of organized and unorganized white labor."[41] In short, the NUL founders and leaders concluded that the ultimate solution to the Negro problem rested on the extent to which white workers accepted the concept of worker solidarity across racial lines.

Washington, unlike the NUL founders and leaders, remained vague in explaining his views on the role of white labor in promoting equal opportunity and equality between the races. In fact, Washington believed organized labor held out few benefits to Negroes, and therefore did not counsel them to seek membership in unions. The NUL was, however, firm in its commitment to organized labor, to Negroes joining unions, and to worker solidarity across racial lines. William L. Bulkley, an NUL founder, wrote that Negroes in New York City need not despair, for "the growth of Socialism, as represented by such men as Eugene V. Debs, promises equality to all men."[42]

The extent to which the other NUL founders shared Bulkley's views on the growing importance of socialism in America is difficult to measure. But countless numbers of urban racial reformers believed, as did Karl Marx, that human beings' social existence determined their consciousness.[43] Therefore scores of Negroes and whites in the Urban League Movement, like a host of the Progressives, endeavored to improve conditions for the urban masses in order to raise their social consciousness. Both the Progressives and the urban racial reformers undertook projects and founded agencies to protect the masses from the abuses of society, and called for more federal regulation of industry and capitalism.

The NUL and the ULM, as authentic products of the Progressive Era, promoted evolutionary reform rather than revolution. It should be clear by now that neither was monolithic in thought and action. The NUL and the Urban League affiliates helped to revolutionize social work among Negroes, changing it from a "street-corner missionary-type work to the up-to-date scientific social service."[44]

Scientific social work won new friends during the Progressive Era, as evidenced by the NUL's insistence that vocational guidance be introduced in the nation's school system. Although a number of the Urban League affiliates established industrial-type programs during the infant years of the ULM, these programs were not at all patterned after those promoted by Washington and his followers. Eugene K. Jones, the NUL executive secretary from 1917 to 1941, characterized the Urban League affiliates' executive secretaries as men "who saw life from a new angle and were preparing new fields for their fellow race members."[45] While the NUL did encourage the Southern-based affiliates to assist the industrial schools in providing better types of training in order to prepare Negro workers for Northern industry, its officials expected the affiliates' executive directors to rely upon scientific social work in the pursuit of their goals. Combining industrial education with scientific social work, the NUL and the affiliates all believed that hard data in the hands of unions and industrial leaders would assist in knocking down the racial barriers that stymied Negro advancement in the economic world.[46]

The degree to which the Southern-based Urban League affiliates assisted the industrial schools in preparing Negroes for Northern industry is outside the scope of this study, which is not primarily concerned with the Urban League affiliates. Moreover, the affiliates were not required to follow the dictates of the NUL, as were the NAACP locals. Hence the Urban League affiliates did or did not cooperate with the Southern-based industrial schools largely because they reflected the personality of the executive directors. It was the executive directors who implemented programs and policies, and they, rather than the local boards, generally initiated programs and policies. Historical studies of the Southern-based Urban League affiliates are needed to implement what little we know of them.

More is known about the NUL than about the Urban League affiliates. Still, historical studies of the NUL have given far more attention to the organization's ideological basis than to the enormous role played by the executive directors in shaping and implementing policies and programs.

The NUL under Jones's direction sought to: (1) accomplish a policy of decentralizing activities and strengthening the local affiliates through coordination of national and local activities; (2) create local employment bureaus within Urban Leagues in states that lacked properly functioning federal and state employment bureaus; (3) introduce vocational guidance in urban school systems; (4) improve the relations of Negro and white workers as well as mend the NUL's relations with the United States Employment Services; (5) enlist the cooperation of trade unions in expanding employment opportunities for Negroes; and (6) transfer workers from areas with few employment opportunities to those where racial barriers were fewer.[47]

As NUL executive director, Lester B. Granger, in contrast to Jones, did not establish a set of specific priorities for the NUL, despite the fact that the problems confronting Negroes in 1910 were much the same as they were in 1941. Granger should have established a set of specific priorities, because by 1941 urban Negroes were less patient about substantive changes in the society than when Jones was named executive director in 1916. More Negroes resided in urban centers in 1941 than in 1916, which not only complicated urban problems but also made Negroes less patient because of their voting power in the North. The only plausible explanation for Granger's spending so little time developing programs was that he loathed having to be concerned with the day-to-day operations of the NUL.

When Granger retired in 1961, he left his mark on the NUL, enlarging its scope to pursue general goals such as: (1) barring federal funds to public and private housing developments that practiced racial discrimination in selling and renting; (2) eliminating segregation from the nation's armed forces; (3) forcing the government to back equal employment opportunity in public and private sectors alike; (4) reforming existing governmental structures; and (5) removing the tax-exempt status from private educational institutions that practiced racial discrimination in the admission of students.

Granger's impact on the programs and techniques of the NUL was personal as well. He differed from Jones in that he did not respect the affiliates' autonomy, and did battle with the local executive directors and boards when provoked or threatened by their actions. While Jones relied primarily upon quiet diplomacy in his dealings with the larger society, Granger combined orchestrated national publicity and persuasion as the tempo of the Negroes' search for equality accelerated between 1941 and 1961. Granger set about to undo Jones's decentralization program, which had made the Urban League Movement both a vital and a permanent fixture in urban America. Granger was, in contrast to Jones, a prima donna who often made decisions without consultation with the Board. The coverage given the NAACP by the news media, added to the NAACP's growing popularity among the urban Negro middle and upper classes until the 1950s, tormented Granger as it had never tormented Jones.

Still, credit must be given Granger for having realized that in order to do the job that had to be done in the field of race relations, there had to be appropriate machinery and, no less important, the involvement of influential whites in the programs of the NUL. Under Granger's direction and leadership, the NUL and the Urban League Movement experienced both horizontal and vertical growth. All told, Granger was not content that the Urban League affiliates act independently of his thinking concerning the appropriate strategies of racial advancement. Unlike some of the affiliates' executive directors, Granger refused to consider the possibility that direct action, rather than fact finding, persuasion, mediation, and the like, was a desirable tactic for pursuing equality during the 1950s. Yet Granger seemed intent upon carving his name in the annals of Negro leaders as an outspoken advocate of full equality, as Walter White had done in his role as NAACP executive secretary.

Granger did not see any advantage in supporting the NAACP, despite his membership in that civil rights organization and his belief that the NUL and the NAACP pursued identical goals—full equality and equal justice. Also Granger resented any statements made by his critics or friends on the Board reminding him of his antagonistic attitude toward the NAACP. In short, Granger's insensitivity to the Board's role as policy-maker, his reluctance to place the NUL in the vanguard of the civil rights revolution of the 1950s, and his suspicions of the NAACP and several of its officials were factors that eventually led to his loss of stature within the Urban League Movement.

A product of the Progressive Era, the NUL did not adjust to the times to the degree that it should have during the Jones-Granger years (1916–61). Yet the presence of the NUL and the Urban League affiliates in urban America serve as vivid reminders to Negroes and white alike that full equality was not a way of life in 1910, in 1961, or today. The NUL and the Urban League affiliates have nonetheless successfully illuminated the problems of Negro life—perhaps their single most notable achievement. And the nation should be thankful that their approach to correcting the glaring inequities in American life has been that of intelligent discussion rather than of inflammatory discourse, and of calm analysis rather than hate.

Whatever the weaknesses of its programs and leaders, the ULM has made significant contributions toward improving interracial understanding. The NUL and the ULM are not to blame for the slowness with which Negroes have realized full equality. Every segment of our society is responsible for the institutionalization of those imponderable features of the racial situation that are our heritage—attitudes hostile, indifferent, or too sentimentally indulgent. Jones, Granger, Young, and Jordan have reminded America of this fact, and also that the road to equality is not through segregation and racial discrimination.

Epilogue—
The New Guard: Young and Jordan

The shooting of Vernon E. Jordan, Jr., president of the NUL, on May 29, 1980, drew national attention to the Urban League Movement. Jordan has become known as one of the nation's most visible, influential, and outspoken civil rights advocates. The emergence of the NUL as a civil rights organization has been an evolutionary process, as previously discussed at length, and Jordan cannot be credited entirely for what has been a remarkable change of course. Eugene K. Jones, Lester B. Granger, and, most important, Whitney M. Young, Jr., each furthered the entry of the NUL into public prominence as a civil rights organization. As the Negro made progress, the NUL leaders spoke in bolder terms and took more direct steps toward the goal of complete equality.

Young's leadership role in the NUL was outstanding. Jordan has described the NUL as it is in 1980 as the work of Young, so that when Jordan became the executive director, few if any structural changes were anticipated. The Young years may well prove to have been the most productive and revolutionary in the history of the Urban League Movement.

It was not until the 1960s that NUL officials received regular invitations to attend White House meetings at which the Negro question was debated. Moreover, the Congress rarely asked NUL officials to testify at its hearings on civil rights or on broad social programs until the Young years. The perception that the NUL was not a civil rights organization during its first fifty years is held only by those unaware of the changes that the social service organization underwent. By the mid-1960s the NUL, under Young's direction, rivaled the NAACP as a major, national civil rights organization. But neither Young nor his predecessors abandoned the Urban League's social service orientation.

The untimely death of Young at the age of 49, and Jordan's selection in 1971 to head the NUL, did not radically alter the course of the Urban League Movement. A *New York Times* announcement of the selection is as follows:

> Vernon E. Jordan, Jr., was born in Atlanta on August 15, 1935. His mother operated a food catering business that helped pay his way through De Pauw University, where he graduated in 1957. After earning a law degree at Howard University three years later, Mr. Jordan worked as a law clerk in the office of Donald Hollowell, a civil rights lawyer. In 1962, as field secretary of the Georgia branch of the NAACP, he began his career as a civil rights activist, leading a boycott of Augusta stores that allegedly refused to hire Negroes. During the Administration of Lyndon B. Johnson, he was appointed to the National Advisory Commission on Selective Service and to the White House Conference titled "To Fulfill these Rights."[1]

Before being named to head the NUL, Jordan was executive director of the United Negro College Fund, located in Manhattan (New York).[2] The evidence suggests that Jordan's background would inevitably thrust both him and the NUL into the midst of the ongoing civil rights struggle.

America has not been disappointed. Indeed Jordan, like Young, has served ably as an advocate of Negro America in housing, family issues, civil rights, equal educational opportunity, desegregation, community organization in urban areas, and improved health care for the poor.

Jordan, like Jones, Granger, and Young, is a product of the times. Whereas Granger and Young seemed wedded to integration as a vehicle to usher Negroes and other minorities into the mainstream of American society, Jordan seems to believe that cultural pluralism is the proper vehicle to achieve the same objective. Hence Jordan has maintained a degree of independence not deemed advisable by his predecessors. He has spurned offers to serve in the highest levels of government, in the belief that his role in the civil rights arena is to monitor and criticize the activities of business and elected officials alike. Above all else, the coverage given the shooting of Jordan by the news media underscores his and the Urban League's enhanced stature in America.

Notes

BIBLIOGRAPHIC NOTE

The primary source for the study of the National Urban League is the Urban League Papers, which are housed in the Manuscript Division of the Library of Congress. This collection contains an abundance of materials for the years 1940–61. The collection has numerous gaps for the years 1910–40, because most of the correspondence, memoranda, and other printed material covering these years were destroyed by the NUL staff when it moved into its new offices during the 1950s. Also housed at the Manuscript Division are the Southern Regional Office Papers, NUL, and they are indeed useful in filling the void in regard to the NUL for the years 1910–40. Fortunately the minutes of the NUL Board were preserved intact, and they are on microfilm at the Library of Congress. The Urban League of Greater New York also has in its files important documents relating to the NUL.

In addition to the materials discussed above, other important sources are NUL publications that include *The Urban League Story, 1910–60: Golden 50th Anniversary Yearbook* (New York, 1961); *The Story of the National Urban League* (New York, 1956); and *The Urban League—Its Story* (New York, 1938). These are housed in the offices of the Urban League of Greater New York.

Other NUL and local Urban League manuscript collections worth examining are located in the local Leagues' main offices as well as at the Manuscript Division, Library of Congress. The papers of three ex-NUL officers are also housed in the Manuscript Division, Library of Congress. Several file boxes of the papers of Jesse O. Thomas, Nelson C. Jackson, and Lester B. Granger are included in the Southern Regional Office collection, NUL. Robert R. Moton's papers, donated to the Tuskegee Library, were of limited value for this study, as well as the Booker T. Washington Papers in the Manuscript Division, Library of Congress.

Of tremendous value were the files of several of the local Urban Leagues. The ones that I examined most carefully were those of the Urban League of Greater New York. Several of the staff members of the Urban League of Greater New York knew Eugene K. Jones and Lester B. Granger personally, and their views of the two men added to my knowledge of the NUL. The papers of the nine local Urban Leagues cited in this study clearly show the divergence of views that has characterized the Urban League Movement. These local Urban Leagues include the Omaha Urban League Files; the Pittsburgh Urban League Files; the Los Angeles Urban League Files; the Urban League of Kansas City (Missouri) Files; the Urban League of Flint (Michigan) Files; the Baltimore Urban League Files; the Winston-Salem (North Carolina) Urban League Files; the Urban League of Portland (Oregon) Files; and the Detroit Urban League Files.

The newspapers used in this study include the *Baltimore Afro-American, Chicago Defender, New York Age, New York Amsterdam News, Pittsburgh Courier, New York World-Telegram, Norfolk Journal and Guide, New York Times, New York Herald Tribune,* and *Washington Post.* Their coverage of the work of the NUL and the local Urban Leagues expanded my knowledge of Negroes' expanding search for equality. And of course the *Messenger,* a Socialist magazine, shed light on the diversity of opinion within Negro America.

Several published studies of the NUL or the Urban League Movement are worth noting. Guichard Parris and Lester Brooks, *Blacks in the City: A History of the National Urban League* (Boston: Little, Brown and Co., 1971), gave undue praise to Lester B. Granger. Nancy J. Weiss's *The National Urban League, 1910–1940* (New York: Oxford University Press, 1974) is a solid history of the NUL, except for the fact that Washington's links to the NUL are overemphasized. Arvarh E. Strickland's *History of the Chicago Urban League* (Urbana: University of Illinois Press, 1966) is the only published study of an Urban League affiliate, and it correctly points out that the NUL has promoted vocational guidance, rather than industrial education, as one possible solution to urban Negroes' employment problems.

Several unpublished studies of the NUL and the Urban League Movement may also be consulted, although there is little to be gained by reading them. They are: Edward S. Lewis, "The Urban League, A Dynamic Instrument in Social Change: A Study of the Changing Role of the New York Urban League, 1910–1960" (Doctoral dissertation, College of Education, New York University, 1960); Raymond W. Smock, "The Rise of the National Urban League, 1894–1920" (paper presented at the Association for the Study of Negro Life and History, New York City, October 4,

1968); Henri A. Belfon, "A History of the Urban League Movement, 1910–1945" (Master's thesis, Fordham University, 1947); and Alexander B. Bolden, "The Evolution of the National Urban League" (Master's thesis, Columbia University, 1932).

Space would not permit me to list the numerous books and articles examined in preparation for writing this study, but the bulk of these are cited in the Notes.

My research was supplemented by written records and by interviews with Edward S. Lewis, Lloyd K. Garrison, Theodore W. Kheel, William H. Baldwin, III, Mrs. Sophia Y. Jacobs, Mrs. Ann Kheel, Frank Montero, Whitney M. Young, Jr., and Mrs. Ira Miller. The exact dates of the interviews are found in the Notes. In addition I consulted several tape-recorded, typed interviews; they are the reminiscences of Will W. Alexander, George S. Schuyler, Roger N. Baldwin, William J. Schieffelin, William E.B. Du Bois, Roy Wilkins, and Judge Waties Waring, housed at the Oral History Research Office, Columbia University. The tape-recorded, typed interviews of Lester B. Granger, Sterling Tucker, Guichard Parris, and Edwin C. Berry are located at the Moorland Research Library, Howard University.

Other Manuscript Collections

Henry H. Arnold Papers, Manuscript Division, Library of Congress.

Frederick Douglass Papers, Douglass Home, Anacosta, Washington, D.C.

United States Army Military Research Collection, Carlisle Barracks, Carlisle, Pennsylvania.

Dwight D. Eisenhower Papers, Eisenhower Library, Abilene, Kansas.

James V. Forrestal Papers, Princeton University Libraries, Princeton, New Jersey.

Air Adjutant General's Files, Modern Military Records Division, National Archives, Washington, D.C.

John Haynes Holmes Papers, Manuscript Division, Library of Congress, Washington, D.C.

James P. Mitchell Papers, Eisenhower Library, Abilene, Kansas.

National Association for the Advancement of Colored People Papers, Manuscript Division, Library of Congress, Washington, D.C.

Brotherhood of Sleeping Car Porters Papers, Manuscript Division, Library of Congress, Washington, D.C.

Army Air Forces Records, Modern Military Records Division, National Archives, Washington, D.C.

Eleanor Roosevelt Papers, Roosevelt Library, Hyde Park, New York.

Franklin D. Roosevelt Papers, Roosevelt Library, Hyde Park, New York.

Eugene J. Lyons and Rocco Siciliano Papers, Eisenhower Library, Abilene, Kansas.

Oswald G. Villard Papers, Houghton Library, Harvard University, Cambridge, Massachusetts.

Harry Wheaton Papers, Eisenhower Library, Abilene, Kansas.

ABBREVIATIONS USED IN NOTES

The National Urban League Papers and those of the Southern Regional Office, National Urban League, were organized when I used them. Therefore they are cited by box numbers. The affiliates' papers are uncatalogued.

Manuscript Collections

BMUL	Baltimore Maryland Urban League Files, Baltimore, Maryland
BOSCP	Brotherhood of Sleeping Car Porters Papers, Manuscript Division, Library of Congress
DDE	Dwight D. Eisenhower Papers, Eisenhower Library, Abilene, Kansas
EFM	E. Frederick Morrow Papers, Eisenhower Library, Abilene, Kansas
EJL and RS	Eugene J. Lyons and Rocco Siciliano Papers, Eisenhower Library, Abilene, Kansas
FDR	Franklin D. Roosevelt Papers, Roosevelt Library, Hyde Park, New York
HHA	Henry H. Arnold Papers, Manuscript Division, Library of Congress
HST	Harry S Truman Papers, Truman Library, Independence, Missouri
JHH	John Haynes Holmes Papers, Manuscript Division, Library of Congress
JOT	Jesse O. Thomas Papers, Manuscript Division, Library of Congress
JVF	James V. Forrestal Papers, Princeton University Libraries, Princeton, New Jersey
LACUL	Los Angeles California Urban League Files, Los Angeles, California
NAACP	National Association for the Advancement of Colored People Papers, Manuscript Division, Library of Congress
NCJ	Nelson C. Jackson Papers, Manuscript Division, Library of Congress
NUL	National Urban League Papers, Manuscript Division, Library of Congress
ONUL	Omaha Nebraska Urban League Files, Omaha, Nebraska
SRO, NUL	Southern Regional Office, National Urban League Papers, Manuscript Division, Library of Congress

ULOFM   Urban League of Flint Michigan Files, Flint, Michigan

ULOGNY   Urban League of Greater New York Files, New York, New York

ULOKC   Urban League of Kansas City Files, Kansas City, Missouri

ULOPO   Urban League of Portland Oregon Files, Portland, Oregon

ULOPP   Urban League of Pittsburgh Pennsylvania Files, Pittsburgh, Pennsylvania

WSUL   Winston-Salem Urban League Files, Winston-Salem, North Carolina

Journals and Periodicals

AJS	*American Journal of Sociology*
AM	*Atlantic Monthly*
Annals	*Annals of the American Academy of Political and Social Science*
APSR	*American Political Science Review*
ASR	*American Sociological Review*
CA	*Colored American*
CC	*Charities and Commons*
C Cor	*Charities and Correction*
CH	*Current History*
Ch C	*Christian Century*
Com Gr	*Common Ground*
CS	*Common Sense*
JNE	*Journal of Negro Education*
JNH	*Journal of Negro History*
JOAS	*Journal of American Studies*
JSF	*Journal of Social Forces*
J Soc H	*Journal of Social History*
MLR	*Monthly Labor Review*
MROW	*Missionary Review of the World*
NR	*New Republic*
PNQ	*Pacific Northwest Quarterly*
ROR	*Review of Reviews*
SASR	*Sociology and Social Research*
SG	*Survey Graphic*
SW	*Southern Workman*
VS	*Vital Speeches*
WW	*World's Work*

CHAPTER 1

1. Edward M. Fee, *The Origin of Vocational-Industrial Education in Philadelphia to 1917* (Philadelphia: University of Pennsylvania Press, 1938), 70.

2. Ibid.

3. Clement Biddle, *The Philadelphia Directory, 1791* (Historical Society of Pennsylvania), 9.

4. Theodore Draper, *The Rediscovery of Black Nationalism* (New York: Viking Press, 1969), 20.

5. Ibid.

6. Fannie Barrier Williams, "Social Bonds in the 'Black Belt' of Chicago," *Charities*, 15 (October 7, 1905), 41.

7. Theodore Hershberg, "Free Blacks in Ante-Bellum Philadelphia," in Allen F. Davis and Mark Heller, eds., *The Peoples of Philadelphia: A History of Ethnics and Lower Class Life, 1790–1940* (Philadelphia: Temple University Press, 1973), p. 111.

8. Benjamin F. Lee, "Negro Organizations," *Annals*, 49 (September 1913), 129.

9. Ibid., 123.

10. Jane H. and William H. Pease, "Black Power: The Debate in 1840," *Phylon*, 29 (Spring 1968), 23. For an in-depth view and a systematic analysis of the Negro Convention Movement consult Howard H. Bell, ed., *Minutes of the Proceedings of the National Negro Convention, 1830–1864* (New York: Arno Press, 1969); and Bell, *A Survey of the Negro Convention Movement, 1830–1861* (Ann Arbor: University Microfilms, 1953).

11. Leon Litwack, "The Emancipation of the Negro Abolitionist," in John H. Bracy, Jr., et al., *Blacks in the Abolitionist Movement* (Belmont, Cal.: Wadsworth Publishing Co., 1971), 67–68. See also Benjamin Quarles, "The Break between Douglass and Garrison," *JNH*, 23 (April 1938), 144–54.

12. Howard H. Bell, "National Negro Convention: Moral Suasion Versus Political Action," *JNH*, 42 (October 1957), 247–60.

13. Cyril E. Griffith, *The African Dream: Martin R. Delany and the Emergence of Pan-African Thought* (University Park: The Pennsylvania State University Press, 1975), 32.

14. See E.A. Forbes, "Can the Black Man Stand Alone? Liberia As It Is Today," *WW*, 18 (October 1909), 12, 115–68; G.W. Ellis, "Political Institutions in Liberia," *APSR*, 5 (May 1911), 213–23; William Innes, *Liberia: or, The Early History and Signal Preservation of the American Colony of Free Negroes on the Coast of Africa* (Ann Arbor: University Microfilms International, 1977); J. Liebenow, *Liberia: The Evolution of Privilege* (Ithaca: Cornell University Press, 1969).

15. Griffith, p. 8.

16. Jane H. and William H. Pease, *Bound with Them in Chains: A Biographical History of the Anti-Slavery Movement* (Westport, Ct.: Greenwood Press, 1972), 144.

17. William E.B. Du Bois, *The Philadelphia Negro: A Social Study* (New York: Schocken Books, 1971), 84.

18. *Statistical View of the United States, Being a Compendium of the Seventh Census, 1850* (Washington: Beverly Tucker, Senate Printer, 1854), Table 160, p. 154, and Table 136, p. 133.

19. Edward T. Ware, "Higher Education in the United States," *Annals*, 49 (September 1913), 209.

20. Du Bois, *The Philadelphia Negro*, pp. 10–31.

21. *Statistical View of the United States, 1850*, Table 42, p. 63.

22. Ibid. p. 8.

23. William H. and Jane H. Pease, "The Negro Convention Movement," in Nathan I. Huggins, et al., *Key Issues in the Afro-American Experience*, 1 (New York: Harcourt Brace Jovanovich, 1971), 193.

24. Laura Josephine Webster, *The Operation of the Freedmen's Bureau in South Carolina* (New York: Russell and Russell, 1970), 64.

25. Report of Reuben Tomlinson, State Superintendent of Education, South Carolina, Monthly Report for February 1867 (hereafter cited as Report of Tomlinson), *Records of the Education Division, Bureau of Refugees, Freedmen, and Abandoned Lands: 1865–71*, Microfilm No. M-803, Reel 29, National Archives, Washington, D.C.

26. Report of Tomlinson, November 1866.

27. Ibid., Monthly Reports for 1867.

28. Report of Edward L. Deane, Semi-Annual Report of July 1, 1870, from the *Records of*

the Education Division, Bureau of Refugees, Freedmen, and Abandoned Lands: 1865–71, Microfilm No. 803, Reel 4, National Archives, Washington, D.C.

29. Report of Tomlinson, May 1869.

30. Edward Magdol, *A Right to Land* (Westport, Ct.: Greenwood Press, 1977), 63.

31. Ware, "Higher Education of Negroes," p. 209.

32. Kelly Miller, "Problems of Race Adjustment," *Dial,* 50 (March 16, 1911), 209–12.

33. "Plea for Higher Education of the Negro," *Report of the Commissioner of Education for the Year 1899–1900* (Washington: Government Printing Office, 1901), 1: 421.

34. Walter L. Fleming, " 'Pap' Singleton, the Moses of the Colored Exodus," *AJS,* 15 (July 1909), 61; see also John G. VanDeusen, "The Exodus of 1879," *JNH,* 21 (April 1936), 121. For a book-length treatment of Negro migration to Kansas consult Nell Irvin Painter, *Exodusters: Black Migration to Kansas after Reconstruction* (New York: Knopf, 1976).

35. Fleming, " 'Pap' Singleton," p. 121.

36. Refer to J. Fred Rippy, "A Negro Colonization Project in Mexico," *JNH,* 5 (January 1921), 66–73; Mozel Hill, "The All-Negro Communities of Oklahoma: The Natural History of a Social Movement," *JNH,* 31 (July 1946), 254–68.

37. Booker T. Washington, "Relation of Industrial Education to National Progress," *Annals,* 33 (January 1909), 1.

38. Ibid., 5.

39. Charles A. Bennett, *History of Manual and Industrial Education, 1870–1917* (Peoria, Ill.: Manual Arts Press, 1937), p. 457.

40. Eugene D. Genovese, *Roll, Jordan, Roll: The World the Slaves Made* (New York: Vintage Books, 1976), 388–98.

41. *Eighth Annual Report of the Commissioner of Labor, 1892* (Washington: Government Printing Office, 1893), 84–85.

42. Jane Addams, "Standards of Education for Industrial Life," *C Cor* (1917), 163.

43. For an in-depth examination of Booker T. Washington and his racial ideology consult the following: August M. Meier, *Negro Thought in America, 1880–1915: Racial Ideologies in the Age of Booker T. Washington* (Ann Arbor: University of Michigan Press, 1963); Louis R. Harlan, *Booker T. Washington: The Making of a Black Leader, 1856–1901* (New York: Oxford University Press, 1972); J. Donald Calista, "Booker T. Washington: Another Look," *JNH,* 49 (October 1964), 240–55. August M. Meier, "Toward A Reinterpretation of Booker T. Washington," *Journal of Southern History,* 23 (May 1957), 220–27.

44. Stephen A. Fox, *The Guardian of Boston: William Monroe Trotter* (New York: Atheneum, 1971), 94. The Niagara Declaration of Principles supported both economic and political equality for Negroes.

45. "Plea for Higher Education of the Negro," 1: 421.

46. William D. Witt Hyde, "A National Platform on the Race Question," *Outlook,* 77 (May 21, 1904), 169–70.

CHAPTER 2

1. Carter G. Woodson, *A Century of Negro Migration* (Washington: Association for the Study of Negro Life and History, 1918), p. 163.

2. *Ninth Annual Report of the Commissioner of Labor, 1902,* p. 89.

3. Matthew Anderson, *Intensive Report: Berean Manual Training School* (Philadelphia: Historical Society of Pennsylvania, undated); see also the Reverend Matthew Anderson, "The Berean School and the Industrial Efficiency of the Negro," *Annals,* 33 (January 1909), 111–18; Richard R. Wright, Jr., "Social Work and the Influence of the Negro Church," *Annals,* 30 (November 1907), 518–19.

4. *Eighth Annual Report of the Commissioner of Labor, 1892,* p. 80.

5. Louis Filler, *Progressivism and Muckraking* (New York: R.R. Bowker Company, 1976), p. 3.

6. Ibid.

7. Lee K. Frankel, "Jewish Charities," *Annals,* 21 (January-June 1903), 389; see also A.T. Pierson, "Mission Work Among Jews," *MROW,* 23 (November 1900), 824–26; L. Meyer, "Jewish Missions at the Close of the Nineteenth Century," *MROW,* 24 (August

1901), 616–19; Jacob Riis, "Real Philanthropy," *Independent,* 52 (May 17, 1900), 1175–76; "Hebrew Charities in New York," *Independent,* 53 (May 16, 1901), 1102.

8. Frankel, "Jewish Charities," p. 404.

9. "The College Settlement of New York," *Outlook,* 69 (October 12, 1901), 348.

10. Isabel Dangaix Allen, "The Savings Bank Militant," *Outlook,* 77 (May 14, 1904), 118.

11. Ibid., p. 119.

12. Isabel Dangaix Allen, "Negro Enterprise: An Institutional Church," *Outlook,* 78 (September 17, 1904), 180.

13. Lee, "Negro Organizations," p. 131.

14. Gladys Sheppard, *Mary Church Terrell, Respectable Person* (Baltimore: Human Relations Press, 1951), 19–23.

15. Refer to Cyrus Field Adams, "Timothy Thomas Fortune: Journalist, Author, Lecturer, Agitator," *CA,* 4 (January-February 1902), 224–28; Robert A. Factor, *The Black Response to America: Men, Ideals, and Organizations From Frederick Douglass to the NAACP* (Reading: Addison-Wesley, 1970), 119–20. For a book-length treatment of Fortune, see Emma Lou Thornbrough, *T. Thomas Fortune, Militant Journalist* (Chicago: University of Chicago Press, 1972).

16. Filler, *Progressivism and Muckraking,* p. 4.

17. Ibid.

18. Frederick C. Howe, "The City as a Socializing Agency," *AJS,* 17 (March 1912), 590.

19. Jane Addams, "Recreation as a Public Function in Urban Communities," *AJS,* 17 (March 1912), 615.

20. Marion Brown, "Is There a Nationality Problem in Our Schools," *Journal of Proceedings and Addresses of the Thirty-Ninth Annual Meeting, National Education Association* (Chicago: University of Chicago Press, 1900), p. 590.

21. For a detailed and analytical view of Negroes in America during the nineteenth century refer to Zane L. Miller, "The Black Experience in the Modern American City," in Raymond A. Mohl and James F. Richardson, eds., *The Urban Experience: Themes in American History* (Belmont, Cal.: Wadsworth Publishing Co., 1973), 43–52. See also Reynolds Farley, "The Urbanization of Negroes in the United States," *J Soc H,* 1 (Spring 1968), 241–58.

22. George E. Haynes, "Conditions Among Negroes in Cities," *Annals,* 49 (September 1913), 109.

23. George E. Haynes, "The Basis of Racial Adjustment," *Survey,* 29 (February 1, 1913), 569.

24. Alexander Johnson, "The Social Work of a Church from a Layman's Viewpoint," *CC* (1913), 147–48.

25. Jane Addams, "Charity and Social Justice," *Survey,* 24 (June 11, 1910), 441.

26. Samuel P. Hays, "The Politics of Reform in Municipal Government in the Progressive Era," *PNQ,* 55 (October 1954), 158.

27. Robert H. Wiebe, *The Segmented Society: An Introduction to the Meaning of America* (New York: Oxford University Press, 1975), 77.

28. Miller, "The Black Experience," p. 51.

29. Howard B. Woolston, "The Urban Habit of Mind," *AJS,* 17 (March 1912), 605.

30. William D. Witt Hyde, "The New England Conscience," *Outlook,* 78 (December 31, 1904), 1088. Refer also to William Jewett Tucker, "The Goal of Equality," *AM,* 112 (September 1913), 489; Arthur Mann, *Yankee Reformers in the Urban Age* (Cambridge: Belknap Press of Harvard University Press, 1954).

31. Ulysses G. Weatherly, "The Racial Element in Social Assimilation," *AJS,* 16 (January 1911), 600.

32. Lester B. Granger, "End of an Era," *Ebony Magazine,* 19 (December 1959), 91.

33. For an insight into how some Progressives viewed capital and labor and how some Progressives sought to balance the powers of capital and labor consult A.M. Simon, *Class Struggles in America* (Chicago: C.H. Kerr, 1903); Graham Adams, Jr., *Age of Industrial Violence, 1910–1915* (New York: Columbia University Press, 1966).

34. William E.B. Du Bois, "The Saving of Black Georgia," *Outlook,* 69 (September 7, 1901), 130.

35. *Who's Who in America,* 1: 1381. Mrs. Wooley was a white American and an ordained Unitarian minister.

36. Fannie Barrier Williams, "Social Bonds in the 'Black Belt' of Chicago," 44.

37. *Who's Who in Colored America,* 1: 231. Wright, a Negro, served as trustee of Wilberforce University (Ohio), a Negro liberal arts college.

38. Maude K. Griffin, "The Negro Church and Its Social Work—St. Mark's," *Charities,* 15 (October 7, 1905), 75.

39. William L. Bulkley, "The School as a Social Center," *Charities,* 15 (October 7, 1905), 76.

40. *Who Was Who in America,* 3: 468.

41. *Who Was Who in Colored America,* 1: 443.

42. Ibid., 378.

43. For a detailed analysis of the work undertaken by some Progressives that directly or indirectly sought solutions to the problems that confronted urban women see, Jane Addams, *Twenty Years at Hull-House* (New York: Macmillan, 1907); Arthur C. Holden, *The Settlement Idea* (New York: Macmillan, 1922); Jane Addams, *My Friend, Julia Lathrop* (New York: Macmillan, 1935).

44. "CIICN Leaflet," (undated), NUL.

45. *New York Age,* May 17, 1906, 1.

46. See Guichard Parris and Lester Brooks, *Blacks in the City: A History of the National Urban League* (Boston: Little, Brown and Company, 1971), p. 11.

47. "Negro Carpenters in New York," *Charities,* 18 (May 18, 1907), 198.

48. Booker T. Washington, *My Larger Education, Being Chapters From My Experience* (Miami: Mnemosyne Publishing Co., 1969), 74.

49. Refer to Herbert Aptheker, ed., *The Correspondence of W.E.B. Du Bois* (Amherst: University of Massachusetts Press, 1973), 1: 118–21.

50. Haynes's study of Negroes in New York City was his Ph.D. thesis, which was published in monograph form in 1912 by the Columbia University Press. George E. Haynes, *The Negro at Work in New York City* (New York: Columbia University Press, 1912).

51. *Who Was Who in America,* 3:383; *New York Times,* January 10, 1960.

52. Minutes of the First Meeting of the Committee on Social Conditions among Negroes, September 29, 1910, NUL. (The NUL Minutes examined for this study are on microfilm and the numbers found in the Notes designate the page number of the document.)

53. Ibid., p. 4.

54. Granger, "End of an Era," p. 93.

55. Editorials, *Opportunity,* 8 (August 1930), 230.

56. Robert C. Dexter, "The Negro in Social Work," *Survey,* 46 (June 25, 1921), 440.

57. Ibid., 439.

58. Robert A. Woods, "Social Work: A New Profession," *CC,* 15 (January 6, 1906), 472.

59. Ibid. Another insight into the Americanization of the urban Negro can be mined from W.I. Thomas, "Race Psychology: Standpoint and Questionnaire, with Particular Reference to the Immigrant and the Negro," *AJS,* 17 (May 1912), 725–75.

60. *Pittsburgh Courier,* November 1, 1912, 1.

61. Ibid.

62. Ibid.

63. Discussion following William H. Baldwin, Jr.'s Address, "The Present Problem of Negro Education," *Journal of Social Science,* 37 (December 1899), 65.

CHAPTER 3

1. "National League on Urban Conditions," *SW,* 40 (November 1911), 599; Lawrence E. Nicholson, "The Urban League and Vocational Guidance and Adjustment of Negro Youth," *JNE,* 21 (Fall 1952), 450.

2. Jane Cassels Record and Wilson Record, "Ideological Forces and the Negro Protest," *Annals,* 357 (January 1965), 95.

3. Address delivered by Eugene K. Jones, Cleveland, Ohio, December 4, 1924, NUL.

4. "Consolidation of Negro Agencies," *Survey,* 27 (October 28, 1911), 1080.

5. *Pittsburgh Courier,* December 30, 1911, 1.

6. *New York Times,* January 28, 1912, 11.

7. "Consolidation of Negro Agencies," 1080.

8. Constitution, National League on Urban Conditions Among Negroes, (undated), NUL.

9. *A Guide to the Microfilm Edition of the Detroit Urban League,* Michigan Historical Collection, Bentley Historical Library, University of Michigan, 1974 (hereafter cited as Microfilm, DUL), 1.

10. "Plan to Practice Business Ethics," *Survey,* 25 (December 31, 1910), 509.

11. Felix Adler, "Bequests for Philanthropy," *Survey,* 26 (July 18, 1911), 561.

12. Frank S. Mead, *Handbook of Denominations in the United States* (Nashville: Abingdon Press, 1970), 23.

13. William H. Baldwin, III, to Jesse T. Moore, Jr., June 20, 1977.

14. *Who Was Who in America,* 1: 78.

15. Charles Flint Kellogg, *NAACP: A History of the National Association for the Advancement of Colored People* (Baltimore: Johns Hopkins University Press, 1967), 1:129..

16. "Boston Conference on the Advancement of Negroes," *Survey,* 26 (April 22, 1911), 120.

17. John Haynes Holmes, "Of New Ideals and the Cities," *Survey,* 25 (December 24, 1910), 501.

18. Ovington to Holmes (undated), Box 39, JHH.

19. Kelly Miller, "The Negro and Education," *Forum,* 30 (February 1901), 694.

20. Ibid., 695.

21. *Who's Who in Colored America,* 3d edition, p. 224. Hall was a board member of the Chicago NAACP.

22. Lee Bennett Hopkins, *Important Dates in Afro-American History* (New York: Franklin Watts, 1961), pp. 146–47.

23. William H. Baldwin, III, to Jesse T. Moore, Jr., June 20, 1977.

24. August M. Meier, "Booker T. Washington and the Negro Press," *JNH,* 38 (January 1953), 33.

25. *Who Was Who in America,* 1:1295.

26. For a conflicting interpretation refer to Nancy J. Weiss, *The National Urban League, 1910–1940* (New York: Oxford University Press, 1974), 59. Weiss stated: "Thus they [Northern black lawyers] joined the NAACP but not the Urban League."

27. *Who Was Who in Colored America,* 6th edition, 399.

28. Ibid., 92.

29. Ibid., 157.

30. Ibid., 20.

31. Ibid., 453.

32. August M. Meier and Elliott Rudwick, *From Plantation to Ghetto* (New York: Hill and Wang, 1970), 223; Weiss, *The National Urban League,* p. 61.

33. Florette Henri, *Black Migration: Movement North, 1900–1920* (Garden City, N.Y.: Anchor Books, 1976), 128.

34. James H. Laue, "The Changing Character of Negro Protest," *Annals,* 357 (January 1957), 122.

35. Thomas R. Dye and L. Harmon Ziegler, *The Irony of Democracy: An Uncommon Introduction to American Politics* (Belmont, Cal.: Wadsworth Publishing Co., 1972), 313.

36. Robert Brisbane, "Black Protest in America," in Mabel M. Smythe, ed., *The Black American Reference Book* (Englewood Cliffs, N.J.: Prentice-Hall, 1976), p. 557.

37. Weiss, *The National Urban League,* p. 62. Weiss wrote: "The second argument for associating Booker T. Washington and the Urban League derived from policy and doctrine. [The] . . . League grew out of organizations that subscribed to Washington's advice to Negroes to make their lives in the rural South."

38. T. Arnold Hill to Jesse O. Thomas, April 30, 1926, SRO, NUL, A–16.

39. "A Way Out: A Suggested Solution to the Problems of Race Relations," adopted at the NUL Annual Conference, Detroit, Michigan, October 16–19, 1919, *Survey,* 43 (November 29, 1919), 184.

40. Jesse O. Thomas to Mr. Alfred Cowles, June 3, 1925, SRO, NUL, A-14. See also Thomas to T. Arnold Hill, May 8, 1926, SRO, NUL, A-18.

41. Refer to Weiss, *The National Urban League*, p. 57. Weiss wrote that Roger N. Baldwin once noted the unfriendliness of the NUL and NAACP officials. An examination of NUL records shows that Baldwin's remark referred to difficulties between Lester B. Granger and Roy Wilkins that marred NUL-NAACP relations during the 1940s. It should be remembered that the Weiss study stops at 1940.

42. Jones to Joel E. Spingarn, January 8, 1915, NAACP, C-384.

43. Memorandum, NAACP to NUL, October 20, 1916, NAACP, C-384.

44. William E.B. Du Bois, "The Study of the Negro Problem," *Annals*, 11 (January 1898), 1.

45. *New York Herald Tribune*, May 13, 1923. See also "Pot-Pourri," *Opportunity*, 4 (June 1925), 193.

46. Herbert J. Seligmann, "Democracy and Jim Crowism," *NR*, 20 (September 3, 1919), 152.

47. *Who's Who in Colored America*, 6th edition, 292. See also L. Hollingsworth Wood, "The Urban League Movement," *JNH*, 9 (April 1924), 119.

48. A transcript of a tape-recorded interview with Lester B. Granger; John Button, Interviewer; Atlanta, Georgia, May 22, 1968 (hereafter cited as Interview of Lester B. Granger), Moorland Library, Howard University, 29.

49. *The National Urban League, Twenty-Fifth Anniversary Souvenir* Booklet, November 1935, ULOGNY, p. 7.

50. "Steps in the Organization of a League Affiliate," (undated), NCJ, 4.

51. Jesse O. Thomas to Eugene K. Jones, September 17, 1926, SRO, NUL, A-18.

52. Jesse O. Thomas to Eugene K. Jones, February 26, 1925, SRO, NUL, A-16.

53. Jesse O. Thomas to Charles S. Johnson, August 4, 1925, SRO, NUL, A-16.

54. Jesse O. Thomas to Eugene K. Jones, May 2, 1925, SRO, NUL, A-16.

55. Interview with Mrs. Sophia Y. Jacobs, May 15, 1977, 11 East 73rd Street, New York City (hereafter cited as Interview with Mrs. Sophia Y. Jacobs). Mrs. Jacobs was president of the New York Urban League and a member of the National Board.

56. William H. Baldwin, III, to Jesse T. Moore, Jr., June 20, 1977. See also Weiss, *The National Urban League*, p. ix. Weiss wrote: "Nor do we know how the actual decision-making process worked. Where did policy originate: in the board or in the executive staff?"

57. See Arnold M. Rose, *The Power Structure: Political Process in American Society* (New York: Oxford University Press, 1967), 161.

58. Michael Harrington, "The Economics of Racism," *Commonweal*, 74 (July 7, 1961), 368.

59. Eugene K. Jones, "Negro Welfare," *Survey*, 37 (December 30, 1916), 371–72.

60. T. Arnold Hill, "Vocational Guidance," *Opportunity*, 8 (August 1930), 246.

61. Robert R. Moton, "Hampton, Tuskegee and Points North," *Survey*, 54 (April 1, 1925), 17.

62. Minutes of the Executive Board of the National Urban League on Urban Conditions among Negroes, February 1, 1918, NUL.

63. Ibid., May 24, 1918, 5–6.

64. Ibid.

65. See Thomas's own statement recalling his earlier life, and that appearing in the *Indianapolis Freeman* (a black newspaper published in Mississippi), JOT, 3.

66. George E. Haynes to Thomas, October 7, 1918, JOT.

67. A.J. Portenar, Special Agent, to Thomas, May 1, 1919, JOT.

68. For commentaries on and analyses of the 1919 racial riots refer to William M. Tuttle, Jr., *Race Riot: Chicago in the Red Summer of 1919* (New York: Atheneum, 1970); Robert T. Kerlin, *The Voice of the Negro, 1919* (New York: Arno Press, 1968); George E. Haynes, "Race Riots in a Democracy," *Survey*, 42 (August 9, 1919), 697–99.

69. Minutes of a Meeting of the Executive Board of the National Urban League, December 16, 1919, NUL.

70. Granger, "End of an Era," p. 92.

CHAPTER 4

1. Minutes of a Meeting of the Executive Board of the National Urban League, June 14, 1920, NUL.

2. Ibid., December 11, 1920, 3.

3. Ibid., September 21, 1923, 3. For an analysis of Coolidge's views on the Negro see John L. Blair, "A Time for Parting: The Negro and the Coolidge Years," *JOAS,* 3 (December 1969), 177–99.

4. Editorials, *Opportunity,* 8 (October 1930), 294.

5. Jesse O. Thomas to Mr. A.F. Herndon, March 1, 1924, SRO, NUL, A–12.

6. *Who's Who in Colored America,* 6th edition, 254.

7. Editorials, *Opportunity,* 8 (October 1930), 295.

8. Ibid.

9. Eugene K. Jones, "Progress: The Eighteenth Annual Report of the National Urban League," *Opportunity,* 7 (April 1929), 121.

10. For an opinion of Randolph's and Owen's views on Du Bois's racial ideology see Editorial, "Du Bois Fails as a Theorist," *The Messenger,* 2 (December 1919), 7–8. This article was chosen because it is my argument that the rise of the NAACP and the NUL represented the ascendancy of the black intelligentsia's racial ideology, of which Du Bois was the premier spokesman.

11. Saunders Redding, *Lonesome Road* (Garden City, N.Y.: Doubleday and Co., 1958), 346.

12. See E.U. Essien-Udom, *Black Nationalism: A Search for Identity in America* (Chicago: University of Chicago Press, 1962), 36; William Pickens, "Africa for the Africans: The Garvey Movement," *Nation,* 113 (December 28, 1921), 750–51; E. Franklin Frazier, "Garvey a Mass Leader," *Nation,* 123 (August 18, 1926), 147–48; Kelly Miller, "After Marcus Garvey, What of the Negro?" *Contemporary Review,* 131 (April 27, 1927), 492–500; R.L. Hartt, "Negro Moses and His Campaign to Lead Black Millions to Their Promised Land," *Independent and Weekly Review,* 105 (February 26, 1921), 205–6.

13. Guy B. Johnson, "The Negro Migration and Its Consequences," *JSF,* 2 (March 1924), 407.

14. Ibid., 408.

15. Monroe N. Work, "The Race Problem in Cross Section: The Negro in 1923," *JSF,* 2 (January 1924), 248.

16. E. Franklin Frazier, "The Garvey Movement," *Opportunity,* 4 (November 1926), 346.

17. Monroe N. Work, "The Race Problem in Cross Section," *JSF,* 248.

18. Amy Jacques-Garvey, ed., *Philosophy and Opinions of Marcus Garvey* (New York: Atheneum, 1970), 18.

19. Minutes of a Meeting of the Executive Board of the National Urban League, February 4, 1920, NUL, pp. 1–2.

20. Eugene K. Jones, "Cooperation and Opportunity," *Opportunity,* 1 (January 1923), 5. A reader chosen by the editor of a university press, whose identity remains unknown, suggested that my failure to acknowledge that *Opportunity* magazine served as an outlet to Negro poets, authors, and playwrights was a gross oversight on my part. I chose not to stress that fact because NUL officials did not make mention of *Opportunity* magazine's service to Negro writers until 1949.

21. "Why We Are," *Opportunity,* 1 (February 1923), 1.

22. T. Arnold Hill to Allen Jackson, November 3, 1926, NUL, 5.

23. See T. Arnold Hill to A.F.C. Fiske, January 28, 1930, NUL, 5; A.F.C. Fiske to T. Arnold Hill, February 30, 1930, NUL, 3.

24. Eugene K. Jones, "The Negro in the North," *CH,* 15 (March 1922), 973.

25. Robert B. Grant, *The Black Man Comes to the City: A Documentary Account from the Great Migration to the Great Depression, 1915–1930* (Chicago: Nelson Hall Company, 1972), 195.

26. See Aaron C. Toodle, President, Wolverine Republican Club, Detroit, Michigan (undated), Detroit Urban League Papers, Detroit Historical Society, Bentley Historical Library, University of Michigan (hereafter cited as DULP, BHL, UM), Reel No. 4; W.P.

Lovett, Executive Secretary, Detroit Citizens League, to John C. Dancy, December 12, 1930, DULP, BHL, UM, Reel No. 4.

27. Clarence Darrow, "The Negro and His Ballot," *Opportunity*, 4 (November 1928), 332.

28. Haynes Walton, Jr., *Black Politics: A Theoretical and Structural Analysis* (Philadelphia: J.B. Lippincott Company, 1972), 105.

29. Pete Daniels, *Deep'n as It Comes: The 1927 Mississippi River Flood* (New York: Oxford University Press, 1977), 105. Daniels did not provide any evidence that he had examined NUL records to learn of its role in the dispute with Hoover and the Red Cross.

30. Minutes of a Meeting of the Executive Board of the National Urban League, May 26, 1927, NUL, p. 3.

31. "Unpublished Report of the Colored Advisory Commission," Robert R. Moton Papers, Box GC–48, Tuskegee Institute Archives, Tuskegee, Alabama. At Hoover's request Moton did not release the original report. A revised version, however, exonerated the Red Cross of any wrongdoing.

32. *New York Times*, April 5, 1931, Section II, 6.

33. Ibid., June 11, 1931, 20.

34. Henry Lee Moon, "How the Negro Voted," *Nation*, 159 (November 25, 1944), 64.

35. John Hope Franklin, "A Brief History of the Negro in the United States," in John P. Davis, ed., *The American Negro Reference Book* (Englewood Cliffs, N.J.: Prentice-Hall, 1966), 68.

36. Frank Knox, "Platform from Repudiated Planks," *VS*, 1 (September 9, 1935), 78–92.

37. Interview with Theodore W. Kheel, former President of the NUL, July 26, 1977, The Carlton House, 680 Madison Avenue, New York City.

38. Minutes of the Meeting of the Executive Board of the National Urban League, October 18, 1933, NUL, p. 2.

39. Harry L. Lurie, "The New Deal Program—Summary and Appraisal," *Annals*, 176 (November 1934), 172.

40. The Honorable Harold Ickes, "The Negro as Citizens," *Crisis*, 43 (August 1936), 244.

41. Eleanor R. Roosevelt, "The Negro and Social Change," *Opportunity*, 14 (January 1936), 23.

42. "Negroes under WPA," *MLR*, 50 (March 1940), 636.

43. Eugene K. Jones to Executive Secretaries, Local Urban Leagues, December 30, 1937, SRO, NUL, A–167.

44. *Pittsburgh Courier*, June 15, 1957 (Magazine Section), 2.

45. Refer to "Special Report on Subversive Activities Aimed at Destroying Our Representative Form of Government," Report Number 2277, U.S. Congress, *House Reports, Miscellaneous*, 77th Congress, 2nd Session, January 5–December 16, 1942, 4 (Washington: U.S. Government Printing Office, 1942), 6.

46. Interview with Edward S. Lewis, May 16, 1977.

47. "Sworn Testimony of Lester B. Granger," Hearing Regarding Communist Infiltration of Minority Groups, Thursday, July 14, 1949, *The Congressional Record*, 81st Congress, First Session (Washington: U.S. Government Printing Office, 1949), 459.

48. Interview with Edward S. Lewis, May 16, 1977.

49. T. Arnold Hill, "Labor: Workers to Lead the Way Out," *Opportunity*, 12 (June 1934), 183.

50. "Statement Setting Forth the Position of the National Urban League on Racial Discrimination in the American Federation of Labor," July 9, 1935, NUL, 5.

51. John M. Corridan, "Craft *vs* Industrial Unionism," *Commonweal*, 25 (November 13, 1936), 66.

52. Refer to "Statement in re: The Wehr Foundry Strike," August 15, 1934, NUL, 4; William V. Kelly to T. Arnold Hill, August 3, 1934, NUL, 4; T. Arnold Hill to Lloyd K. Garrison, August 13, 1934, NUL, 4.

53. Lloyd K. Garrison to T. Arnold Hill, August 27, 1934, NUL, 4.

54. Interview with Lloyd K. Garrison, May 17, 1977.

55. Ibid.

56. T. Arnold Hill, "National Urban League—Which Way after 1935?" *SW*, 65 (May 1936), 136.

57. Interview with Edward S. Lewis, May 17, 1977.

58. William H. Baldwin, III, to Jesse T. Moore, Jr., June 20, 1977.

59. Minutes of a Special Meeting of the Steering Committee of the National Urban League, March 15, 1940, NUL, Appendix 1, p. 1.

60. Ibid., 2.

61. Ibid.

62. Minutes of a Meeting of the Executive Board of the National Urban League, November 14, 1940, NUL.

63. Transcript of a tape-recorded interview with Sterling Tucker, ex-executive secretary of the Washington (D.C.) Urban League, October 18, 1969; James Mosby, Interviewer (hereafter cited as Interview of Sterling Tucker); Moorland Library, Howard University, 6.

64. Interview of Lester B. Granger, May 22, 1968, 35.

65. Granger, "End of an Era," p. 98.

CHAPTER 5

1. Granger, "End of an Era," p. 96.

2. Tape-recorded interview with Roy Wilkins; William Ingersoll, Interviewer (hereafter cited as Interview of Roy Wilkins); March 22, 1960, New York City, Oral History Research Office, Columbia University, 78.

3. Tape-recorded interview with W.E.B. Du Bois; William Ingersoll, Interviewer (hereafter cited as Interview of W.E.B. Du Bois); 1960, New York City, Oral History Research Office, Columbia University, 78.

4. *Pittsburgh Courier,* December 28, 1940, 3; see also "Memorandum on the National Defense Housing Program and Negro Working Population," October 22, 1940, NUL, 3, pp. 3–4.

5. Louis Ruchames, *Race, Jobs and Politics* (New York: Columbia University Press, 1953), 16.

6. Tape-recorded interview with Will W. Alexander; Dean Albertson, Interviewer (hereafter cited as Interview of Will W. Alexander); August 6, 1952, New Hope Farm, Chapel Hill, North Carolina, Oral History Research Office, Columbia University, 257–58.

7. Ibid., 668–71.

8. Jervis Anderson, *A. Philip Randolph: A Biographical Portrait* (New York: Harcourt Brace Jovanovich, 1972), 243.

9. Ibid., 252.

10. Interview of Will W. Alexander, 677.

11. The definitive study of the 1941 proposed March on Washington Movement is Herbert Garfinkel, *When Negroes March* (New York: Atheneum, 1969). Other sources worth consulting include A. Philip Randolph, "Why Should We March," *SG*, 31 (November 1942), 488–89. The Randolph files at the Roosevelt Library, Hyde Park, New York, also contain valuable information.

12. Samuel I. Rosenman, ed., *The Public Papers and Addresses of President Franklin D. Roosevelt* (New York: Harper and Brothers, 1941), 215–17.

13. Granger, "End of an Era," 98.

14. Tape-recorded and typed interview with George S. Schuyler; William T. Ingersoll, Interviewer (hereafter cited as Interview of George S. Schuyler); May 17, 1960, Oral History Research Office, Columbia University, 353.

15. Interview of Will W. Alexander, 692.

16. Interview of Roy Wilkins, 98.

17. Interview of Lester B. Granger, 64.

18. Louis Kesselman, "The Fair Employment Practices Commission Movement in Perspective," *JNH*, 31 (January 1946), 32.

19. Minutes of a Meeting of the Executive Board of the National Urban League, November 25, 1942, NUL, p. 2.

20. Interview of Lester B. Granger, 7.

21. A transcript of a tape-recorded interview with Guichard Parris, Staff, National Urban League; Vincent J. Brown, Interviewer (hereafter cited as Interview of Guichard Parris); November 3, 1967, New York City, Moorland Library, Howard University, 7.

22. William H. Baldwin, III, to Jesse T. Moore, Jr., June 20, 1977.

23. *Norfolk Journal and Guide*, December 27, 1941, 5.

24. Minutes of a Meeting of the Executive Board of the National Urban League, November 25, 1941, NUL, pp. 3–4.

25. Interview of Lester B. Granger, 48.

26. Granger, "End of an Era," 95.

27. A Summary of the Hearing of the President's Committee on Fair Employment Practices held in New York, New York, February 16 and 17, 1942, NUL, 3.

28. William H. Baldwin, III, to Paul McNutt, January 13, 1943, NUL, 15; see also Baldwin to President Franklin D. Roosevelt, January 13, 1943, NUL, 15.

29. Interview of Will W. Alexander, 678–82.

30. *Norfolk Journal and Guide*, March 6, 1943.

31. Minutes of the Executive Board of the National Urban League, June 8, 1943, NUL, p. 1.

32. *Norfolk Journal and Guide*, November 13, 1943, 1.

33. Interview with Frank Montero, May 17, 1977, the Tishman Realty Corporation, 666 Fifth Avenue, New York City. Montero was one of the NUL's and ULOGNY's fundraisers.

34. Minutes of a Meeting of the Executive Board of the National Urban League, June 9, 1943, NUL, p. 3.

35. Ibid., November 9, 1943, 3.

36. Ibid.

37. William H. Baldwin, III, to Jesse T. Moore, Jr., June 20, 1977.

38. Ibid.

39. Minutes of a Meeting of the Executive Board, National Urban League, December 14, 1943, NUL, p. 3.

40. Ibid., January 11, 1944, 2–3.

41. Ibid., January 9, 1943, 4.

42. Interview with Edward S. Lewis, May 15, 1977.

43. Randolph to the Reverend John Haynes Holmes, October 23, 1941, JHH, 39.

44. Randolph to D.B. Robertson, President, BLEF Union, February 27, 1941, BOSCP, 5.

45. Malvina C. Thompson, Secretary to Mrs. Roosevelt, to A. Philip Randolph, September 20, 1941, Box 34, Eleanor Roosevelt Papers (hereafter cited as ER Papers, RL), Roosevelt Library.

46. F.A. La Guardia to Randolph, September 18, 1941, JHH, 39.

47. "Open Letter to Mr. Roosevelt from Citizens' Committee to Save Colored Locomotive Firemen's Jobs," January 27, 1943, JHH, 53.

48. Franklin O. Nichols to Granger, September 18, 1943, SRO, NUL, A–68.

49. NLUCAN, *Bulletin* (January 1915), ULOGNY.

50. William L. Evans, "Federal Housing Brings Residential Segregation to Buffalo," *Opportunity*, 20 (April 1942), 106.

51. Granger to the Honorable John M. Carmody, January 27, 1941, NUL, 3.

52. Granger to Carmody, October 17, 1943, NUL, 3.

53. Minutes of the First Regular Monthly Meeting of the Executive Board of the National Urban League, March 10, 1942, NUL, pp. 4–5.

54. Granger to Duffy, October 22, 1941, NUL, 3.

55. Reverend Leo R. Smith, Assistant Chancellor, Diocese of Buffalo, New York, to Granger, October 31, 1941, NUL, 3.

56. Louis Martin, "Prelude to Disaster: Detroit," *Com Gr*, 4 (Autumn 1943), 21–22.

57. For detailed commentaries on and analysis of the Detroit Riot see "Two Sides of a Street: Federal Housing Project Intended for Negroes," *Time*, 39 (March 9, 1942), 14; "Detroit Has A Race Riot as Whites Bar Negroes from New Homes in U.S. Housing Unit," *Life*, 12 (March 16, 1942), 40–41; "Strangers that Sojourn; Housing Unit Built for Negroes in Detroit Causes Riot," *Commonweal*, 35 (March 20, 1942), 224–26.

58. *Norfolk Journal and Guide,* March 7, 1942, 1.

59. Ibid.

60. Ibid., March 14, 1942, 1.

61. Ibid., March 21, 1942, 1.

62. H.L. Nieburg, "Violence, Law and the Informal Polity," *Journal of Conflict Resolution,* 3 (June 1969), 207.

63. Robert M. Fogelson, "Violence and Grievances: Reflections on the 1960s Riots," *Journal of Social Issues,* 26 (Winter 1970), 160.

64. Michael Lipsky, "Protest as a Political Resource," *APSR,* 42 (December 1968), 1158.

65. Louis Martin, "Prelude to Disaster: Detroit," 23.

66. Julius A. Thomas to Granger, June 22, 1943, NUL, 31.

67. See "Race War in Detroit," *Life,* 15 (July 5, 1943), 93–100; Thomas Sancton, "Race Riots," *NR,* 109 (July 5, 1943), 9–13; J. Edgar Hoover, "Memorandum for the Attorney General," July 8, 1943, Official File, 93–C, FDR, 17; Jonathan Daniels, "Memorandum for the President," July 23, 1943, Official File, 93–C, FDR, 17; C.F. Retts, "Re: Detroit Race Riot," July 12, 1943, Official File, 93–C, FDR, 17; Philleo Nash to Mr. Jonathan Daniels, "The Detroit Election," November 10, 1943, Official File, 4245–G, FDR, 10.

68. H. Randolph Moore, "Negro-White Relations During Demobilization," *SASR,* 28 (July-August 1944), 464–70.

69. Minutes of a Meeting called by Mr. Baldwin to discuss Detroit Riot, etc., June 23, 1943, NUL, 31; see also "News Release on the Detroit Riot: June 24, 1943," NUL, 31.

70. *New York Times,* July 3, 1943, 16.

71. Alfred B. Lewis, "Reducing Racial Tensions," *Opportunity,* 21 (October 1943), 157.

72. *New York Times,* July 3, 1943, 16.

73. "National Urban League Report of Detroit Race Riots," June 28, 1943, Reel 10, Microfilm, DUL.

74. "A Statement to Detroit Youth from the Committee on Interracial Problems," June 29, 1943, Reel 10, Microfilm, DUL.

75. *New York Times,* August 3, 1943, 1. See also Parris and Brooks, *Blacks in the City,* 297; Adam Clayton Powell, Sr., *Riots and Ruins* (New York: R.R. Smith, 1945), pp. 42, 45–46.

76. See "Riots in Harlem," *NR,* 109 (August 16, 1943), 220–22; W.C. Headrick, "Race Riots, Segregated Slums," *CH,* 5 (September 1943), 30–34; Oswald G. Villard, "War Between the Races," *CC,* 60 (July 7, 1943), 795–96; "Racial Explosives; Animosity Fuse Still Burning but Trouble May Be Averted," *Newsweek,* 24 (August 21, 1944), 38–39.

77. Francis Biddle, "Memorandum for the President," July 15, 1943, Official File, 4245–G, FDR, 10.

78. Biddle to Granger, August 23, 1943, Official File, 4245–G, FDR, 10.

79. Anderson, *A. Philip Randolph,* p. 252.

CHAPTER 6

1. *Annals of the Congress of the United States, Second Congress* (Washington: Gales and Seaton, 1849), 1301.

2. Adjutant and Inspector General's Office, "General Orders," February 28, 1820, in Morris J. MacGregor and Bernard C. Nalty, eds., *Blacks in the United States Armed Forces: Basic Documents,* 1 (Wilmington: Scholarly Resources, Inc., 1977), 218; see also Jack D. Foner, *Blacks and the Military in American History* (New York: Praeger Publishers, 1974), 27.

3. *United States Statutes at Large,* 13 (1863–65), 11. The Act of February 24, 1864, repealed the Act of March 3, 1863. The 1863 Act empowered the President to call out the national forces, but it did not specifically call for the arming of Negroes.

4. Oswald G. Villard, "The Negro in the Regular Army," *AM,* 91 (June 1903), 722.

5. *Congressional Record,* 45th Congress, 1st. Session (1877), 238.

6. E.K. Davis to General Benjamin F. Butler, 7 December 1876, National Archives Microfilm, National Archives (hereafter cited as NAM, NA).

7. Sherman to Cameron, February 21, 1877, NAM, NA.

8. Cameron to Butler, February 5, 1877, NAM, NA.

9. *Military Laws of the United States,* 1 (Washington: Government Printing Office, 1921), 383.

10. W.B. Hazen, Brigadier and Brevet Major General, Chief Signal Officer, U.S. Army, to the War Department, Office of Chief Signal Office, July 23, 1884, Military Archives, Division of National Archives (hereafter cited as MA, DONA). See also *Army and Navy Journal,* July 23, 1884; Ibid., June 21, 1884.

11. Robert Todd Lincoln, Secretary of War, to W.B. Hazen, Brigadier and Brevet Major General, September 12, 1884, *Army and Navy Register,* 4 October 1884.

12. Davis to Chief of Staff, 20 October 1904, MA, DONA.

13. Memorandum, "The Employment of Negroes as Soldiers in the Regular and Volunteer Forces in the United States," June 1907, MA, DONA.

14. *Digest of Opinions of the Judge Advocates General of the Army* (1912), p. 1004.

15. Ibid., p. 1044.

16. *Military Laws of the United States,* 2 (1912), 1098.

17. Major General George Van Horn Mosely, Acting Chief of Staff, to Walter White, September 1931, Military Records, National Archives.

18. F.H. Payne, Acting Secretary of War, to Walter White, 11 August 1931, Military Records, National Archives. See also Charles H. Houston to General Douglas MacArthur, 9 August 1934, NAACP; Robert R. Moton to President Herbert Hoover, 27 October 1931, Moton Papers, Tuskegee Institute.

19. "If War Comes," *Opportunity,* 17 (April 1939), 98.

20. "The Negro and War," *Opportunity,* 18 (May 1940), 131.

21. "Where Democracy Fails," *Opportunity,* 19 (January 1941), 3.

22. "Negro Medical Officers," *Opportunity,* 19 (June 1941), 163.

23. Lawrence D. Reddick, "The Negro Policy of the United States Army, 1775–1945," *JNH,* 24 (January 1949), 24.

24. "Army," *Time,* 26 (October 28, 1940), 19.

25. Interview of George S. Schuyler, 355.

26. Ibid.

27. "War Department Policy in Regard to Negroes," October 15, 1940, NUL, 3.

28. Interview with Edward S. Lewis, May 16, 1977.

29. *Pittsburgh Courier,* October 26, 1940, 3.

30. Interview of George S. Schuyler, 513.

31. *Pittsburgh Courier,* November 23, 1940, 5.

32. E.S. Adams, the Adjutant General, "War Department Policy in Regard to Negroes," October 16, 1940, in MacGregor and Nalty, *Blacks in the United States Armed Forces,* 5:32–33.

33. "Blunder and Precedent," *Time,* 36 (November 4, 1940), 20.

34. Interview of Lester B. Granger, 21.

35. Ibid., 21, 24.

36. "A Negro Pursuit Squadron," *Opportunity,* 29 (April 1941), 99.

37. *Pittsburgh Courier,* August 23, 1941, 1.

38. "Negroes at War," *Life,* 12 (June 15, 1942), 86.

39. Rio Ottley, "The Negro Press Today," *Com Gr,* 3 (Spring 1943), 11.

40. Ibid.

41. Ibid.

42. Franklin O. Nichols, "War Programs and Racial Objectives," *Opportunity,* 20 (October 1942), 296.

43. Ibid.

44. Interview of Roy Wilkins, 85.

45. Transcribed tape recording of an interview with Roger N. Baldwin; Thomas F. Hogan, Interviewer, April 16, 1963 (hereafter cited as Interview of Roger N. Baldwin); New York City, Oral History Research Office, Columbia University, 84.

46. *Norfolk Journal and Guide,* March 20, 1943, 1.

47. War Department, *Leadership and the Negro Soldier* (Washington: U.S. Government Printing Office, 1943), pp. 1–104.

48. *Norfolk Journal and Guide,* September 2, 1944, 1.

49. Memorandum, J.A. Ulio, Major General, to Commanding Generals, July 8, 1944, NUL, 21.

50. *Norfolk Journal and Guide,* September 9, 1944, 16.

51. "Chronological Summary, Events at Freeman Field," HHA, 224, p. 5.

52. *Norfolk Journal and Guide,* August 26, 1944, 1.

53. "Alleged Racial Discrimination at Deming Army Air Field," 24 August 1945, Box 348, Army Air Forces, Modern Military Records Division, National Archives (hereafter cited as MMRD, NA). A subsequent hearing restored Baker's rank of sergeant.

54. See "Racial Conditions at Freeman Field," 18 April 1945, HHA, 224; "Disorder Occurring at Brookley Field, Alabama," (1945), Air Adjutant General's Files, Box 348, MMRD, NA.

55. "Report of Board of Officers on Utilization of Negro Manpower in the Post-War Army," 17 November 1945, United States Army Military Research Collection, Carlisle Barracks, Pennsylvania.

56. *New York Times,* March 5, 1946, 10.

57. *Norfolk Journal and Guide,* May 11, 1946, 11.

58. Ibid., November 9, 1946, 8.

59. Ibid., September 28, 1946, 20.

60. Manet Fowler, "The Challenge in the Crime," *Opportunity,* 24 (Fall 1946), 170.

61. See *Congressional Record,* 80th Congress, 2nd Session, Part 4, 4312–4314.

62. Minutes of a Meeting of the Executive Board of the National Urban League, April 14, 1948, NUL, p. 3.

63. Ibid.

64. *Congressional Record,* 80th Congress, 2nd Session, Part 4, 4768–4770.

65. *Chicago Defender,* May 8, 1948, 1.

66. Granger to Forrestal, April 23, 1948, NUL, 4; see also Forrestal to Granger, February 12, 1948, JVF, 31.

67. "Introductory Statement by Lester B. Granger, Chairman," April 26, 1948, NUL, 2. For a thorough account of Forrestal's relationship with Granger, consult Boxes 31, 63, and 89, JVF.

68. Minutes of a Meeting of the Executive Board of the National Urban League, May 11, 1948, NUL, p. 3.

69. Interview of Roy Wilkins, 94; see also *Public Papers of the Presidents, Harry S Truman* (Washington: Government Printing Office, 1953), 141.

70. Interview of George Schuyler, May 17, 1960, 542.

71. Interview of Lester B. Granger, May 22, 1968, 33.

72. Ibid., 32.

73. Leo Bogart, et al., *Social Research and the Desegregation of the U. S. Army* (Chicago: Markham Publishing Co., 1969), 19.

74. *Pittsburgh Courier,* April 8, 1950, 1.

75. Charles C. Moskos, Jr., "Racial Integration in the Armed Forces," in Marcel L. Goldschmid, *Black Americans and White Racism* (New York: Holt, Rinehart and Winston, 1970), 298.

76. Robert R. Moton, "The Negro and the World War," *WW,* 36 (May 1918), 75.

77. "The Negro in the United States Navy," *Crisis,* 47 (July 1940), 200.

78. John W. Davis, "The Negro in the United States Navy, Marine Corps, and Coast Guard," *JNE,* 12 (Summer 1943), 346.

79. Harry L. Binesse, "Negroes in the Navy," *Commonweal,* 42 (September 21, 1945), 546.

80. *Norfolk Journal and Guide,* September 23, 1944, 1.

81. Ibid., February 10, 1945, 1.

82. Interview of Lester B. Granger, 29.

83. Minutes of a Meeting of the Executive Board of the National Urban League, April 9, 1945, NUL.

84. *Pittsburgh Courier,* October 20, 1945, 2.

85. Interview of Lester B. Granger, 30.

86. *Pittsburgh Courier,* November 17, 1945, 1.

87. "Granger Report Presented Appeal," January 7, 1946, NUL, 2.

88. "The President's Committee on Equality of Treatment and Opportunity in the Armed Services," 28 March 1949, HST, 10.

89. Ibid.

90. "Text of the Report of the Conference Group of Negro Leaders to Secretary Forrestal," September 8, 1948, NUL, 22, p. 4.

91. The definitive study of the desegregation of the armed forces is Richard M. Dalfiume, *Desegregation of the U.S. Armed Forces* (Columbia: University of Missouri Press, 1969), 26–28.

92. *New York Times,* August 8, 1948, 18.

93. Ibid. For an opposing view see Dalfiume, *Desegregation of the U.S. Armed Forces,* 165. Dalfiume wrote that "Walter White and the NAACP did not disavow Randolph's proposal completely."

94. Granger, "End of an Era," 94.

95. Dalfiume, *Desegregation of the U.S. Armed Forces,* pp. 165, 168, 176, 179, 193.

CHAPTER 7

1. *Norfolk Journal and Guide,* January 1, 1945, 1.

2. Herbert R. Northrup, *The Negro in the Aerospace Industry* (Philadelphia: University of Pennsylvania Press, 1968), 19.

3. "Industrial Democracy," *Time,* 40 (November 23, 1943), 93.

4. James MacGregor Burns, "The Butte Experiment," *CS,* 13 (June 1943), 190.

5. *Pittsburgh Courier,* September 1, 1945, 1. See also Walter F. White, *A Rising Wind* (Garden City, N.Y.: Doubleday, Doran and Co., 1945), 143. Southern House Members, Senators, and Northern Conservative Republicans in the Congress voted to end FEPC funding.

6. *Norfolk Journal and Guide,* March 10, 1945, 3.

7. Memorandum, "Racial Aspects of Reconversion," August 27, 1945, HST, 43, pp. 27–29.

8. "A Report to the Adjustment Problems of Negro Veterans in 50 Cities," March 1946, NUL, 6.

9. A.A. Liveright to Harry S Truman, July 24, 1946, HST, 39.

10. "Urban League Asks Full Use of Negro Building Trades Workers," June 12, 1946, NUL, 2, 1.

11. Harry S Truman, *Memoirs by Harry S Truman,* 2 (Garden City, N.Y.: Doubleday, 1955), p. 180.

12. *Code of Federal Regulations, 1943–48* Compilation (Washington: U.S. Government Printing Office, 1949), p. 590. See also "Executive Order 9808," *Federal Register,* 13 (December 7, 1946), 14153.

13. Carey McWilliams, "Spectrum of Segregation," *SG,* 36 (January 1947), 22.

14. Marion Greene, "Forum: Should We Oppose the Truman Civil Rights Program?" *Forum,* 109 (June 1948), 357.

15. Truman, *Memoirs,* 2: 182.

16. Ibid.

17. Eugene K. Jones to Harry S Truman, December 9, 1946, Official File, HST, 13.

18. "Executive Order 9980," *Federal Register,* 13 (July 28, 1948), 4311–13.

19. Ibid., 4311.

20. "Special Message to the Congress on Civil Rights," February 2, 1948, in *Public Papers of the Presidents: Harry S Truman* (Washington: U.S. Government Printing Office, 1964), 124.

21. *Norfolk Journal and Guide,* September 3, 1949, 18. Julius A. Thomas, the NUL's Industrial Relations Secretary, compiled the report and presented it to the delegates attending the 1949 Annual Convention.

22. *New York Times,* September 6, 1949, 18.

23. The Reminiscences of William J. Schieffelin (hereafter cited as Interview of William J. Schieffelin), February 1949, Oral History Research Office, Columbia University, 78. The *World Telegram,* a New York newspaper, smeared Schieffelin as a "pink," a "fellow traveller," and a "subversive."

24. *Pittsburgh Courier,* January 27, 1951, 1.

25. Ibid.

26. William C. Berman, *The Politics of Civil Rights in the Truman Administration* (Columbus: Ohio State University Press, 1970), 179–80.

27. "Executive Order 10210," *Federal Register,* 16 (February 6, 1949), 1051.

28. Refer to *Federal Register,* 16 (1951), 1815, 2675, 3025, 4419, and 8789. The Executive Orders were Numbers 10216, 10227, 10231, 10243, and 10281.

29. Memorandum to the Attorney General, "Re: The President's Committee on Government Contract Compliance," June 3, 1953, Official File, DDE, 440, p. 2.

30. "Executive Order 10308," *Federal Register,* 16 (December 6, 1951), 12303.

31. Memorandum to the Attorney General, "Re: The President's Committee on Government Contract Compliance," p. 2.

32. Granger to Truman, July 5, 1951, NUL, 3. See also *New York Times,* July 8, 1951,

33. Executive Order 10216 prohibited the AEC and its contractors and subcontractors from denying jobs to individuals on account of race, color, creed, or national origin.

33. "AEC Segregates," *NR,* 124 (May 7, 1951), 7.

34. Minutes of a Meeting of the Board of Trustees of the National Urban League, September 21, 1950, NUL, p. 3.

35. Ibid., 4.

36. Minutes of a Luncheon Meeting of the Board of Trustees of the National Urban League, March 15, 1951, NUL, p. 3.

37. Minutes of a Luncheon Meeting of the Board of Trustees of the National Urban League, September 20, 1951, NUL, 4–5.

38. Charles T. Steele to Board of Directors, Louisville Urban League, Memorandum, "Atomic Energy Plant, Paducah, Kentucky," April 12, 1951, Louisville Urban League Files (hereafter cited as LUL Files), p. 1.

39. Ibid., 2.

40. Curlee Brown, Business Agent, Carpenters Local 1912, to Mr. Clarence Mitchell, NAACP, January 1952, SRO, NUL, A-146.

41. Alston to Mr. John T. O'Brien, Director of Information, Office of Rent Stabilization, January 29, 1952, SRO, NUL, A-146.

42. Eugene A.R. Montgomery, South Carolina Conference, NAACP, to Nelson C. Jackson, Southern Field Director, NUL, February 16, 1951, SRO, NUL, A-146.

43. Thomas to Nelson C. Jackson, February 2, 1951, SRO, NUL, A-140.

44. Charles T. Steele to Board of Directors, April 12, 1951, 3.

45. Memorandum, Harold O. DeWitt to Nelson C. Jackson, "Field Visit-Savannah River Project," May 8–18, 1951, SRO, NUL, A-140, p. 2.

46. Ibid., p. 13.

47. Nelson C. Jackson to Granger, Memorandum, "Attendance at Meeting Called by the NAACP in Washington, D.C., May 23," May 31, 1951, SRO, NUL, A-128, p. 1.

48. Harry L. Alston to Nelson C. Jackson, Memorandum, "Fifth Field Trip to the Savannah River Project, August 22–25, 1951," September 4, 1951, SRO, NUL, A-128, p. 2.

49. Eugene A.R. Montgomery, Local NAACP Secretary, to Harry L. Alston, Southern Regional Office, NUL, September 25, 1951, SRO, NUL, A-134, p. 1.

50. Harry L. Alston to Nelson C. Jackson, Memorandum, "Seventh Field Trip to the Savannah River AEC Project Area, September 29–30, 1951," October 3, 1951, SRO, NUL, A-134, p. 2.

51. Ibid., 5.

52. *Norfolk Journal and Guide,* September 27, 1951, 3.

53. Julius A. Thomas to Harry L. Alston, January 25, 1952, SRO, NUL, A-140.

54. Alston to Thomas, January 29, 1952, SRO, NUL, A-140.

55. Alston to Nelson C. Jackson, January 30, 1952, SRO, NUL, A-140.

56. *Norfolk Journal and Guide,* December 8, 1951, 4.

57. Minutes of a Luncheon Meeting of the Board of Trustees of the National Urban League, March 15, 1951, NUL, p. 2.

58. Minutes of a Meeting of the Board of Trustees, September 20, 1951, NUL, p. 5.

59. Minutes of a Meeting of the Board of Trustees, January 17, 1952, NUL, p. 3.

60. Sebastian C. Owens, Acting Executive Secretary, to Nelson C. Jackson, February 22, 1952, Urban League of Denver Colorado Files (hereafter cited as the ULODC Files).

61. Westbrook McPherson, Executive Director, to Nelson C. Jackson, February 14, 1952, the New Orleans Louisiana Urban League Files (hereafter cited as NOLUL Files).

62. Wesley R. Brazier, Executive Director, to Nelson C. Jackson, Feburary 21, 1952, LACUL.

63. Marion M. Taylor to Nelson C. Jackson, February 20, 1952, ONUL.

64. Louis Mason, Jr., Director, Industrial Relations, to Nelson C. Jackson, April 23, 1952, ULOPP, p. 1.

65. Inge Powell Bell, *CORE and the Strategy of Non-Violence* (New York: Random House, 1968), 102.

66. Carleton Mabee, "Two Decades of Sit-Ins: Evolution of Non-Violence," *Nation,* 193 (August 12, 1961), 78. Another excellent source is August M. Meier and Elliott Rudwick, "How CORE Began," *Social Science Quarterly* (hereafter cited as *SSQ*), 49 (March 1969), 789–99.

67. Carleton Mabee, "Two Decades of Sit-Ins," 78.

68. See "CORE Challenges Housing Policy," *Ch C,* 79 (February 1962), 158. Refer also to James Farmer, *Freedom—When?* (New York: Random House, 1966); August M. Meier, *CORE: A Study in the Civil Rights Movement, 1942–1968* (New York: Oxford University Press, 1973).

69. Holmes to White, November 18, 1946, JHH, 100.

70. Wilkins to the Honorable Hubert T. Delany, November 1, 1949, JHH, 138.

71. Delany to Wilkins, November 9, 1949, JHH, 138, 2.

72. Ibid., 3.

73. Ibid., 2.

74. "NAACP Strategy Is Questionable," *Ch C,* 68 (March 28, 1951), 389.

75. Minutes of a Meeting of the Board of Trustees of the National Urban League, January 19, 1950, NUL, p. 6.

76. Ibid., May 21, 1953.

77. Granger to the Executive Staff, Memorandum, "Flint, Michigan," March 4, 1952, SRO, NUL, A-139, 2.

78. Eason to Nelson C. Jackson, February 20, 1952, ULOFM.

79. Ibid., March 4, 1952, ULOFM.

80. Transcript of a recorded interview with Sterling Tucker, Director, Washington, D.C., Urban League (hereafter cited as Interview of Sterling Tucker); Vincent J. Brown, Interviewer, July 7, 1967; Spingarn-Moorland Research Center, Howard University, 7.

81. Ibid., 25.

82. Ibid., 40.

83. Interview of Lester B. Granger, 36.

84. Interview with Mrs. Sophia Y. Jacobs.

85. Interview with Mr. Lloyd K. Garrison, May 17, 1977.

86. Minutes of a Meeting of the Executive Board of the National Urban League, November 18, 1947, NUL, 3.

87. Interview of Lester B. Granger, 73.

88. Mary S. Bedell, "Employment and Income of Negro Workers, 1940–1952," *MLR,* 76 (June 1953), 601.

89. *Chicago Defender,* March 13, 1948, 1.

90. "Activities of the Department of Industrial Relations—1948," December 16, 1948, NUL, 6, 4.

91. "Gentleman's Agreement, St. Louis Public Schools," *Time,* 54 (July 4, 1949), 15; see also "Race Riot in St. Louis," *Life,* 27 (July 4, 1949), 30–31.

92. "Summer Crisis Arrives in Race Relations," *Ch C,* 66 (July 13, 1949), 836; see also Constance M. Green, *The Secret City: A History of Race Relations in the Nation's Capital* (Princeton: Princeton University Press, 1967), 292–93.

93. "An Urgent Call to Action to Enforce the Rights of All Citizens—Without Discrimination," July 8, 1949, HST, 68, 2.

94. Ibid., 4.

95. Ibid., 1–16.

CHAPTER 8

1. Interview with Theodore W. Kheel, July 26, 1977.

2. For an opposing view consult Weiss, *The National Urban League,* p. ix.

3. Interview with Mrs. Sophia Y. Jacobs.

4. Interview with Edward S. Lewis, May 16, 1977.

5. Interview with Mrs. Ira Miller, Administrative Assistant to the ULOGNY's executive secretary, May 19, 1977, New York Urban League Offices, 1500 Broadway, New York City.

6. Interview with Mrs. Sophia Y. Jacobs.

7. Granger to the Editor of the *Chicago Defender,* January 28, 1944, SRO, NUL, A-70.

8. "Report on Memphis," November 18, 1943, SRO, NUL, A-70, 1.

9. Granger to Mr. M.W. Bonner, January 18, 1944, SRO, NUL, A-70.

10. "Report on Memphis," November 18, 1943, p. 2.

11. Ibid., 3.

12. Ibid., 5.

13. Granger to William Y. Bell, Jr., January 18, 1944, SRO, NUL, A-70.

14. Ibid.

15. Memorandum, Executive Secretary to the President and Members, Board of Directors, Urban League of Portland, Oregon, "Recurrence of Racial Trouble at Roosevelt," February 4, 1952, ULOPO, p. 1.

16. "Willie Johnson Incident, Roosevelt High School," February 6, 1951, ULOPO; refer also to "Confidential Report on Roosevelt High Incident," February 8, 1951, ULOPO, pp. 1–5.

17. "Recurrence of Racial Trouble at Roosevelt," February 4, 1952, ULOPO, p. 3.

18. Grondahl to Rehmus, February 5, 1952, ULOPO, p. 2.

19. Interview of Sterling Tucker, July 7, 1967, 30.

20. Interview with Theodore W. Kheel, July 26, 1977.

21. Interview with Frank Montero.

22. Ibid.

23. Ibid.

24. Interview of Lester B. Granger, 23.

25. Ibid., 43.

26. Interview with Mrs. Sophia Y. Jacobs.

27. Interview with Edward S. Lewis.

28. Interview with Frank Montero.

29. *Current Biography* (New York: H.W. Wilson, 1952), 157.

30. Roy Wilkins to New York City NAACP Members, June 1, 1943, NAACP, 87.

31. *Pittsburgh Courier,* May 22, 1954; see also *Chicago Defender,* May 22, 1954, 1.

32. See Memorandum, "For Discussion with Select Members of the Board," April 19, 1954, NUL, 7, 1.

33. Ibid., 2.

34. Ibid., 3.

35. *New York Amsterdam News,* June 19, 1954, 1.

36. Ibid.

37. Ibid.

38. Minutes of the 44th Annual Meeting of the National Urban League, June 10, 1954, NUL, 4, p. 4.

39. Ibid., 7.

40. Memorandum, R. Maurice Moss to Nominating Committee, "Statement for Committee Use at the May 26th Meeting," May 26, 1954, NUL, 7, 4.

41. Minutes of the 44th Annual Meeting of the National Urban League, June 10, 1954, NUL, p. 4.

42. Memorandum, Lester B. Granger to Executive Secretaries, Local Urban Leagues, June 24, 1954, NUL, 7, p. 1.

43. Ibid., 2.
44. Minutes of a Meeting of the Board of Trustees of the National Urban League, February 18, 1954, NUL, 6, 5.
45. Ibid., 6.
46. Ibid., 5.
47. *New York Amsterdam News,* June 12, 1954, 1, 6.
48. Ibid., June 26, 1954, 1, 6.
49. Ibid., July 3, 1954, 1, 20.
50. Interview with Lloyd K. Garrison.
51. Ibid.
52. Memorandum, Guichard Parris to Mr. Dowdal H. Davis, July 1, 1954, NUL, 7, 2.
53. Carter Wesley to Granger, July 19, 1954, NUL, 7, 1.
54. *Chicago Defender,* May 27, 1954, 5.
55. Ibid.
56. Ibid., July 3, 1954, 2.
57. *New York Amsterdam News,* June 12, 1954, 1.
58. Granger to Joe [complete name not given on letter], July 30, 1954, NUL, 7.
59. *New York Amsterdam News,* June 12, 1954, 1.
60. *Chicago Defender,* June 19, 1954, 1, 2.
61. *New York Amsterdam News,* July 24, 1954, 14.
62. Ibid., July 31, 1954, 14.
63. Refer to P. Goldman, "Significance of African Freedom for the Negro American," *Negro History Bulletin,* 24 (October 1960), 2–5.
64. *New York Amsterdam News,* July 10, 1954, 14.
65. Ibid., July 3, 1954, 20.
66. Granger to Charles S. Zimmerman, Secretary-Manager, Dressmakers Union Local 22, August 18, 1954, NUL, 7, 1.
67. Ibid.
68. Ibid., 3.
69. Interview with Mrs. Sophia Y. Jacobs.
70. Ibid.
71. Interview with Frank Montero.
72. Memorandum, Regina M. Andrews, Board Secretary, to Trustee Members and Delegate Members of the National Urban League, August 23, 1955, NUL, 5, 1–2.
73. *Who's Who in Finance and Industry* (Chicago: Marquis Who's Who, Inc., 1967), 397.
74. Interview with Mrs. Ann Kheel, July 26, 1977, the Carlton House, 680 Madison Avenue, New York City.
75. Interview with Theodore W. Kheel.
76. Ibid.

CHAPTER 9

1. Interview of Lester B. Granger, 22.
2. "A Documented Report on Housing," submitted by the National Urban League to President Eisenhower, June 18, 1954, EFM, 11, 3.
3. Memorandum, Reginald A. Johnson, "HHFA Housing Minority Families Conference," December 21, 1954, EFM, 11, 1.
4. Minutes of a Meeting of the Board of Trustees, March 20, 1952, NUL, p. 3.
5. Ibid., September 17, 1953, 10.
6. Ibid.
7. Ibid., October 15, 1953, 4.
8. Ibid., January 21, 1954, 9.
9. Memorandum, "The President's Committee on Government Contract Compliance," June 3, 1953, DDE, 440, 5.
10. Minutes of a Meeting of the Board of Trustees of the National Urban League, January 21, 1954, NUL, 7.
11. "Conference with Mr. David McDonald, President, United States Steel Workers of America," February 9, 1954, NUL, 9, 1.

12. Minutes of a Meeting of the Board of Trustees of the National Urban League, January 21, 1954, NUL, p. 11.

13. Ibid., March 17, 1954, p. 6.

14. Ibid., September 17, 1953, p. 6.

15. *New York Times,* September 8, 1954, 35.

16. Walter Reuther to President Dwight D. Eisenhower, March 6, 1953, DDE, 201.

17. Interview of Lester B. Granger, 12.

18. "A Statement by the National Housing Conference on Mr. Cole's Alleged Candidacy," February 10, 1953, DDE, 210.

19. "Slogan of Public Housing and Slum Clearance Has Implanted Untruth, Representative Cole Declares," November 12, 1952, DDE, 1.

20. Eisenhower to Reuther, April, 1, 1953, DDE, 201.

21. Granger to Eisenhower, June 18, 1954, EFM, 11.

22. Minutes of a Meeting of the Board of Trustees, National Urban League, September 9, 1954, NUL, p. 1.

23. Ibid.

24. Granger to Eisenhower, August 4, 1955, EFM, 11.

25. Memorandum, Albert Cole, HHFA Administrator, to Maxwell Rabb, November 23, 1955, DDE, 212.

26. Original Draft of Memorandum, Albert Cole, HHFA Administrator, to Maxwell Rabb, September 10, 1955, DDE, 212.

27. Memorandum, Reginald A. Johnson to Lester B. Granger, "The Battle of Levittown, New Jersey," June 20, 1953, NUL, 14.

28. Open Memorandum, J. Wood, Special Assistant for Housing, NAACP, "Conference with Norman Mason, Administrator, HHFA, March 11, 1959," March 13, 1959, DDE, 1160, 1.

29. Val J. Washington to Mr. Wilton B. Persons, the White House, April 14, 1959, DDE, 1160.

30. Albert M. Cole to Algernon D. Black, Chairman, National Committee Against Discrimination in Housing, December 19, 1954, EJL and RS, 42, 2–3.

31. Levitt to Maxwell Rabb, September 20, 1955, DDE, 909.

32. Memorandum, Reginald A. Johnson to Lester B. Granger, "Federal Housing Administration," August 12, 1959, NUL, 5, 1.

33. Ibid., p. 2.

34. See *New York Times,* February 3, 1959, 23; Ibid., March 15, 1959, 8:1; Ibid., March 14, 1959, 6.

35. Ibid., February 3, 1959, 23.

36. Refer to Memorandum from Presidential Assistant E. Frederick Morrow, July 12, 1957, in Branyan Larsen, ed., *The Eisenhower Administration 1953–1961: A Documentary History,* 2 (New York: Random House, 1971), 1106; Val Washington to President Eisenhower, July 18, 1957, DDE, 1160.

37. *New York Times,* July 13, 1960, 20.

38. "Colored Teachers in Charleston Schools," *Crisis,* 22 (June 1921), 58.

39. Refer to *Missouri ex rel. Gaines v. Canada,* 305 U. S. 337 (1938).

40. Thomas A. Webster, Executive Director, to Mr. Walter White, June 30, 1939, ULOKC.

41. Ibid.

42. Minutes of a Meeting of the Executive Board of the National Urban League, April 14, 1948, NUL, p. 2.

43. *New York Times,* May 16, 1952, 23.

44. Minutes of a Meeting of the Board of Trustees of the National Urban League, November 19, 1953, NUL, 5.

45. *New York Times,* July 23, 1954, 13.

46. The reminiscences of Judge Waties Waring (hereafter cited as Interview of Judge Waties Waring); Interviewers, Harlan B. Phillips and Louis M. Starr; December 5, 1958, Oral History Research Office, Columbia University, 364.

47. Minutes of a Meeting of the Board of Trustees of the National Urban League, July 22, 1954, NUL, p. 7.

48. Ibid., January 9, 1949, NUL, pp. 2–3.

49. Memorandum, Howard H. Murphy, Chairman, Education Committee, to the Board of School Commissioners, April 7, 1949, BMUL, 1–7.

50. "Statement Before the Governor's Commission on Negro Higher Education," December 13, 1949, BMUL, pp. 4–5.

51. Memorandum, Lester B. Granger to Executive Secretaries of Affiliate Organizations, October 15, 1954, NUL, 28, 1.

52. Lester B. Granger to Local Executives of Leagues in the Southern and Border States, October 18, 1955, NUL, 28, 1.

53. *New York Times,* September 4, 1956, 26.

54. Granger to Mr. R.L. Scheetz, Norfolk Community Chest, October 6, 1956, NUL, 48, 2.

55. "Statement Regarding Current Attacks on Urban League," May 16, 1956, NUL, 47, 1.

56. *New York Times,* September 6, 1957, 10.

57. "Statement from the National Urban League," signed by Theodore W. Kheel and Lester B. Granger, September 24, 1957, NUL, 6.

58. Telegram, Theodore W. Kheel, President, NUL, to the Honorable Dwight D. Eisenhower, October 3, 1957, NUL, 3, 2.

59. Kheel to Holmes, June 21, 1957, JHH, 195.

60. Interview with Theodore W. Kheel.

61. Interview with Sophia Y. Jacobs.

62. Minutes of a Meeting of the Board of Directors of the Urban League of Greater New Orleans, May 28, 1954, Urban League of New Orleans (Louisiana) Files (hereafter cited as ULONO Files), p. 2.

63. Ibid., September 23, 1954, ULONO Files.

64. Harry L. Alston to Samuel D. Harvey, November 13, 1956, WSUL.

65. Alston to Harvey, November 16, 1956, SRO, NUL, 182, 1.

66. Harvey to Alston, November 8, 1956, WSUL.

67. Daniels to M.T. Puryear, January 18, 1957, Memphis Urban League Files.

68. "The Urban League of Portland," 1957, ULOPO, p. 1.

69. *New York Times,* September 8, 1958, 16.

70. Walter White, "Eisenhower and Civil Rights," April 1, 1948, Box 115, Harry Wheaton Files (hereafter cited as HW Files), Eisenhower Library, 2.

71. *Federal Register,* September 8, 1954, 5655.

72. Ibid., January 19, 1955, 409.

73. Refer to "Second Report of the President's Committee on Government Employment Policy," (1958), EJL and RS, 20, 1–19.

74. Mitchell to Maxwell Rabb, April 2, 1953, DDE, 440.

75. Refer to Case No. 27, May 15, 1956; Case No. 30, May 15, 1956; Case No. 134, September 20, 1955, DDE, 441, 1–5.

76. Interview with Mrs. Sophia Y. Jacobs.

77. Interview with Theodore W. Kheel.

78. Interview of Judge Waties Waring, 78.

79. Refer to "Remarks at Meeting of Negro Leaders, Sponsored by National Newspaper Publishers Association, May 12, 1958," in *Public Papers of the Presidents, Dwight D. Eisenhower* (Washington: U.S. Government Printing Office, 1958), 391–93.

80. Robinson to Eisenhower, May 13, 1958, DDE, 731, 1.

81. Eisenhower to Robinson, June 4, 1958, DDE, 731.

82. *New York Times,* May 14, 1958, 2.

83. Telegram, the Reverend Martin L. King, Jr., to the President, May 29, 1958, DDE, 731.

84. "Report and Recommendations on Meeting with the Reverend Martin Luther King," June 10, 1958, EJL and RS, 42.

85. Ibid.

86. Ibid.

87. *Pittsburgh Courier,* July 5, 1958, 1, 2.

88. Memorandum, Lester B. Granger to NUL Board of Trustees, et al., "June 23rd Conference with President Eisenhower," June 26, 1958, EJL and RS, 42, 1.

89. *Pittsburgh Courier,* June 28, 1958, 2.

90. Memorandum, Granger to NUL Board, "June 23 Conference," p. 2.

91. *New York Times,* September 11, 1959, 19.

92. Memorandum, Guichard Parris to Executives of Local Leagues, March 8, 1960, NUL, 4.

93. *Public Papers of the Presidents, Dwight D. Eisenhower,* 296.

94. "Urban League Comments on President Eisenhower's Recommendation for Biracial Conferences," March 21, 1960, NUL, 7, 1.

95. Roberts to Eisenhower, March 18, 1960, DDE, 194.

96. "Information from the President's Committee on Government Contracts," January 19, 1959, Box 140, James P. Mitchell Papers (hereafter cited as JPM Papers), Eisenhower Library, 1.

97. Interview with Theodore W. Kheel.

98. Interview with Mrs. Sophia Y. Jacobs.

99. "Statement on the National Urban League's Attitude to Situation Regarding the Discriminatory Hiring Practice Against Negro Applicants for Electricians' Jobs," May 21, 1960, NUL, 7, 1.

100. Minutes of a Meeting of the Board of Trustees, National Urban League, May 19, 1960, NUL, p. 3.

101. Ibid., 5.

102. Interview of Lester B. Granger, 66.

103. *Pittsburgh Courier,* January 7, 1961.

104. *New York Times,* September 7, 1960, 34.

105. Interview with Theodore W. Kheel.

106. Interview of Lester B. Granger, 48.

107. Interview with Theodore W. Kheel.

108. Interview of Guichard Parris, 21.

109. Interview of Edwin Berry, 11.

CHAPTER 10

1. Frederick Douglass's views of the Negro problem and what he saw as the appropriate strategies of racial advancement can be mined from the *Douglass Monthly,* June 1858 to August 1863, 5 vols.; Philip S. Foner, ed., *Frederick Douglass: Selections from His Writings* (New York: International Publishers, 1945); Frederick Douglass, *From Slave to Statesman: The Life and Times of Frederick Douglass* (New York: Noble and Noble, 1972); Philip S. Foner, ed., *The Life and Writings of Frederick Douglass* (New York: International Publishers, 1950–75), 5 vols.; The Papers of Frederick Douglass, Manuscript Division, Library of Congress; and the *New National Era, 1870–74.*

2. "Address at the Fourth Congregational Church, Washington, D.C., April 16, 1883," Frederick Douglass Papers, Douglass Home, Anacosta, Washington, D.C.

3. R. Lawrence Moore, "Flawed Fraternity—American Socialist Response to the Negro, 1901–1911," *Historian,* 32 (November 1969), 1–18.

4. Pierre Van der Berghe, *Race and Racism in Comparative Studies* (New York: Macmillan Co., 1973), 53.

5. Ibid.

6. William J. Wilson, *Power, Racism, and Privilege* (New York: Macmillan Co., 1973), 53.

7. Ibid.

8. William H. Baldwin, Jr., "Publicity as a Means of Social Reform," *North American Review,* 173 (December 1901), 848.

9. Ibid.

10. John Graham Brooks, *An American Citizen: The Life of William Henry Baldwin, Jr.* (Boston: Houghton-Mifflin Co., 1910), 248.

11. William H. Baldwin, Jr., "Publicity as a Means of Social Reform," 853.

12. William H. Baldwin, Jr., "The Present Problem of Negro Education," 52–53.

13. Ibid., 56.

14. Ibid.

15. Brooks, *An American Citizen,* 223.

16. *New York Times,* January 8, 1905, 8.

17. Ibid.

18. Refer to Discussion following William H. Baldwin, Jr.'s, Address, "The Present Problem of Negro Education," 65.

19. Du Bois to Mr. Samuel May, Jr., December 10, 1907, in Aptheker, ed., *Correspondence of W.E.B. Du Bois,* 1: 138.

20. Kelly Miller, "Is the Color Line Crumbling?" *Opportunity,* 7 (September 1929), 285.

21. The monograph linking the NUL to Washington's racial ideology and tactics for racial advancement is that of Weiss, *The National Urban League,* pp. 60–64.

22. William H. Baldwin, Jr., "Publicity as a Means of Social Reform," 853.

23. Ibid.

24. Walter Rauchenbusch, "The Ideals of Social Reformers," *AJS,* 2 (July 1896), 215.

25. Editorial, "The Interracial Conference," *Opportunity,* 7 (February 1925), 36.

26. Eugene K. Jones, "Negro Welfare," *Survey,* 37 (December 30, 1916), 371–72.

27. Kelly Miller, "The Harvest of Race Prejudice," *Survey,* 53 (March 1, 1925), 711.

28. Editorial, "The Negro College," *Opportunity,* 1 (March 1923), 3.

29. Du Bois to Mr. Barry C. Smith, April 13, 1935, in Aptheker, *Correspondence of W.E.B. Du Bois,* 2: 61.

30. Minutes of a Meeting of the Executive Board of the National Urban League, November 9, 1943, NUL, 4.

31. Monroe N. Work, "Taking Stock of the Race Problem," *Opportunity,* 2 (February 1924), 45.

32. Interview of Lester B. Granger, 46.

33. "The Cleveland Conference," *Opportunity,* 3 (January 1925), 18. Johnson made these remarks during an address to the delegates in attendance at the NUL's annual convention.

34. See Du Bois to Professor Paul Hanus, June 19, 1916, in Aptheker, *Correspondence of W.E.B. Du Bois,* 1: 216.

35. Roy Wilkins, "The Negro Wants Full Equality," in Rayford W. Logan, ed., *What the Negro Wants* (Chapel Hill: The University of North Carolina Press, 1944), 116–17.

36. Basil Matthews, *Booker T. Washington, Educator and Interracial Interpreter* (Cambridge University Press, 1948), 288; refer also to H.A. Overstreet's Book Review of Matthew's monograph, "Man Farthest Down," *Saturday Review,* 3 (November 20, 1948), 18.

37. Elliot M. Rudwick, "Booker T. Washington's Relations with the National Association for the Advancement of Colored People," *JNE,* 29 (Spring 1960), 134.

38. Ovington to Du Bois, April 11, 1914, in Aptheker, *Correspondence of W.E.B. Du Bois,* 1: 194.

39. Gunnar Myrdal, *An American Dilemma: The Negro Problem and Modern Democracy* (New York: Harper and Row, 1944), 831. See also Houston A. Baker, Jr., *Long Black Song: Essays in Black American Literature and Culture* (Charlottesville: University Press of Virginia, 1972), 94.

40. Editorial, "The Interrracial Conference," 36.

41. Editorial, "Vocational Opportunity," *Opportunity,* 8 (May 1930), 135.

42. William L. Bulkley, "The Industrial Conditions of Negroes in New York City," *Annals,* 27 (May 1906), 133.

43. Karl Marx, *A Contribution to the Critique of Political Economy* (Chicago: Charles H. Kerr and Co., 1904), 11–12.

44. Eugene K. Jones, "Cooperation and Opportunity," *Opportunity,* 1 (January 1923), 5.

45. Ibid.

46. "The Cleveland Conference," 18.

47. Ibid.

EPILOGUE

1. *New York Times,* June 17, 1971, 37.

2. Ibid., January 28, 1970, 81.

Index

DATE DUE

NO 7 '85			
GAYLORD			PRINTED IN U.S.A.